HOW CORRUPT IS BRITAIN?

How Corrupt is Britain?

Edited by David Whyte

www.plutobooks.com

First published 2015 by Pluto Press
345 Archway Road, London N6 5AA

www.plutobooks.com

Copyright © David Whyte 2015

The right of the individual contributors to be identified as the authors of this work has been
asserted by them in accordance with the Copyright, Designs and Patents Act 1988.

British Library Cataloguing in Publication Data
A catalogue record for this book is available from the British Library

ISBN 978 0 7453 3529 2 Hardback
ISBN 978 0 7453 3530 8 Paperback
ISBN 978 1 7837 1284 7 PDF eBook
ISBN 978 1 7837 1286 1 Kindle eBook
ISBN 978 1 7837 1285 4 EPUB eBook

This book is printed on paper suitable for recycling and made from fully managed and
sustained forest sources. Logging, pulping and manufacturing processes are expected to
conform to the environmental standards of the country of origin.

10 9 8 7 6 5 4 3 2 1

Typeset by Stanford DTP Services, Northampton, England
Text design by Melanie Patrick
Simultaneously printed by CPI Antony Rowe, Chippenham, UK
and
Edwards Bros in the United States of America

Contents

Contents

Preface

Liberal thought contends that the United Kingdom is a mature parliamentary democracy, with a House of Commons elected by universal suffrage that is subject to scrutiny and revision by a second chamber, with both chambers underpinned by a powerful unwritten constitution that ensures that neither become too overweening.

Over time Parliament itself, with the assent of the electorate, has created a host of parliamentary and extra-parliamentary bodies, with trusted appointees who hold to account the judiciary, the police, the security forces, the corporations and other powerful organisations in society.

In sum, those living in contemporary Britain are the beneficiaries of a model liberal democratic social order with checks and balances evolving over centuries ensuring everyone, rich and poor alike, lives in a law-governed society in which the corruption of the powerful is an aberration, a threat to the system, and not to be tolerated.

The collection of essays in *How Corrupt is Britain?* fundamentally challenges this contention. The essays emerged out of a conference of the same title that the Centre for Crime and Justice Studies co-sponsored with University of Liverpool in May 2013. The conference brought together some of the leading experts and campaigners on state and corporate corruption in Britain. As the day progressed a picture was drawn that contrasted sharply with the view that Britain nears the end of an inexorable march towards a transparent liberal democracy.

How Corrupt is Britain? demonstrates that, rather than an aberration, corruption is endemic in powerful institutions in contemporary Britain, both public and private, and is sustained by a culture of impunity that has emerged over generations. Indeed, the main bodies that are supposed to bring the corrupt to book, Parliament and the police, are implicated in corrupt practices to such a degree that it is difficult to conceive how they might be able to hold others to account.

It is a common refrain in contemporary politics that those in power no longer have the trust of the 'the people'. Much of the material source of this distrust can be found in *How Corrupt is Britain?* The breadth of corruption detailed is remarkable and the lack of accountability of the powerful in British society palpable.

Will McMahon, Deputy Director
Centre for Crime and Justice Studies

Acknowledgements

There are a large number of people who helped, encouraged and inspired the production of this book. I would like to thank everyone who came to Liverpool on 10 May 2013 to the conference 'How Corrupt is Britain?' I am particularly grateful for the support of the Centre for Crime and Justice Studies. Thanks especially to Will McMahon, the co-organiser of the conference, who wrote the preface to this book and has worked closely with me on this project from the beginning. Thanks also to Sam Harding, Sylwia Szydlowska and Richard Garside for their work in promoting the conference, and to Tammy Mcgloughlin and Rebecca Roberts for helping publish a series of short papers from the conference in *Criminal Justice Matters*. Among my colleagues at the University of Liverpool who supported the event, a big thanks goes to Rachel Barrett and Steph Tully for their work in promoting and organising the day. Thanks also to the speakers whose work appears in this book. I am also grateful to Steve Acheson, Tom Anderson, Deborah Coles, Carole Duggan, Ken Fero, Penny Green, Ciara Kierans, Carolyn Jones, Colin Leys, Peter North, Rizwaan Sabir, Enrico Tortolano and Hilary Wainwright. The conference was supported by the University of Liverpool School of Law and Social Justice, and the Lipman Miliband Trust.

I am grateful for the support of David Castle at Pluto who has been important in shaping the development of the book and has always been patient as deadlines inevitably got pushed back. Numerous friends and colleagues have offered encouragement and inspiration. Steve Tombs and Vickie Cooper and several anonymous reviewers diligently read and commented on earlier versions of the Introduction, and I have tried to do justice to their insights. Thank you. The biggest thanks of all go to the contributors of this book who have generously given up their time, energy and expertise for a project that I hope has all been worth it in the end.

David Whyte

Introduction: A Very British Corruption

David Whyte

'We Are Not Afghanistan or Russia!' Or Are We?

The idea that British institutions are fair and democratic is one of the foundation stones of our self-imagined national heritage. Historically we have construed corruption as something that is exclusively a problem in developing or economically 'primitive' societies, rather than our own. Yet the almost daily reporting of all manner of corruption cases in our most prominent and powerful institutions is beginning to unravel the idea the British establishment is predicated on civilised values of 'fairness', 'openness' and 'transparency'. As the façade shatters, it reveals the residual racism in the claim that we are not corrupt like other countries in the Global South, or indeed that we are not like our Southern European counterparts. If we have corruption in British public life, we have always been led to believe, it is only found at the margins.

It seems that the margins are getting wider. In the past couple of years alone we have seen several national newspapers involved in routine phone-tapping and payoffs to police officers; we have seen allegations of systematic price-fixing in the energy supply industry; and a major European Commission investigation into the alleged role in price manipulation by key corporate players in the oil industry, including BP and Shell. In the food retail industry, we have had a major meat labelling scandal in which horsemeat was sold as 'beef' by supermarkets and major brands in Britain. As this book goes to press, GlaxoSmithKline (GSK) has just been fined £297 million – and senior executives given suspended jail sentences and deportation orders for bribing Chinese officials. An investigation into similar conduct by Rolls-Royce executives in Indonesia and China is ongoing.[1] The banking sector has been mired in all manner of grand corruption scandals. Low-end estimates show that LIBOR and

1

related rate-fixing alone involved frauds that were comparable to the combined losses of WorldCom and Enron.[2] Those frauds led to fines of £290 million being imposed on Barclays and over £700 million on the Royal Bank of Scotland. In a different set of cases, HSBC, Lloyds and Barclays have collectively been made to pay fines of well over $3 billion for money-laundering and sanctions-busting offences in the United States.[3] In November 2014, the Royal Bank of Scotland and HSBC were among five banks fined hundreds of millions of pounds for fixing foreign exchange markets. Barclays awaits news of its fine for the same offence.[4]

A seemingly endless catalogue of police evidence-falsification cases has been exposed in recent years. Some of the evidence that has reached the public domain relates to historical cases, such as the fabrication of statements that were used against striking miners the 1980s, an alleged police whitewash of the Jimmy Savile case, fabricated evidence *en masse* following the Hillsborough disaster, and a review of the Stephen Lawrence case by Mark Ellison QC that revealed corruption in the original investigation. Further, there have been recent revelations of illegal covert operations used to target, infiltrate and smear other community campaign groups, including the friends and family of Stephen Lawrence.[5] A great deal of reported evidence relates to contemporary cases. A Scotland Yard investigation into the fabrication of police evidence surrounding the so-called 'plebgate' incident involving former government chief whip Andrew Mitchell led to one officer being convicted and a public apology by the commissioner of the Metropolitan Police. The Met's sexual assault unit, Sapphire Command, has been condemned by the Independent Police Complaints Commission for encouraging victims to withdraw rape allegations to boost detection rates through 'criminality or neglect'.[6] There is even evidence of corruption at the heart of the Met's own dedicated anti-corruption unit.[7] Yet what we know now represents only a fraction of what we could know about police corruption. The BBC has reported Metropolitan Police insiders admitting that a major four-year investigation into Met corruption ended in the shredding of a 'lorry-load' of evidence.[8]

In recent months, we have also witnessed a steady stream of lobbying scandals inside Parliament which include boasts by former Conservative MP Tim Collins, now an executive at public relations firm Bell Pottinger that his company could access the highest levels of government;[9] former Conservative Party co-treasurer Peter Cruddas who allegedly promised access to the prime minister in exchange for regular corporate donations to the party;[10] and Lord Laird, Lord Cunningham, Lord Mackenzie and Patrick Mercer all offering to conduct parliamentary work in exchange for payment.[11]

A particular concern about corruption in politics has been focused on the development of health policy and the personal gains accrued by some politicians. One investigation by Social Investigations has noted that 142 peers with close links to private healthcare companies were eligible to vote on the government's Health and Social Care Act 2012, the law that opened up the NHS to further private outsourcing. Such links included owning shares, occupying positions on the boards of private healthcare companies, being paid as consultants and working as senior advisers to health investment groups.[12] This type of work is now business as usual for many senior politicians. The former health secretary Patricia Hewitt, for example, after standing down as an MP, was recruited as a special consultant to Boots UK Limited and as a senior adviser to Cinven Ltd, the same company that bought 25 private hospitals from BUPA in 2008.[13] Other recent beneficiaries of the private healthcare sector include former health secretary Alan Milburn[14] and former chancellor of the Exchequer Alistair Darling, who has also been on Cinven's payroll.[15]

Amidst the apparently routine accusations of parliamentary corruption, it is easy to forget that the two most recent changes of party in UK government took place against a backdrop of parliamentary corruption. Labour's election victory in 1997 took place following a major 'cash for questions' scandal in parliament; and an expenses fraud involving MPs from all of the major political parties provided the backdrop to the 2010 general election.

And so it goes on and on: endless case after case; endless scandal after scandal. In a recent interview, a spokesperson for the anti-corruption NGO Transparency International (TI) told listeners to Radio 4's *Today* programme that although a string of corruption cases reflects badly on the British system of government: 'we are not Afghanistan or Russia'.[16] Perhaps he had not been following the news for a while. Certainly his comments seemed a little complacent given the spectacular litany of corruption cases involving British public institutions and corporations that are reported almost every day.

Perhaps his own perceptions had simply been informed by his own organisation's index of corruption. The *TI Corruptions Perception Index* for 2013 places the United Kingdom at 14th out of 177 countries, Russia is placed at 127th and Afghanistan at 176th. It sounds like a pretty good record. Indeed it sounds like conclusive evidence that we are not Afghanistan or Russia. However, when this headline figure is reported in the newspapers (as it is every year), the methods that the survey uses are generally not acknowledged. This is not merely a pedantic or petty academic point, but is a point that is crucial to our understanding of what the *Index* is: a measure of corruption that is not objective, but subjective. The *TI Perception Index* merely measures the impressions of a large group of observers and experts around the world that TI selects for the survey. In the sense that it is based on 'perceptions' of groups of people who are 'perceived' to be experts, the *Index* can be said to be doubly subjective.

League tables like the *TI Index* can make us complacent. The cherished idea that we are a country of fair play, open politics and clean business has been remarkably resilient as the pile of corruption scandals grows higher and higher. Although elite corruption is apparently threatening to become a national stereotype, the assumption that 'we are not Afghanistan or Russia' is a persistent one. The assumption normally follows two lines of argument. The first is that there is no routine bribery in the police or in other public services. The second is that we have relatively robust mechanisms of accountability built into the system, in the form of checks and balances and strong independent regulators.

Perhaps bribery is not everyday in British police forces, public services or in government; money does not change hands to avoid a discretionary traffic violation or to secure the statutory protection of the police. We do know, however, that it does exist: money does change hands at some times for some purposes. We do not know how wide a practice it is in the Metropolitan Police, thanks to the destruction of the 'lorry load' of evidence referred to earlier in this Introduction. Yet there is more than enough evidence from parliamentary inquiries into the role of News International and other media groups into 'phone-hacking' to show that private investigators and journalists have in a very wide range of circumstances regularly made payments for information to former and serving police officers, and to other public officials. The phone-hacking scandal is essentially a bribery scandal. The pursuit of individual interest in the form of bribing of public officials is the corruption that the most prominent experts[17] and watchdog organisations such as TI tend to focus on, but it is probably a relatively peripheral part of a much larger problem of institutional corruption in the United Kingdom.

Certainly, countless faceless and nameless individuals will have benefited indirectly as a result of their involvement in corruption, and some no doubt have been paid, as part of the various forms of corruption that this book explores. Yet the British corruption problem, as we shall see in this book, is much bigger than this: it is the pursuit of institutional interests that characterises British corruption.

Indeed, it is the pursuit of *institutional* interests that, as we shall see later in this Introduction, also undermines our system of checks and balances, and the autonomy and independence of regulatory agencies and processes. As the contributors to this book collectively explore, the watchdogs that are supposed to guard against corruption have been fatally weakened as a result of the slow and pernicious onward march of a neoliberal political economy.

The evidence gathered here will show us that corruption is not merely a minor accidental flaw of the political and economic systems that we live in, but is actually a routine practice that is used for maintaining and extending the power of corporations, governments and public institutions. The weight of this evidence fundamentally questions the extent to which the current rulers of the United Kingdom can be trusted to make decisions that are in the public interest. The cumulative force of the chapters in this book impels us to ask: can we now say that we are entering an era of 'turbo-corruption'?[18] At the very least, it is time we started talking openly and seriously about our very own, quintessentially British, brand of corruption.

The Corruption of the 'Weak'

Britain is probably not alone in its apparent unwillingness to concede that we have a corruption problem. The cracks in the claims that Western states make about their relative clean and transparent ways of doing business and politics have been widening for some time. Following the collapse of Enron and WorldCom, anthropologists Dieter Haller and Cris Shore declared that:

> Europeans and Americans cannot assume that grand corruption is something that belongs primarily to the non-Western 'Other' or to public-sector officials in defective state bureaucracies [but] can also be found in the very heart of the regulated world capitalist system.[19]

Narratives of 'corruption' and economic backwardness (normally presented as the polar opposites of civilised, enlightened values of 'fairness', 'openness' and 'transparency') have endured in the historical narratives of the European colonial powers. Those narratives typically invoke the primitiveness of less-developed states as a justification for political or military domination.[20] Non-British ways of trading and doing business and so on were, in British colonial mythology, plagued by corruption, cheating and subterfuge; foreigners never play by the rules (meaning they don't play by our rules).[21] In British history, the notion was mediated to provide a narrative of morality that underpinned colonial strategy and allowed the British Empire to claim the pursuit of virtue as its rationale for colonial domination.[22] International financial institutions (IFIs)[23] currently invest a lot of time and effort on initiatives that are not fundamentally different from colonial counter-corruption narratives,[24] and alert us to the possibility that our perception of corruption is shaped by an enduring prejudice.[25]

Guarantees that counter-corruption measures are in place are now used prescriptively as a precondition of grant aid, debt relief or of membership of international bodies. Counter-corruption policy in this form is often imposed by the same international institutions (such as the World Bank and the United Nations Development Programme)[26] that impose structural adjustment polices demanding the removal of protective economic policies and encourage privatisation and 'market' reform. This contemporary counter-corruption movement therefore involves a much larger enterprise that goes beyond the eradication of corruption in business and political life as such. Increasingly, this movement can be understood as a moral crusade which organises international opposition to non-mainstream or deviant economic practices. The world of anti-corruption is therefore a 'stage in which moral projects are intertwined with money and power'.[27] (See also Chapter 12.)

A central idea that is found in contemporary counter-corruption narratives is that corruption is predominantly a public sector problem, precipitated by the unnecessary concentration of economic decision making in the hands of governments. The World Bank definition of corruption is simply 'the abuse of public office for private gain'. The World Bank definition explicitly covers bribery, as well as 'patronage and nepotism, the theft of state assets, or the diversion of state revenues'. Chapter 1 sets out a different approach to defining corruption that locates the problem not in the 'public' or 'private' sector as such, but in the distortion of the public realm by private interest.

In so far as the World Bank definition is preoccupied with 'public' policies, revenues and bureaucracies, the 'private' sector is conveniently distanced from the definitional terrain of corruption; private sector corruption should only become a matter of concern if its corruption encroaches on the public sector. The formal separation between the 'public' and 'private' domains here is therefore reduced to the problem of public officials colluding in the capture of state assets. The problem is pathological: that is, corruption occurs when states deviate from the normal path of economic development. And this pathology is generally explained by the presence of a core of corrupt state officials.

A key World Bank document on 'state capture' summarised this position:

> the capture economy is trapped in a vicious circle in which the policy and institutional reforms necessary to improve governance are undermined by collusion between powerful firms and state officials who reap substantial private gains from the continuation of weak governance.[28]

It is clearly the case that many governments are vulnerable to predatory attempts to 'capture' public policy-making processes. However, the presumption made in the 'state capture' perspective is that corruption results from 'weak governance'. Indeed, this very same starting point is shared almost unanimously across opinion makers in the field of corruption. TI notes 'the highest levels of corruption are in countries plagued by conflict and poverty.'[29] In so far as this perspective explains corruption as a problem that is created by poor governance in 'weak' developing states (and undoubtedly this is part of the story, but it is certainly not the full story), it obscures any possibility that World Bank policies themselves might influence the conditions in which corruption can exist. It also obscures the possibility that corruption is a problem that also pervades the 'strong' governments of the Global North.[30]

The IFI agenda on corruption should therefore be read with caution, since it can be understood as an attempt to organise a consensus around the need to reform 'weak' states with economies that are targeted for structural adjustment. It is a strategy that has been neatly summed up by Sampson: '[i]n the world of anti-corruption, one can pursue virtue and integrity while being ruthless and partisan'.[31] Being against 'corruption' allows state officials to construct a moral narrative that legitimates all manner of political interventions at local and national levels, as well as globally.[32] It is a contradiction that this book will unravel further in the context of the British system of government, which still claims to uphold a formal division between public and private while at the same time progressively breaching this division.

The Corruption of the 'Strong'

The location of corruption in the transgression of the 'public' and 'private' divide in 'weak states' leads to very prescriptive ways of dealing with the problem. From a perspective that is preoccupied with corruption as a public sector problem, it is the public sector itself that becomes the problem. Corruption of the market can, from the perspective generally accepted in the counter-corruption policies of the IFIs, be eradicated by encouraging more open competition, expressed in the decisions of competing, self-interested market participants. This is a distinctly neoliberal perspective. From the neoliberal perspective, competition and deregulation, rather than overbearing state controls on capital, are likely to reduce corruption. Thus, as the influential corruption scholar Susan Rose-Ackerman has noted, privatisation can reduce corruption by removing certain prohibitions from state control. The eradication of corruption is not *necessarily* guaranteed by 'deregulation'. However, if such measures stimulate market mechanisms, then corruption is gradually removed from an economic system. In other words: '[I]f the economy is fully competitive, then no corruption can occur.'[33]

There is a certain logic to this, albeit one that is tautological: if there are fewer rules, then the rules will be broken less. The idea that the capitalist markets can rid societies of corruption simply by outsourcing, however, is at best a chimera, and at worst a cynical 'moral deflection device',[34] a crude ideological sledgehammer of an argument.

One location where this strategy was most clearly discernible in recent years was during the occupation of Iraq following the 2003 invasion. It was hardly reported or analysed in any of the 'embedded' mass media coverage at the time, but in the wake of the invasion, the language and practice of counter-corruption for a brief moment dominated the US-led coalition's moral justification for occupation. Just after Saddam Hussein fled Baghdad, George W. Bush proclaimed to the Iraqi public: 'You will be free to build a better life, instead of building more palaces for Saddam and his sons .... You deserve better than tyranny and corruption....'[35] Central to the core economic project of the government of occupation, the Coalition Provisional Authority (CPA),[36] was the promise to end government theft and corruption.[37] The problem of corruption in Iraq was defined by the occupiers as resulting from 'the centrally planned economy, nationalisation of the oil sector and the intrusion of the state into economic life'.[38] The post-invasion rhetoric that proselytised about Saddam's corruption in fact became a means to condemn the previous regime's rejection of a liberal market economy and champion the neoliberal transformation of the post-Saddam economy.

It is now well documented that the 'reconstruction' process in Iraq was based explicitly on a crude application of a trickle-down economic model. The strategy – to stimulate development by ensuring the speedy entry of foreign capital into the economy – is comparable to the classic neoliberal 'shock therapy' experiments in Chile and Indonesia. Indeed, as

Naomi Klein has documented in her book *The Shock Doctrine*,[39] the cynical use of mass public disorientation to impose new economic settlements that ultimately transfer power from the populace to elites is a common neoliberal strategy. In a series of key economic experiments, new market rules and political settlements, and the launch of huge public privatisations, have occurred in the midst of emergencies and conflict situations. Naomi Klein's conclusion is that the orchestration of 'disaster capitalism' is profoundly undemocratic. Her conclusion is without doubt an accurate one. Indeed, the examples she discusses to illuminate her case, from the opening-up of the Iraqi economy to post-Katrina New Orleans, are predicated upon various forms of corporate cronyism and corruption.

In those contexts we generally find the protagonists of economic reform railing against the 'inefficiency' or 'corruption' of the system which must be eradicated to pave the way for 'democratic' or 'market' reforms. And time and time again, we find even more profoundly corrupt economic systems put in their place, which generally bear little resemblance to either democracy or a 'free' market system.

In Iraq, the key effect of sudden economic transformation was the creation of a system of government procurement in which both public and private sector actors were free to engage in embezzlement, bribery and fraud. According to the monitoring group Iraq Revenue Watch, the lack of accounting, auditing or rudimentary controls on expenditure by the CPA paved the way for corruption and waste of billions of dollars of oil revenues.[40] US government sources identified a total of $8.8 billion of Iraqi oil revenue that disappeared, unaccounted for, in this period.[41] The real figure of cash that flowed, unrecorded, into the pockets of contractors and officials is certain to be much larger. Those funds were very deliberately used to establish a form of corruption that provided the necessary incentives for a remarkable corporate invasion. The corruption that flourished under the auspices of the temporary government of occupation provided a structural advantage for Western firms seeking to penetrate the Iraqi economy. The corruption of the reconstruction economy was thus not merely a result of aberrations or flaws in the system, but a central and constituent part of the panoply of domination.[42]

In other contexts we can read an almost identical story. In his analysis of sub-Saharan Africa, politics professor Richard Robison leaves no doubt that in the parts of Africa that have experienced the most fundamental reforms, the corruption of the economy 'has been integral to the way economic and social oligarchies and state elites, the agents and beneficiaries of the new market societies, have established their ascendancy'.[43]

A detailed study of the restructuring of the Indonesian economy shows that market reforms were used by incumbent networks of power to consolidate predatory state and private oligarchies.[44] In Russia, the development of corruption, in the form of the immense political influence held by the oligarchies and the immediate and widespread graft that characterised the post-1991 public sector, enabled the formation and consolidation of an elite that remains dominant. The case of Argentina's economic restructuring following the 2002 economic crisis is vastly different from those already noted, but the routine corruption in the organisation of the state and the private sector has close similarities to the Russian case. Most obviously, the speed and scale of privatisation led to a concentration of power among elites.[45]

There is, therefore, a growing, persuasive body of evidence which shows clearly that the seeds of corruption in the Global South are sown in the 'neoliberal' structural adjustment strategies imposed by key IFIs including the World Bank. Corruption can be understood as part of 'the neo-liberal harvest',[46] in which unrestrained self-interest and aggressive economic self-maximisation are constructed as the logical aims of economic policies. IFI structural adjustment strategies pursue such aims through the imposition of privatisation and so-called 'open' markets in forms that render developing economies vulnerable to predatory foreign corporations.

Those same conditions of structural adjustment blur any distinctions between the interests of 'public' and 'private' elites. Imposing the kinds of market reform that bring an economy in line with the neoliberal order invariably means that the dividing line between 'public' and 'private' becomes more and more blurred. There is a contradiction, then, in strategies of counter-corruption which seek to tackle what anthropologist Tone Sissener has called 'the non-respect of the distinction between public and private',[47] while at the same time designing policies and strategies that encourage the incursion of private wealth accumulation into the public sphere. It should not be surprising that counter-corruption narratives disseminated by the IFIs are wholly concerned with open competition and local governance. To ask questions about corruption which locates its origins in the pathological weaknesses of governance in underdeveloped states and in underdeveloped markets in underdeveloped states directs us away from a much bigger corruption story: that the policies of the strongest states have, for the best part of a century, created the conditions of oligarchy in most industrial sectors. Indeed the key trend in the 'globalisation' of business is the internationalisation of the *concentration* of capital; that is, the elevation of domestic oligopolies – markets or industries dominated by a small number of large corporations – that allows them to operate on an international level.[48] One recent analysis has shown that 737 super-corporations and powerful individuals control 80 per cent of the world's economy.[49]

Rather than simply being understood as the peripheral consequence of various neoliberal experiments, corruption is an ever-present feature. Moreover, various forms of corruption are used as a means to maintain the strategically dominant position of particular elite groups. In other words, corruption in those contexts can be understood as a form of power-mongering: a means of maintaining economic and political dominance.

The Private Sector Takeaway

The chapters in Part I of this book together show how neoliberal corruption is produced when market ideas and practices penetrate the heart of the public sector. Contemporary understandings of corruption must therefore start with an understanding of what has changed in the relationship between the 'public' and 'private'. It has been fashionable in critiques of capitalist globalisation to conclude that the rise of the power of the corporation has been achieved at the expense of nation states. As corporate power grows, so state power wanes. Yet this characterisation of the relationship between states and corporations, portrayed in simple antagonistic terms as one type of institution pitted against the other, is too easy. It is also naïve.

The post-2008 crash was a moment when, in most liberal democracies, the illusion of the global triumph of corporate power over the nation state was shattered as governments around the globe scrambled to save their banks.[50] When the UK chancellor of the Exchequer Alistair Darling completed his £500 billion bank bail-out deal in October 2008, he did so before it could be debated in Parliament. This decision, perhaps the most high-impact political decision in recent memory, has ensured that Britain will remain in a perpetual fiscal and public sector funding crisis for a long time to come. The deal was thrashed out behind closed doors between leading bankers, politicians and senior civil servants. But was this corruption? Certainly it was never reported as such, and there has never been any serious questioning in the mainstream news media of this process as an illegal or unconstitutional one. It is nothing short of incredible that in liberal democracies like the United Kingdom, so much public funding could be so simply transferred from government to the 'private' sector with a settlement which was, according to Darling's autobiography, negotiated with a hand-picked group of elite bankers over a Balti takeaway.[51]

Whether we can think of such deals as being 'corrupt' or not, the point is that 'corruption' itself cannot simply be understood in narrow terms. It is precisely because the constitutional distinction between 'public' and 'private' can be so spectacularly breached that corruption cannot be defined naïvely as 'the abuse of public office for private gain'. We live in a social system in which the unity of interest between government and corporations is now assumed. The flagship neoliberal policies that have been enthusiastically pursued by all UK governments since 1979 are based upon this same article of faith: that there is an indivisible unity of interest between public and private. It is an article of faith that has been used to rationalise the rash of privatisations that all liberal democracies have experienced. An increasingly visible manifestation of the very same article of faith is the 'revolving door' that often facilitates the movement of personnel between public and private sectors, and provides the social networks that are ultimately used to concentrate power in social elites. In some industrial sectors, revolving door appointments have made it almost impossible to draw a formal distinction between 'public' and 'private' interest (see Chapter 10).

One reason that this common bond between public sector organisations and private corporations appears as such a powerful force is simply because the neoliberal project has been so successful in remaking the public sector in the image of the market. The project to bring market discipline to the public sector on a grand scale – with its contemporary British origins in the Thatcher governments of the 1980s – has always contained a militant anti-state ideology at its core. Put into practice, this anti-statism is measured by the extensive programme of privatisation of public utilities and services in this period, and a constant stream of political invective about the need to reduce the size and scope of 'the state'. Thanks largely to this 'anti-statist' movement, the private sector, only peripheral in terms of public service provision in the 1980s, now enjoys a commanding position in public utilities, public transport and telecommunications, not to mention welfare, health and education. One investigation has reported that the current value of schools to the private sector is approximately £7.2 billion, the health system is worth around £24.2 billion, prisons around £4 billion. The rapidly transforming market in welfare will be worth approximately £5 billion over the seven years from 2012–19.[52]

Welfare and housing provision, public transport, the utilities and most local authority functions have been made irrevocably vulnerable by the creeping neoliberalism that has infected those areas of the public sector (see Chapter 9). Managerialist techniques, linked with an ever-growing range of 'performance indicators', have since the 1980s been rolled out to serve successive governments' political objectives. The neoliberal reform of public services over the past 40 years has sought to inject the 'enterprise' culture of the private sector into the public sector, a process that is inextricably linked to the customerisation of the public sector.[53]

In the late 1990s and 2000s, the Labour government pursued exactly the same management processes and arguably intensified the use of key performance indicators introduced under the previous Conservative governments.[54] Public services were reconstructed using an entrepreneurial mode of practice, shaping its sets of relations, ways of thinking and modes of conduct with techniques from the business sector that aimed to make the public sector efficient and calculative.

Those managerialist techniques (known collectively as the New Public Management) were rolled out to serve political objectives; to reorganise public services using principles of market discipline. The reforms of public services sought to inject the 'enterprise' culture of the private sector into, and to 'customerise', the public sector.[55] Of course, one of the consequences of what became a mass migration of peripheral public services into the private sector was that the opportunities for corrupt practices in public services were hugely magnified.

The myth of 'consumer choice' – justified by public choice theory (see Chapter 3) – did not make the public sector any more accountable, but merely presented new opportunity for the growth of a managerial class that could profit from its 'enterprise'. But more importantly, this misleading notion of public choice obfuscated the carefully engineered shift of power to the private sector. There are endless examples of the cynical manipulation of choice by the new private providers.

One investigation by *Spinwatch* in 2011 found that internal NHS documents were cynically using the principle of 'choice' to force consumers to opt for private providers of health care. The investigation found that that NHS Partners Network, a lobby group representing private health care companies such as BUPA, Care UK, Circle and United Health, lobbied the NHS Co-operation and Competition Panel[56] to demand an inquiry into more private sector access to NHS contracts. The lobbying – which included hospitality at a £250 per head gala dinner – was successful, and an inquiry was forthcoming. The inquiry delivered. It put on the political agenda new possibilities for the NHS to encourage more private sector involvement. Its report cynically concluded that 'we understand that patients will "remove themselves from the waiting list" either by dying or by paying for their own treatment at private sector providers'.[57]

Privatisation programmes have from their early days been marred with obvious conflicts of interests, and have brought to the surface new questions about the appropriate relationship between parliamentary decision making and the pursuit of private interest.[58] Perhaps one of the most obvious examples is found in the private finance initiative and its variants (see Chapter 9). As economic commentator Patrick Glynn and his colleagues have argued:

> [t]he sudden deregulation of entire new areas of economic activity that were once under exclusive control of the state can vastly expand room for misconduct, opening the door to fraud and all sorts of abuses by firms trying to take advantage of the opportunities created by capitalism.[59]

They make those comments in the context of economies that are in the midst of economic transition, restructuring and privatisation. The United Kingdom, not normally described as a 'transition' economy, has certainly faced a transition from public to private ownership in many key sectors. And this process has certainly opened some doors to corrupt practices.

In welfare, new markets have been exploited by unscrupulous companies. Perhaps most notorious amongst them is A4e, a company that derives almost all of its turnover from running government welfare-to-work schemes. A4e has been investigated numerous times by the DWP for 'irregularities' since becoming the government's favoured welfare contractor, and has been forced to forfeit government payments on five occasions. A criminal investigation into fraud at the firm, following a series of whistle-blower allegations, forced the firm's chair and government policy adviser, Emma Harrison, to resign in 2012. Other allegations about fraud in welfare contracts include evidence put to the Public Accounts Committee that the company Working Links had also been forced to repay monies overcharged to the public purse.[60]

Central to the New Public Management was the introduction of a range of benchmark standards and targets against which the performance of a service or even a particular part of the organisation could be measured. It is in this intensification of the need to achieve results that we also find the seeds of fraudulent practices. In their book *State Crime*, Penny Green and Tony Ward argue that:

> The growing obsession with quantitative targets in western bureaucracies can encourage ... deviance, such as the manipulation of hospital

waiting lists in the UK. Target-setting has combined with an increasingly entrepreneurial culture to encourage a number of instances of fraud.[61]

There is no claim being made here that performance indicators necessarily lead to corrupt practices, but in the absence of adequate scrutiny it is inevitable that any pressure for results will increase the likelihood of institutional pressures to achieve results using any means available.

There is compelling evidence that the pressure to meet targets set by performance indicators has combined with a new entrepreneurial culture to produce fraudulent results. Health economist Allyson Pollock has pointed out that in the NHS, GP contracts encourage pharmaceutical interventions, as doctors are reimbursed for the number of treatments administered. Lucrative markets for 'big pharma' have been expanded in ways that provide opportunities for fraud.[62] Indeed, the British Medical Association (BMA) has gone public about what it described as 'highway robbery', in which drug companies exploit loopholes in NHS pricing rules in order to rebrand drugs, resulting in an artificial inflation of prices, in some cases multiplying the market value by 20 times.[63] An investigation by the *Telegraph* estimated that artificial pricing in this case may have inflated the costs of up to 20,000 drugs.[64]

The use of NHS waiting list targets as key performance indicators has similarly created pressures on hospital managements to massage the figures. In a series of cases, patients have been found to be removed from lists en masse when they are deemed 'unavailable for treatment'. One investigation by Audit Scotland in February 2013 found performance-driven waiting lists led to the removal of patients across a large number of health boards in Scotland.[65] Hundreds of patients were removed from waiting lists because they were 'unavailable' within an hour of being contacted. This included people who were unable to travel to the proposed appointments, enabling health boards to delay their treatment without breaching Scottish government performance targets. One health board was reported as marking a patient unavailable because of equipment shortages.[66] In some cases, waiting list managers were told to do 'whatever was required to clear the list'.[67] The twist in the tale of this type of routine list fixing is that the quick and dirty solution to meeting targets is to pay private hospitals to absorb the waiting list surplus.

In this sense, the effect of the New Public Management has not simply been to introduce new techniques of managing public sector services, but more importantly, to force the evolution of entirely new relationships between public and private sectors, and between customers and providers. And as we have seen, as power is concentrated through those new relationships, it is this concentration that creates new pressures and opportunities for fraudulent practices in government.

There has been no successful transition to a corruption-free Britain since the major periods of economic restructuring in the 1980s and 1990s. As we shall see in more detail throughout this book, corruption scandals now straddle all sectors of the public sector and the privatised economy.

Getting the Job Done

This Introduction has noted that the continuing UK privatisation bonanza is justified by 'anti-state' rhetoric. To note this is not to imply that the incursion of business into the field of politics and government has in any general sense actually precipitated a diminution of state power. Indeed, one of the great myths of the Margaret Thatcher period was that governments actually sought a 'roll-back' of the state.[68] Notwithstanding the great public sector sell-off, there occurred in the same period a process of centralising power that certainly took different forms across different parts of government and the public sector. Indeed, although the total number of public sector employees as a proportion of the total workforce has been in steady decline since 1977, the number of general government[69] employees has remained stable.[70] This is one indication that, if there has been a process of state roll-back, it has not occurred in the centres of administrative power.

For some institutions, an expansion of state expenditure enhanced their autonomy and power. Police officer numbers – which have showed a steady rise across the United Kingdom since the Thatcher period[71] – may well be a measure of the political prioritisation of this institution, just as they indicate a measure of the political impunity they have been granted (see Chapter 5). The prison estate (partly privatised) has expanded to accommodate a doubling of prisoner population since the 1980s.[72] Defence expenditure shows a similarly stable picture, with slow but consistent growth from the 1970s to the current period.[73]

Although some sections of the public sector have maintained or expanded their power and influence, the anti-statist propaganda that has been at the heart of all British governments since that of Thatcher was not merely political bluster; as welfare and security/policing budgets rose, many public services were either squeezed by real-terms spending cuts, or faced privatisation. But the key tool in disciplining the public sector was not merely budgetary. There was a major political campaign to reconstitute rather than reduce the power of state institutions throughout the 1980s and 1990s.

A limited range of similar techniques of performance measurement to those noted earlier have been introduced in police forces and the military, but in the military they do not correspond to the level of micro-reporting expected in other public sector organisations, and they have not triggered the transformation of practice or create fundamentally new ways of working.[74] While the pressure to use a range of performance measurement techniques in police forces was formalised following the introduction of the Police Reform Act 2002, the performance culture has not created the same demands. In June 2010, Home Secretary Theresa May, within weeks of the Coalition taking power, announced that performance indicators in policing would be 'abolished'. Stating boldly that the role of the police would be simply to 'cut crime',[75] May expressed a favoured political trope: that it is the job of government to get out of the way and let the police get on with the job. Now, police forces are experiencing significant resource cuts as part of the current government's 'austerity' measures. Yet at the same time, policing remains a special case – a service that cannot be exposed to the same level of scrutiny as other public services. Policing in other words is given some exemptions from the normal standards of public accountability.

The recently completed exposé of the Special Branch SDS squad by journalists Rob Evans and Paul Lewis demonstrated how a secret police unit was authorised at the highest level of government to covertly infiltrate political opposition and campaign groups. Their investigation found that the SDS was effectively given *carte blanche* by commanding officers to use 'any means necessary'. It was revealed as common practice for officers to develop sexual relationships with female campaigners and to use drugs in order to build their credibility in those groups. In one case, it is alleged that an officer carried out a firebomb attack on a department store to improve his cover. Such practices were tolerated and indeed encouraged at the highest level of command.[76] The institutional response to a wave of cases of police misconduct provides some indication that police corruption continues to be treated as a special case (see Chapters 5 and 6).

There have always been pressures on police forces to meet particular targets, and this has played in ways that have often intensified the pressure to get results, or to 'get the job done'. The fraudulent practice of police 'cuffing' (in which officers make crimes disappear from official figures by either recording them as a 'false report' or downgrading their seriousness) is perhaps the most widely used by many forces.[77]

Of course, huge security markets have been opened up, particularly in prisons and peripheral policing services, and private companies in those new markets have been the subject of a sustained chain of corruption cases. Yet the core of policing and security remains a special case – not to be exposed to the same level of scrutiny and accountability as other public services.

The general principle of impunity for policing, military and security services is intimately related to the way that those institutions are provided with the autonomy to go about their business.[78] In the public sector, policing and security institutions enjoy a comparatively insulated status.

As Chapter 7 shows, a range of deceptive and covert practices were used by military and security forces as part and parcel of the conflict in Northern Ireland, and that those practices were tolerated at the highest levels of government. State deception was used to mask collusion with paramilitaries, and as recent evidence has shown, murders and terrorist attacks were carried out with the approval of senior military and government officials. In many cases, going by the book was simply an operational obstacle to 'getting the military job done'.[79] Chapter 4 refers to James Morton's similar argument that in the police, corruption protects 'the Job'. The principle of deception is central to the *modus operandi* of the security state. This is the principle that has also shaped the rise to dominance of a largely illegal state-funded surveillance network in the United Kingdom. Information released by the whistle-blower Edward Snowden has shown us how the UK government intelligence service GCHQ has been harvesting personal data from millions of individuals' personal communications as part of the 'Prism' and 'Tempora' programmes.[80]

The institutionalisation of illegal data collection in the security sector is intimately related to the way that those institutions are provided with the autonomy to go about their business. This very same autonomy has resulted in the stunning examples of police fraud that we have seen enter the public sphere recent years. The conveyor belt of police evidence-rigging cases outlined in this Introduction, then, must be understood in the context of a set of institutions that are not to be meddled with: nothing should stand in the way of the police getting the job done.

As part of a reconstitution of state power in the neoliberal period, the institutional standing of some was clearly bolstered, not least in policing and security institutions, and those at the heart of the political establishment (see Chapter 10). In the private sector, the power of some institutions and entire industrial sectors has also been enhanced, as others have been diminished. The politically driven rise of the City of

London since the early 1980s (see Chapters 11 and 12) at the expense of British-based manufacturing industry is a clear example of this. It is openly admitted in governments across the capitalist world now that in the most economically powerful sectors of business, such as banking and finance, there are firms that are simply 'too big to fail'.[81] The political support for the relative autonomy of the police and security services, coupled to a regulatory structure that guarantees virtual impunity for some practices, all adds up to a situation in which those institutions, just like the banks, are deemed 'too big to fail'.

There has been a steady accumulation of formal police powers to arrest people and to search individuals and premises since the mid-1980s. At the same time, the system of self-regulation that is designed to provide accountability for abuses of those powers has remained ineffective.[82] Police forces and security institutions are protected by a very particular structure of impunity that places the primary responsibility for investigation of a particular institution with the same institution. Any corruption uncovered in the military and security forces will most likely be investigated by the Ministry of Defence (MoD) Police. This is the reason that few cases ever reach the public domain. In 2012, MoD police arrested three former armed forces officers in an investigation into what was described in one newspaper report as 'the biggest-ever Armed Forces corruption probe'.[83] The case has not been reported in any newspaper or news service since. The case appears to have disappeared without trace. One reason for the mysterious disappearance of such cases is down to the practice of dealing with misconduct in the armed forces behind closed doors in hearings presided over by other military officers.

The system of investigating police misconduct is ruled by a similar principle. In allegations of corruption, the same force that is the subject of the complaint will normally investigate in the first instance, before deciding whether to pass the case to the watchdog body, the Independent Police Complaints Commission (IPCC). This acts as a remarkably effective filtering mechanism. Data published by the IPCC shows that of 8,542 allegations of corruption recorded by police forces between 2008 and 2011, only 21 cases actually resulted in an investigation by the IPCC.[84] In other words, much less than one in every 400 reported complaints of corruption in the police are likely to be subject to full investigation. (For a longer discussion of the role of the IPCC, see Chapter 6.) In those public institutions accountability is sacrificed to preserve the autonomy to get the job done. The result is an enduring structure of impunity.

The following section explores in more detail how a structure of impunity has extended into the deepest levels of government, not least the government's international relations strategy, and has even reached into the work of the regulatory watchdogs at the heart of government.

Structures of Impunity

At the starting point in this inquiry into the structure of business impunity we are confronted with some fairly stark questions. How, for example, do we explain the blanket impunity given to senior executives in the finance sector? When Andrew Bailey became head of the new bank regulator the Prudential Regulation Authority, he pointed out that no senior director had faced charges or been disqualified for conduct in the wake of the financial crisis.[85] We might also ask how serious repeat offending in the financial services sector has been largely tolerated for 30 years at least (see Chapter 13)?

This section will argue that a shift in the way that the public interest is conceptualised in government has profound implications for how corruption is tolerated at the heart of government. In doing so, it will reinforce a point that has already been developed in this Introduction: that neoliberal strategies have successfully fused once-separate ideas of what constitutes the 'public' and 'private' interest.

Clearly some governments now explicitly recognise public and private interests as intimately entwined. In his speech to the annual Conservative Party Conference in 2012, David Cameron proclaimed:

> When I became Prime Minister I said to the Foreign Office: those embassies you've got ... turn them into showrooms for our cars, department stores for our fashion, and technology hubs for British start-ups. Yes, you're diplomats but you need to be our country's sales force too. ... And to those who question whether it's right to load up a plane with business-people – whether we're flying to Africa, Indonesia, to the Gulf or China ... whether we're taking people from energy, finance, technology or yes – defence ... I say – there is a global battle out there to win jobs, orders, contracts ... and in that battle I believe in leading from the front.

To support the prime minister in this current effort to turn the UK government into a commercial 'showroom', a number of senior executives of British companies are named by the Department for Business, Innovation and Skills as UK government 'trade envoys'. On the current list of UK government appointed business trade envoys are individuals representing a large number of companies that have been implicated in very serious corruption. They include HSBC (fined a record $1.9 billion for US money laundering offences in December 2012 and currently under investigation for rigging the Euribor borrowing rate)[86]; Prudential (one of the firms most implicated in the UK pension frauds in the 1980s; see Chapter 13); AMEC, Laing O'Rourke and Balfour Beatty (construction firms recently revealed by the UK Information Commissioner as having illegally paid for a 'blacklist' of trade unionist building workers operated by a secret company);[87] and Ernst & Young (the accounting firm that last year agreed to pay $123 million to the US government in a non-prosecution deal over its participation in 'the promotion of abusive tax shelters to rich individuals':[88] see Chapter 11).

In December 2013, David Cameron flew 131 business leaders to China on a UK government trade mission. The delegation to China included representatives of companies that have been involved in bribery and fraud allegations connected to Chinese officials. Among them were Andrew Witty, chief executive of pharmaceuticals giant GSK, and Patrick Horgan, representing Rolls-Royce. The former company has been convicted of, and the latter is still facing investigation for, large-scale bribery.[89] The GSK case was ongoing during the delegations visit, and a formal UK Serious Fraud Office (SFO) investigation into the Rolls-Royce allegations was launched three weeks after the delegation's trip to China.[90] Also represented in the prime minister's delegation to China was ICAP, the broker that was fined $87 million a couple of months before the trip for its role in the LIBOR rate-fixing scandal.[91]

However, when Cameron was pressed on this trip to make a statement about the GSK charges, he mounted a bizarre defence of the company, responding, 'All I'll say is that from all my dealings with GSK I know that they are a very important, very decent and strong British business.'[92] There is no grand claim being made here that the current government includes those corporations in its trade delegations out of a cynical desire to support or devalue the seriousness of the charges that face them. The reason they remain part of government trade delegations is more mundane: if governments were to vet companies for their criminal records, or their involvement in unethical practice, then those trade delegations would be sizeably diminished.

Yet the effect of their inclusion certainly undermines the basic principle that private corporations or their executives should be held accountable for their crimes. The institutional phenomena of ever closer public–private ties and the revolving door apparently in this context supports a latent indication that such crimes are not taken seriously at the highest levels of government. Indeed, the current prime minister has fairly regularly lobbied foreign governments to mitigate the punitive response to some serious corporate crimes. The UK government's *amicus curiae* brief to the US Supreme Court called on the court to review appeals court rulings against BP over the 2010 Gulf of Mexico oil spill to avoid undermining confidence in the 'vigorous and fair resolution of disputes', warning that foreign corporations would not invest in the United States 'if companies are exposed to liability for losses they did not cause'. In this case, BP had already pleaded guilty to 14 criminal charges relating to the causes of the Deepwater Horizon explosion, which killed eleven people and caused major pollution in the Gulf of Mexico. The company admitted to charges deriving from findings that senior executives withheld documents and provided false and misleading information in response to the US government's request for oil flow-rate information, and manipulated internal estimates that understated the amount of oil escaping from the well.[93]

Lobbying for clemency in such cases is a practice of government that is not confined to the present one. The consistent interventions of the UK government under Blair, Brown and Cameron to stick up for BAE Systems whenever it is accused of paying bribes in arms constitute a paradigm example of this enduring practice.

If nothing else, those examples offer clear indications of a politics of impunity that pervades British government. It is a politics that does not merely raise its head from time to time in high-profile diplomatic excursions, but is now etched into the theory and practice of regulation. Neoliberal ideas have taken hold in ways that have powerfully reshaped our notion of the public interest. The latest twist in the story of the UK government's reverence for BP underlines how far we have come in this respect. In October 2014 John Manzoni, a former BP executive who recently joined the civil service, was chosen to be the first chief executive of the civil service, with a specific remit of injecting private-sector management techniques into the management of government. An internal BP investigation had cleared Manzoni of 'serious neglect or intentional misconduct' in the Deepwater Horizon disaster, but concluded that he had failed to take the necessary steps to consider and mitigate known risks long before the disaster occurred.[94] Those criticisms apparently did not hinder his appointment or reflect badly on his managerial abilities.

The baseline idea that reshapes our notion of the public interest is that controls on business, or 'red tape', get in the way of economic efficiency and economic growth. This basic assumption has provided impetus to the championing of 'light touch' regulation by all political parties in government since the mid-1980s. And a basic assumption of a unity of interests between the 'public' interest and those of 'business' has been the principle underpinning business regulation for at least the past 40 years. The particular form that 'light-touch regulation' takes in the current government was significantly shaped by a series of policy interventions by business leaders themselves rather than politicians or public servants. Labour's favoured practice of appointing key figures from business to design how we should regulate business set the pattern for a politics of impunity. In 2004, Gordon Brown appointed Philip Hampton, chair of J. Sainsbury, and also the former finance director of Lloyds Bank, to review business regulation. His report, which recommended a *carte blanche* withdrawal of government inspection from all business watchdogs, undermined regulatory scrutiny of business across the board, from workplace safety and environmental standards to financial fraud.[95] Poachers, gamekeepers, turkeys and Christmas all come to mind.

As Seamus Milne has noted recently, 'Who can seriously doubt that politicians were encouraged to champion light touch regulation before the crash by the lure and lobbying of the banks, as well as by an overweening ideology?'[96]

In July 2008, Gordon Brown asked Winfried Bischoff, the former chair of Citigroup and now chair of Lloyds, to co-chair, with Chancellor Alistair Darling, a report 'on the future of UK financial services'. The report, published seven months after the October 2008 crash, concluded that 'the international financial services sector has been a major contributor to the wider UK economy, and we envisage this remaining the case in the future'.[97] Therefore, as the report further stated, the United Kingdom's future success would be based not on stricter regulation but 'on partnership: between the financial services industry and the wider domestic economy; and between the UK, emerging economies and their financial centres'.[98] With this kind advice – derived from the leaders of financial service companies themselves – there is little wonder that government policy on controlling the finance industry has prompted no major interruption of business as usual within the City of London. Nor has it dealt with the issue of rising inequality and soaring levels of executive pay (see Chapter 14).

This is an especially pervasive dimension of the revolving door. The door that has allowed characters like Philip Hampton and Winfried Bischoff into the heart of government has a very special function: it allows key policy decisions about how to regulate business to be made by the business world itself. Moreover the terms on which all of the major British privatisations have been conducted have, as James Meek's book *Private Island* makes clear, generally been determined by private consultants and key industry figures.[99] The result, for the public who rely on the energy supply sector, water, the railways and the NHS, has been unnecessary rising bills and endless costs imposed on the taxpayer.

Key figures from the world of business occupy key positions in business watchdogs with alarming alacrity (see Chapters 10 and 11). John Griffith-Jones, former senior partner at KPMG, is now the chair of the new Financial Conduct Authority, tasked with cleaning up corruption in the City of London. Griffith-Jones had been head of the accountancy firm when it had failed to pick up on the HBOS's reporting and credit risk problems in its audit of the bank before it collapsed.[100] John Whiting, former partner of PwC, became director of the Office of Tax Simplification in July 2010. On receiving this appointment he admitted to having 'campaigned for a simpler tax system for years'.[101]

This 'revolving watchdog' has moved equally fast in the opposite direction: especially, it seems, at the now disbanded Financial Services Authority (FSA). The most notable examples include Sally Dewar, the FSA's former head of risk who joined JP Morgan in 2011; Margaret Cole, the FSA's managing director, who joined PwC in 2012; and Hector Sants, FSA chief executive who joined Barclays Bank in January 2013 (see also Chapter 10). In the big-earning sectors of the economy, there are always revolving door opportunities.

What we are witnessing is not merely a revolving door between government and industry, but a revolving door into the places where policies and laws are written and enforced. This evidence suggests that private interests are increasingly setting the parameters of their own scrutiny and control. In other words, they are establishing the coordinates of those structures of impunity. The claim that liberal democracies can preserve the neutrality of government and 'state', and ensure their insulation from corporate interests in this context, is now barely credible.

A Political Economy of Institutional Corruption

In many ways, what is being described here is a situation that predates the current period. Crime and corruption in large corporations and some state institutions has always been tolerated, and indeed is in many cases embedded in the normal practice of those organisations. Few historians would be surprised by this litany of present-day corruption cases. The history of the British establishment is, in many ways, a history of corruption. Key debates have centred on the shift from court-centred corruption in the 16th century to parliament-centred corruption in the 18th century.

While there are debates about the extent to which this can be blamed on the rising merchant class, or the attempt by the feudal lords to maintain influence, there is one thing that historians are agreed on: the politics of corruption has been a crucial form of ruling class power-mongering for centuries. Indeed, historian Linda Levy Peck argues that throughout the 18th century 'corrupt practices were instrumental in maintaining coalitions of interest between royal ministers and the House of Commons, and welded together the aristocracy and major financiers into a single oligarchy'.[102] At this point in the early 21st century we are experiencing a peculiar moment of crisis in the UK state, the seeds of which have been planted over the past 40 years at least. It is a crisis that is likely to last for some time.

In this Introduction, we have begun to analyse this slowly germinating crisis as part of a wider 'political economy' in which institutions both public and private are shaped by particular economic strategies, and vice versa: in which economic strategies are shaped by political strategies. This book is primarily concerned with mapping a political economy of neoliberal corruption; it seeks to map how the dominant ideas that give shape to both the political and economic spheres have produced a new opportunity structure for institutional corruption. There are four features of this political economy of corruption that will be described in more detail in the chapters that follow.

First, corruption is always related to the way that dominant notions of the 'public interest' are constructed and then put into practice in policy and politics. In the neoliberal period there has been a concerted attempt to encourage policies and practices that wholly reinvent the meaning of the 'public interest'. In the early sections of this Introduction it was shown how corruption, viewed from the neoliberal perspective, is produced when there is a particular violation of the distinction between private and public interest; and this violation occurs when the state monopolises economic activity, or where economies are 'over-regulated'. This line of argument contends that overbearing state interference inevitably leads to a 'corruption' of the natural balance of market forces.[103] Yet what appears to be unfolding in many of the cases explored in this book is a different type of violation: the development of neoliberal policies that reduce the aims of 'public policy' and 'public interest' to the pursuit of the interests of private profit-making corporations. A clear distinction between public and private, then, might still be made in constitutional or political theory, but this distinction is increasingly difficult to discern in political practice. As we have seen, the most visible example of the way that the public interest is being coupled to the interests of business is found in the revolving door of senior appointments between business and government. It is this dynamic – a more open attempt to subsume the public interest to the interest of private corporations – that has brought the rationales, practices, and even the morals and values, of the private sector into the public sector, and at the same time is further undermining the independence of policy-making and regulatory processes.

Second, the opportunities for corruption in a given society are related to the structure of regulation that applies to particular practices. Although some individuals may be caught and criminalised for institutional corruption (as in the current round of prosecutions of bankers for LIBOR offences), such cases are rare and tend not to penalise the most senior architects and beneficiaries. A structure of impunity continues to protect 'special case' state institutions policing and security. In the neoliberal period, this structure of impunity has certainly extended further into the corporate sector. We are yet to see what the current crisis in the IPCC will lead to, but the reforms offered thus far are unlikely to do much to break the structure of police impunity (see Chapter 6).

Third, levels of corruption are related to the way that institutional power is concentrated in a given social system. Neoliberalism concentrates power in particular institutions in both the public and private sectors. We must be careful to avoid an over-simplified zero-sum analysis of the relationship between public and private institutions, which sees the power of corporations rise as the power of the state declines. During the neoliberal period, some state institutions have maintained or extended their power; and not all business sectors have flourished. The rise to dominance of finance capital has enabled some sectors of the economy to develop new practices and new commercial activities which continue relatively unhindered despite the huge potential risks attached to them. There are some corporations and some industries that have been constructed as untouchable or 'too big to fail', and are therefore relatively immune from invasive state controls. Further, there are some public institutions, such as police forces and security agencies, that have become more insulated, or have sustained their 'moral capital'[104] under current political and economic conditions, and at the same time have exploited the conditions of neoliberalism to extend their powers. The consequences are profound in terms of the ways in which inequalities of power have been embedded, and opportunities to challenge power have been neutralised.

Fourth, corruption is produced when the means of particular policies and practices are subjugated to the ends. The subjugation of means to ends in the production of outcomes in both the private and the public sectors is perhaps one of the least acknowledged and yet is certainly the most socially damaging feature of neoliberal capitalism. This process, as the chapters of the book will show, profoundly alters the ways that institutions are structured and the practices that are developed to meet particular outcomes. This has been a theme that cuts across much of the analysis in this Introduction and in the chapters to follow. The ends are subjugated to the means when police officers falsify evidence with the purpose of 'getting the job done'; when bribes are made to secure lucrative foreign contracts; and when waiting list figures are falsified to achieve impossible targets. The renewed focus on very specific measurables in the state sector, and the intensification of profit-seeking in the private sector, as ends in themselves, have devalued the integrity of the means by which those ends are achieved (even when they are clearly socially damaging or illegal). As this book will show, corruption and institutional fraud are very often the means to achieve a crudely measured end.

Analysed in the context of a wider political economy, then, corruption appears not merely as an *effect* of power, but is a *means* by which institutions maintain and concentrate power. None of the examples of corruption analysed in this book can be explained merely as the result of opportunistic individual pursuit of gains; in each case, it is the competitive advantages and strategies of *institutional* domination that are enhanced by corrupt practices. The point that corruption is a systematic power-mongering strategy that enhances the power of institutions is supported when we analyse the form that corruption takes in Britain. Bribery is not the *principal* motivation of police officers in any of the cases of corruption mentioned in this Introduction or in the various contributions to this book.[105] In most cases, if police or public officials did receive payment, this payment could only be measured indirectly in the form of promotion or career protection. This is the type of corruption that we can observe in some so-called 'strong' states. It is a brand of corruption that characterises the British neoliberal state: a corruption that means individual police officers may be less open to bribes and are more likely to be involved in forms of corruption that protect and extend *institutional* power.

In so far as it directs its gaze at British institutions, the purpose of this book is to stimulate debate on how corruption arises, develops and is sustained at the *core* rather than the periphery of the global social order. And yet the function and effect of corruption is the same whether we find it in the core or the periphery. One point is made *ad nauseum* in relation to the 'weak' or 'under-developed' states of the Global South:

that corruption allows elites to accumulate wealth and consolidate their power as elites. There is actually a great deal of analysis of the relationship between corruption and *class* power in African, Asian and Latin American nations, a form of class power normally described as kleptocracy.[106] We don't talk very much about the relationship between class power and corruption in the context of 'strong' or 'developed' states of the Global North. And yet this very clearly is the function of the political economy of institutional corruption in Britain: to extend and embed the class power of elites.

Corruption as Class Power

It is only when we compare the structure of impunity protecting the perpetrators of institutional misdeeds with the harsh punitiveness that now faces the poor in Britain that we fully understand how corruption operates as a form of class power. The rise in the number of convictions that have led to the doubling of the UK prison population since the 1980s, noted earlier, is clearly not explained by a rise in convictions of rich members of the elite. The majority of custodial sentences handed down by the courts in England and Wales have consistently been for property-related crimes (burglary, robbery, theft, handling stolen goods, fraud and forgery).[107] Yet it is not the grand property theft of the elite that is being punished here. In the year ending 2013, the UK Serious Fraud Office prosecuted 20 individuals.[108] By contrast, in the same year the Crown Prosecution Service prosecuted just under 40,000 burglars.[109]

The way that different social groups are policed – or not – is the most obvious and visible manifestation of the way capitalist states in the Global North ensure that the class power of elites is guaranteed in this 'age of fraud' or 'turbo-corruption'. It is an observation that is almost too obvious to mention because we take it for granted: the vast policing resources that we have in Britain are not mobilised to deal with elite corruption, but to control groups that fall much further down the social hierarchy (see Chapter 4). Despite its glaring obviousness, this is an observation that is never seriously debated in public discussions and debates about institutional corruption. The class bias – and the racism – of policing in Britain is most obvious to the communities and organisations that actively oppose police corruption and racism (see Chapters 5 and 6). Struggles around corruption are very often struggles to expose the practices that provide a shield of impunity to perpetrators (see Chapters

7 and 8). Invariably those struggles against corruption are therefore a challenge, not merely to the order of policing, but to the more general order of things. Struggles to oppose the power that is concentrated in particular state institutions are invariably struggles against the use of class power. If the immediate function of the structure of impunity that we find in policing is to guarantee that the legitimacy of policing remains intact, it has a more socially significant function: to ensure the sustainability of a social order that police forces are expected to protect. And at this particular moment, the social order in Britain has a particularly unequal character.

The corruption that appears to be institutionalised in politics, in policing and security and in the finance sector has not disrupted the orderly progression of a system that guarantees equally shocking levels of inequality. Social class inequalities have been institutionalised in early 21st-century Britain at levels that could not have been imagined even in Margaret Thatcher's wildest dreams. As Chapter 14 reports, in the 1980s the salary of the average company CEO equated to fifteen or twenty times the national average wage, a multiplier that is obscene enough on its own terms. Yet today CEOs on average collect 160 times the pay of the average wage earner. The commanding position in the British state is occupied by a financial plutocracy that rules from the City of London (see Chapters 11 and 12). The corrupting consequences of this commanding status of finance capital – the centrifugal force around which political strategies and social policies must now be organised – is exemplified by the revolving door in politics (see Chapter 10) and the commissioning of all major public building projects (see Chapter 9).

The immunity that the financial services industry now enjoys, even in the face of the most clear-cut habitual repeat offending (see Chapter 13), looks increasingly like a mirror image of the self-regulation mechanisms that protect the police and security services.

The chapters in this book focus our attention on a very specific regime of (neoliberal) power that has been cultivated, nurtured and forcefully imposed in the UK state since the 1980s. It is a regime of power that encourages a particular political economy of corruption. What is significant in the contexts that we explore is that those strategies are pursued through established institutions that often have very long histories (see Chapter 8). It is in many of those institutions that we now find particular rationales (see Chapter 3) that reshape the way we think about the world, and this shapes a new morality (see Chapter 2) of profiteering that would have been considered shocking and unthinkable not so long ago. It is no longer shocking to think of healthcare or education as spheres of activity that must be open to huge corporations to develop new forms of profit extraction.

Just as corruption is becoming viewed as a characteristic of the political and business elite in the United Kingdom, so it has provoked widespread revulsion and resistance. In the past few years we have seen the emergence of new movements to challenge corporate tax evasion, criminality in journalism and new community groups that challenge police power. Simmering under all of the contributions that follow are campaigns and movements to dismantle the conditions that have institutionalised corruption in the UK state and in the British corporate sector. Many of the contributors to this book are involved in organisations that have been instrumental in exposing and opposing the institutional corruption in Britain. Those organisations include Corporate Watch, Democratic Audit, the High Pay Centre, the Hillsborough Family Support Group, the Hillsborough Justice Campaign, Inquest, the Northern Police Monitoring Project, the Pat Finucane Centre, Spinwatch and the Tax Justice Network. A challenge to the institutional corruption of the core has begun, and this challenge will undoubtedly gather momentum as corruption is continually revealed as a central mode of power-mongering in contemporary Britain.

Notes

1   Binham, C. (2014) 'SFO secures extra funds to pursue Rolls-Royce investigation', *Financial Times*, 19 January. www.ft.com/cms/s/0/e8d7939e-811a-11e3-b3d5-00144feab7de.html#axzz2y6TsgtJ7

2   The London Interbank Offered Rate (LIBOR) is the rate at which inter-bank lending is calculated. It is estimated that the rate is tied to a market of $350–500 trillion in derivatives and related financial instruments. One bank, Citigroup, has calculated that in the first quarter of 2009, a fall by 0.25 per cent would earn the bank $936 million in a quarter. The same analysis has shown that the same bank had understated its borrowing costs by an average of 0.12 percentage points from August 2007 to August 2008. For a more detailed analysis of this case, see Snider, C. and Youle, T. (2010) 'Does the LIBOR reflect banks' borrowing costs?' 10 April 2010. Available at SSRN: http://ssrn.com/abstract=1569603 or http://dx.doi.org/10.2139/ssrn.1569603. Even if a much small level of under-reporting is replicated across all of the 18 member banks in LIBOR, the annual costs of LIBOR rate fixing would still probably be measured in the range of tens of billions of dollars.

3   In April 2013, US regulators subpoenaed a number of banks and brokers in an investigation into the manipulation of ISDAfix, another inter-bank rate. ISDAfix is a benchmark set by 15 of the world's largest banks and used

to calculate the costs of interest rate swaps, a market estimated to have a value of over $300 trillion. There are ongoing investigations into the rigging of ISDAfix by the US Commodity Futures Trading Commission, the UK Financial Conduct Authority and German regulator BaFin.

4   Goodway, N. (2014) 'Barclays excluded from FCA deal in bid to cut FOREX fine', *Independent*, 12 November.

5   Evans, R. and Lewis, P. (2013a) *Undercover: The True Story of Britain's Secret Police*, London: Faber & Faber.

6   Independent Police Complaints Commission (2013) 'IPCC finds failings in the working practices of Southwark Sapphire Unit between July 2008 and September 2009', press release, 26 February. www.ipcc.gov.uk/news/ipcc-finds-failings-working-practices-southwark-sapphire-unit-between-july-2008-and-september

7   Evans, R. and Lewis, P. (2013b) 'Metropolitan police anti-corruption unit investigated over payments', *Guardian*, Tuesday 22 May.

8   Mark Ellison QC's review of the Stephen Lawrence case focused on this investigation, conducted between 1994 and 1998, known as Operation Othona. The review noted: 'We have very recently been informed that in 2003 there was "mass-shredding" of the surviving hard copy reports generated by Operation Othona' (2014). *The Stephen Lawrence Independent Review: Possible Corruption and the Role of Undercover Policing in the Stephen Lawrence Case, Summary of Findings*, HC 1094, London: Home Office.

9   In a story published on 6 December 2011, the *Independent* reported that Collins had been filmed by the Bureau of Investigative Journalism claiming that he had successfully lobbied David Cameron to speak to the Chinese premier on behalf of a client within 24 hours of being requested to do so. This case, incidentally, didn't prevent Nick Clegg, the deputy prime minister, from appointing the Bell Pottinger executive Stephen Lotinga as his director of communications three years later. Lotinga was named by Collins as a key fixer who could facilitate access to senior Liberal Democrats: www.telegraph.co.uk/news/politics/10745156/Nick-Clegg-employs-cash-for-access-lobbyist.html

10   On 25 March 2012 the *Sunday Times* released a video showing Cruddas offering access to the prime minister or the chancellor of the Exchequer for donations in the region of £250,000. In the video Cruddas says, 'Two hundred grand to 250 is Premier League .... what you would get is, when we talk about your donations the first thing we want to do is get you at the Cameron/Osborne dinners. You do really pick up a lot of information and when you see the prime minister, you're seeing David Cameron, not the prime minister. But within that room everything is confidential – you can ask him practically any question you want. If you're unhappy about something, we will listen to you and put it into the policy committee at number 10 – we feed all feedback to the policy committee.' Following the release of the video Cruddas resigned from his position as Tory co-treasurer. In June 2013 Cruddas won a libel case against Times Newspapers for defamation and malicious falsehood. The Times Newspapers appeal against this ruling is ongoing.

11   BBC News online, 2 June 2013, www.bbc.co.uk/news/uk-politics-22742327

12   Social Investigations Report, '142 peers have financial links to companies involved in private health care', 26 March 2012. http://socialinvestigations. blogspot.co.uk/2012/03/141-peers-have-financial-links-to.html

13   See her business profile at Bloomberg Businessweek: http://investing.business-week.com/research/stocks/private/person.asp?personId=42375726&priv-capId=19685&previousCapId=19685&previousTitle=Cinven%20Limited

14   Molloy, C. (2013) 'Milburn, the NHS, and Britain's "revolving door"', *Open Democracy*, 23 May, www.opendemocracy.net/ournhs/caroline-molloy/milburn-nhs-and-britains-revolving-door.

15   Kelly, M. (2013) 'Alistair Darling paid thousands by NHS privatisation company', newsnetscotland.com, http://newsnetscotland.com/index.php/scottish-news/7709-alistair-darling-paid-thousands-by-nhs-privatisation-company. One impressive audience member at the second televised Scottish Referendum debate in August 2014 attacked Darling for his links to private healthcare, telling him: 'When you're at your fancy dinners I hope you feel Aneurin Bevan sitting on your shoulders' (*Herald*, 26 August 2014).

16   Robert Barrington, executive director of Transparency International UK, *Today*, BBC Radio 4, 10 May 2013.

17   See for example Rose-Ackerman, S. (1999) *Corruption and Government: Causes, Consequences and Reform*, Cambridge: Cambridge University Press, p, 18.

18   Following the bombastic term used by right-wing theorist Edward Luttwak, 'turbo-capitalism'; Luttwak, E. (2000) *Turbo-Capitalism: Winners and Losers in the Global Economy*, New York: Harper Perennial.

19   Shore, P. and Haller, D. 'Sharp practice: anthropology and the study of corruption', in Haller, D. and Shore, P. (eds) (2005) *Corruption: Anthropological Perspectives*, London: Pluto, pp. 1–2.

20   Haller and Shore (2005).

21   Bayley, C. (1989) *Imperial Meridian: The British Empire and the World 1780–1830*, Harlow, Essex: Pearson.

22   Chomsky, N. (2004) *Hegemony or Survival: America's Quest for Global Dominance*, London: Penguin, pp. 44–5.

23   The term IFI normally denotes the 'Bretton Woods' institutions: the World Bank and the International Monetary Fund. The term as used here refers to those institutions.

24   Brown, E. and Cloke, J. (2004) 'Neoliberal reform, governance and corruption in the South: assessing the international anti-corruption crusade', *Antipode*, vol. 36, no. 2, pp. 272–94.

25   Carrier, J. (1997) 'Introduction', in Carrier, J. (ed.), *Meanings of Market: The Free Market in Western Culture*, Oxford: Berg.

26   Ibid.; see also Le Billon, P. (2005) 'Corruption, reconstruction and oil governance in Iraq', *Third World Quarterly*, vol. 26, no. 4–5, pp. 685–703.

27   Sampson, S. (2005) 'Integrity warriors: global morality and the anti-corruption movement in the Balkans', in Haller and Shore (2005).

28   Hellman, J., Jones, G. and Kaufmann, D. (2000) '"Seize the state, seize the day"': state capture, corruption, and influence in transition', Policy Research Working Paper 2444, Washington: World Bank Institute.

29 Transparency International, *Corruption Perceptions Index: In Detail*, video at 1.03–1.08, www.transparency.org/cpi2013/in_detail

30 This position on 'state capture' is replicated across IFIs; see for example an IMF paper, Hellman, J. and Kaufmann, D. (2001) 'Confronting the challenge of state capture in transition economies', *Finance and Development*, vol. 38, no. 3.

31 Sampson (2005), p. 129.

32 Gupta, A. (2005) 'Narrating the state of corruption', in Haller and Shore (2005).

33 Rose-Ackerman, S. (1978) *Corruption: A Study in Political Economy*, Cambridge: Academic Press, p. 208.

34 Dine, J. (2007) 'The capture of corruption: complexity and corporate culture', *McGeorge Global Business & Development Law Journal*, p. 269.

35 *Guardian*, 10 April 2003.

36 Provisional Authority, the temporary administration installed by the US, UK and Australian governments under the authority of UN Security Council resolution 1441.

37 Whyte, D. (2007) 'The crimes of neoliberal rule in Occupied Iraq', *British Journal of Criminology*, vol. 47, no. 2, pp. 177–95.

38 Government of Iraq (2005) *Iraq National Development Strategy 2005–2007*, Baghdad: Government of Iraq.

39 Klein, N. (2008) *The Shock Doctrine: The Rise of Disaster Capitalism*, London: Penguin.

40 Iraq Revenue Watch (2004) 'Iraq fire sale: CPA rushes to give away billions in Iraqi oil revenues', briefing no. 7, New York: Open Society Institute.

41 Special Inspector General for Iraq Reconstruction (2005) Report to US Congress, 30 January.

42 Whyte (2007), see also Herring, E. and Ragwala, G. (2006) *Iraq in Fragments: The Occupation and its Legacy*, New York: Cornell University Press, pp. 252–7.

43 Robison, R. (2009) 'Strange bedfellows: political alliances in the making of neo-liberal governance', in Hout, W. and Robison, R. (eds), *Governance and the Depoliticisation of Development*, London: Routledge, p. 22.

44 Hadiz, V. and Robison, R. (2005) 'Neoliberal reforms and illiberal consolidations: the Indonesian paradox', *Journal of Development Studies*, vol. 41, no. 2, pp. 220–41.

45 Pablo Saba, R. and Manzetti, L. (1997) 'Privatization in Argentina: the implications for corruption', *Crime, Law and Social Change*, no. 25, pp. 335–6.

46 Wiegratz, J. (2012) 'The neoliberal harvest: the proliferation and normalization of economic fraud in a market society', in Winlow, S. and Atkinson, R. (eds), *New Directions in Crime and Deviancy*, London: Routledge.

47 Sissener, T. (2001) *Anthropological Perspectives on Corruption*, Bergen, Norway: Chr. Michelsen Institute, p. 4.

48 Bellamy Foster, J., Chesney, R. and Jonna, J. (2011) 'The internationalization of monopoly capital', *Monthly Review*, vol. 63, no. 2.

49 Vitali, S., Glattfelder, J. B. and Battiston, S. (2011) 'The network of global corporate control', *PLoS ONE*, vol. 6, no. 1: e25995. doi:10.1371/journal.pone.0025995

50 Whyte, D. (2013) 'Market patriotism: the liberal mask slips', in Fisher, R. (ed.) *Managing Democracy, Managing Dissent*, London: Corporate Watch.

51 Darling, A. (2012) *Back from the Brink: 1000 Days at Number 11*, London: Atlantic.

52 Boffey, D. (2012) 'Public services, big earners: a sector-by-sector analysis', *Guardian*, 25 February.

53 Du Gay, P. and Salaman, G. (1992) 'The cult(ure) of the customer', *Journal of Management Studies*, vol. 29, no. 5.

54 Clarke, J., Gewirtz, S. and McLaughlin, E. (eds) (2000) *New Managerialism, New Welfare*, London: Sage and Open University Press;

55 Du Gay and Salaman (1992).

56 The NHS Co-operation and Competition Panel is the regulatory body that encourages competition in health care.

57 Cave, T. (2011) 'Private healthcare group lobbied competition body for NHS inquiry', *Spinwatch*, 29 July, www.spinwatch.org/index.php/evel-spin-off/item/5347-private-healthcare-group-lobbied-competition-body-for-nhs-inquiry

58 For example, an investigation of the privatisation of British Telecom in 1987 found 101 MPs and 34 MPs' wives had purchased shares in the company. The beneficiaries were mostly Conservative MPs who had voted for privatisation in the House of Commons. Some, perhaps most notoriously Keith Best, were found to have illegally posted multiple applications. While Best was sent to jail for his frauds, he was released almost immediately on appeal after having spent a long weekend in Brixton Prison. See Doig, A. (1990) *Westminister Babylon: Sex, Money and Scandal in British Politics*, London: W. H. Allen.

59 Glynn, P., Kobrin, S. and Maim, M. (1997) 'The globalisation of corruption', in Elliot, K. A. (ed.), *Political Corruption – Economic Aspects*, Washington DC: Institute for International Economics, p. 11.

60 *Independent*, 28 September 2012.

61 Green, P. and Ward, T. (2004) *State Crime: Governments, Violence and Corruption*, London: Pluto, p. 14.

62 Pollock, A. (2004) *NHS Plc: The Privatisation of Our Health Care*, London: Verso, pp. 220–5.

63 'Drug companies committing "highway robbery"', *Commisioning GP*, 17 July 2013, www.commissioning.gp/news/article/1040/drug-companies-committing-highway-robbery/17/

64 *Telegraph*, 20 June 2013.

65 Auditor General for Scotland (2013) *Management of Patients on NHS Waiting Lists*, Edinburgh: Auditor General for Scotland.

66 Auditor General for Scotland (2013).

67 *Herald*, 21 December 2012.

68 Coleman, R., Sim, J., Tombs, S. and Whyte, D. (2009) 'Introduction', in Coleman, R., Sim, J., Tombs, S. and Whyte, D. (eds), *State, Crime, Power*, London: Sage.

69 The figures cited here follow the ONS definition of 'general government' which comprises all levels of government (central, state, regional and

local) and includes core ministries, agencies, departments and non-profit institutions that are controlled and mainly financed by public authorities.

70 Cribb, J., Disney, R. and Sibieta, L. (2014) *The Public Sector Workforce: Past, Present and Future*, IFS Briefing Note BN145, London: Institute for Fiscal Studies.

71 Berman, G. (2013) *Police Service Strength*, Standard Note SN0063, London: House of Commons Library.

72 Sim, J. (2009) *Punishment and Prisons: Power and the Carceral State*, London: Sage.

73 Berman, G. (2013) *Defence Expenditure*, Standard Note SN/SG/113, London: House of Commons Library.

74 Although ironically, academic Michael Levi has pointed out that one casualty of New Public Management reforms in the police was the investigation and detection of fraud at precisely the same time that 'out-sourcing of public sector contracts generated more corruption and public sector fraud enquiries for the police'. Levi, M. (2008) 'Policing fraud and organised crime', in Newburn, T. (ed.), *Handbook of Policing*, Cullompton: Willan, p. 532.

75 *Independent,* 29 June 2010.

76 Evans and Lewis (2013a).

77 Young, M. (1990) *An Inside Job. Policing and Police Culture in Britain*, Oxford: Claredon Press; Burrows, J., Tarling, R., Mackie, A., Lewis, R. and Taylor, G. (2000) *Review of Police Forces's Crime Recording Practices*, Home Office Research Study 204, London. Home Office; Patrick, R. (2009) 'Performance management, gaming and police practice: a study of changing police behaviour in England and Wales during the era of New Public Management', PhD thesis, University of Birmingham.

78 Independent Police Complaints Commission (2012) *Corruption in the Police Service in England and Wales: Second Report – A Report Based on The IPCC's Experience from 2008 To 2011*, London: The Stationery Office.

79 Rolston, B. (2005) 'An effective mask for terror: democracy, death squads and Northern Ireland', *Crime, Law and Social Change*, vol. 44, no. 2.

80 Harding, L. (2014) *The Snowden Files: The Inside Story of the World's Most Wanted Man*, London: Vintage.

81 Sorkin, A. (2009) *Too Big To Fail*, New York: Viking.

82 Sanders, A. and Young, R. (2008) 'Police powers', in Newburn, T. (ed.), *Handbook of Policing*, Cullompton: Willan.

83 Hughes, C. (2012) 'Four arrests in armed forces corruption probe', *Mirror*, 12 January.

84 IPCC (2012).

85 *Guardian*, 16 April 2013.

86 Viswanatha, A. and Wolf, B. (2012) 'HSBC to pay $1.9 billion U.S. fine in money-laundering case', Reuters online, 11 December, 18:15, www.reuters.com/article/2012/12/11/us-hsbc-probe-idUSBRE8BA05M20121211; Titcomb, J. (2014) 'Three banks accused of rigging Euribor', Telegraph online, 20 May, www.telegraph.co.uk/finance/newsbysector/banksandfinance/10843666/Three-banks-accused-of-rigging-Euribor.html

87 Whyte, D. (2013) 'Policing for whom?' *Criminal Justice Matters*, issue 94, December.

88 Novack, J. (2013) 'Ernst & Young pays $123 million, avoids tax shelter prosecution', *Forbes* online, 3 January, 18:31, www.forbes.com/sites/janetnovack/2013/03/01/ernst-young-pays-123-million-avoids-tax-shelter-prosecution/

89 *Guardian*, 23 October 2013.

90 BBC News online (2013) 'Rolls-Royce: Serious Fraud Office launches probe', 23 December, 13.09: www.bbc.co.uk/news/business-25490876

91 BBC News online (2013) 'Libor: ICAP fined $87m and three traders charged with fraud', 25 September, 19.02: www.bbc.co.uk/news/business-24250750

92 Reuters, 3 December 2009, http://uk.reuters.com/article/2013/12/03/uk-britain-china-trade-gsk -idUKBRE9B217T20131203

93 Department of Justice Office of Public Affairs (2013) 'BP Exploration and Production Inc. pleads guilty, is sentenced to pay record $4 billion for crimes surrounding Deepwater Horizon incident', press release, 29 January, www.justice.gov/opa/pr/bp-exploration-and-production-inc-pleads-guilty-sentenced-pay-record-4-billion-crimes

94 Neville, S. (2014) 'Former BP man secures role as Whitehall's first chief executive', FT.Com, 2 October, www.ft.com/cms/s/0/a0a9a8c4-4a18-11e4-bc07-00144feab7de.html#axzz3GDYVmBPu

95 Tombs, S. and Whyte, D. (2010) *Regulatory Surrender: Death, Injury and the Non-Enforcement of Law*, Liverpool: Institute of Employment Rights.

96 Milne, S. (2013) 'Corporate power has turned Britain into a corrupt state', *Guardian*, 4 June.

97 HM Treasury (2009) 'UK International Financial Services – the future: a report from UK based financial services leaders to the government', London: HM Treasury, p. 6.

98 HM Treasury (2009), p. 7.

99 Meek, J. (2014) *Private Island*, London: Verso.

100 Alan MacDougall (managing director, Pirc), letter to editor, *Financial Times*, 9 April 2013, www.ft.com/cms/s/0/b5ac2584-a056-11e2-88b6-00144feabdc0.html#axzz2Q8jOPVQW

101 *Telegraph*, 21 July 2010.

102 Levy Peck, L. (1990) 'Corruption and political development in early modern Britain', in Heidenheimer, A., Johnston, M. and LeVine, V. (eds), *Political Corruption: A Handbook*, New Brunswick: Transaction.

103 Shore, P. and Haller, D. 'Sharp practice: anthropology and the study of corruption', in Haller and Shore (2005).

104 This phrase is borrowed from Steve Tombs: 'Thinking about white-collar crime' in Lindgren, S. (ed.) (2001) *White Collar Crime Research. Old Views and Future Potentials*, BRA report, Stockholm: National Council for Crime Prevention:

105 Although the revelation of the Metropolitan Police 'mass-shredding' of documents from a Met investigation into corrupt practices noted earlier is relevant here, the review by Mark Ellison QC revealed evidence that much of the material from 'Operation Othona' contained details of 'police officers

... sharing reward payouts with informants, selling confidential police intelligence to criminals' (*Independent*, 24 March 2014).

106 For differing takes on this perspective, see Simon Fan, C. (2006) 'Kleptocracy and corruption', *Journal of Comparative Economics*, vol. 34, no. 1, pp. 57–74; and Bayart, J. F. and Ellis, S. (1999) *The Criminalization of the State in Africa*, Bloomington, Ind.: Indiana University Press.

107 Ministry of Justice (2013) *Criminal Justice Statistics Quarterly Update to March 2013 England and Wales*. London: National Statistics.

108 Masters, B. (2013) 'Serious Fraud Office reports rising costs and fall in conviction rates', *Financial Times* online, 17 July, www.ft.com/cms/s/0/8462c362-ee34-11e2-a325-

109 Ministry of Justice (see note 107).

Part I

Neoliberalism and Corruption

1

Moving Beyond a Narrow Definition of Corruption

David Beetham

In his introduction to this collection David Whyte refers to the World Bank's definition of corruption as 'the abuse of public office for private gain', and he challenges the limitation of corruption implicit in this definition to the personal gain of office holders. Like him, I want to propose a wider conception which serves better to capture the different concerns of the contributors to this volume. These concerns include the following:

- the capture of regulators and public officials by the corporate sector and its consultants
- the ever-revolving door between government and business
- the preferential access to ministers and officials enjoyed by the wealthy and powerful
- corporate funding of political parties and politicians' private offices in return for favours
- the use of tax havens and other mechanisms to deprive the public purse of revenue
- cover-ups of wrongdoing by officials to protect their personal reputation and position
- police collusion in illegal information gathering by journalists.

Of these, perhaps only the last two could fit into a narrow World Bank definition of corruption as 'the abuse of public office for private gain', and we therefore need a wider conception of corruption if we are to capture what is distinctively worrying about these various practices. For that wider conception I propose 'the distortion and subversion of the public realm in the service of private interests'. Crucial to this conception is the idea of a public realm which is more than simply the sum of public offices and their occupants. It includes the idea that the activities of government should serve a general or public interest rather than a set of private ones, and that there should be a transparent public debate to determine where the general interest lies. Such a debate is short-circuited by many of the practices outlined above, which systematically favour a limited set of special interests at the expense of more general ones. These practices make money, and the personal contacts and influence money can buy, a major determinant of public policy, even if the money does not directly line the pockets of office holders themselves. It is for this reason that we need a wider conception of corruption which goes beyond the narrow World Bank definition quoted above. To suggest that this is too normative a conception ignores the fact that any conception of 'corruption' must have a normative element, as the World Bank term 'abuse of office' itself entails.

Once we have articulated what is disturbing about the practices listed – what I call 'the distortion and subversion of the public realm in the service of private interests' – we need to explain why they have gained such a foothold in UK politics over the past few decades. The explanation lies in the privatisation of public services begun under Margaret Thatcher and continued by governments of all complexions ever since. Some services have been wholly privatised (public utilities), others contracted out by central or local government or public bodies like the NHS, while the construction and management of public infrastructure and buildings have been funded through the private finance initiative (PFI) programme. This record of privatisation is identified in the Introduction to this book as key to many of the concerns of the contributors to this volume.

Privatisation has itself been responsible for distortions of the public interest in the provision of essential public services, in which taxpayers have formed an impotent cash-cow for private profit. The utility providers constitute a de facto monopoly, inadequately regulated, which squeezes consumers in the interest of shareholders and directors' fat remuneration packages. The privatisation of the railways has led to a fragmentation of services, the most expensive train fares in Europe and more than double the level of taxpayer subsidy that was provided under British Rail. Private service contractors are free to walk away from their contracts if they prove unprofitable, as has happened with the rail infrastructure company, with the modernisation of the London underground, with the failure of complex IT systems, and also in the health and local government sectors.[1] Or they provide an inadequate service, which can never be challenged because their terms of service are subject to commercial confidentiality clauses and immune from freedom of information scrutiny. Failures or fraudulent practices by private companies in the delivery of services, such as by G4S, Serco and Atos, prove no barrier to lucrative new contracts. Even PFI contracts can be sold on to third parties which use high interest charges and offshore jurisdictions to avoid paying corporation tax – a procedure that undermines the already questionable arithmetic on which the supposed advantage of the PFI system was originally based (see also Chapter 9).[2] And the process of privatisation itself can deprive taxpayers of much-needed revenue, as happened with the selling off of the Royal Mail, where the same company as advised the government on the price for shares was given a major allocation, and was thus able to benefit from the almost doubling in their price shortly after trading started.[3]

Such defects give the lie to the neoliberal dogma that the market is always superior to the public sector. In his book *The Great Divestiture*, Massimo Florio showed how the supposed gains in productivity and efficiency arising from privatisation had proved illusory, and that it brought all kinds of negative consequences for social welfare and the United Kingdom's industrial development.[4] Yet beyond the direct distortions of the public interest involved in so much privatisation, the process has also served to undermine the capacity and integrity of government itself. The hollowing out of government at central and local levels that result from so much outsourcing deprives government of the skills, experience and personnel that flow from providing services directly, and gives the private sector a key advantage when negotiating service contracts. It also leads to the burgeoning government use of private consultancies and business personnel in key positions, who will invariably recommend further privatisation and outsourcing as the solution to any public sector problem.[5]

More serious even than the loss of capacity is the loss of government integrity. With private firms hovering like vultures over the easy prey afforded by the guaranteed income of taxpayer-funded contracts, there is a ready market for the employment of newly retired ministers, civil servants and military commanders who can bring their inside knowledge and contacts to bear on the commissioning process. And the latter, in turn, while still in office have a considerable incentive to conduct themselves with an eye to their future well-remunerated employment as consultants or directors in the private sector. Hence the rapidly revolving door between government and business, which is documented in detail but inadequately policed by the so-called Advisory Committee on Business Appointments (ACoBA; see also Chapter 10). A glance at its website is enough to reveal the large numbers regularly marching through this revolving door.[6]

Then there is the huge corporate lobbying industry, enjoying in the words of a Commons Public Administration Select Committee Report, 'privileged access and disproportionate influence ... which is related to the amount of money they are able to bring to bear on the political process'.[7] Their money funds political parties, think tanks enjoying charitable status and politicians' private offices, and can effectively purchase seats in the second chamber of parliament.[8]

These practices may not meet the World Bank's narrow definition of corruption, but they certainly count as such if we expand the conception in the way I have proposed. They all fit squarely as examples of the distortion and subversion of the public realm in the service of private interests, once we understand 'the public realm' to include more than the sum of public offices, and 'private interests' to involve more than the personal advantage of office holders themselves.

To be sure, the public is slowly waking up to the perverse effects of market penetration into the heart of the public sector. People are aware that they are being ripped off by the utility providers and the rail companies. They don't want further privatisation or marketisation in the NHS. Through the activities of the Occupy Movement and UK Uncut they know about the scandals of corporate tax avoidance and the widespread use of tax havens. They are unhappy about the power of corporate lobbying and the revolving door, with former ministers selling themselves, in the words of former Labour government minister Stephen Byers, 'like a cab for hire'.[9] Yet they lack a coherent narrative which links these different phenomena together, explains their common causes and systematic effects. This would involve not only the kind of analysis offered here, but a changed evaluation of government – not as a negative obstacle to economic and social well-being, but as a necessary contributor to it.[10]

It would also require an even fuller conception of the public realm than was articulated at the outset of this chapter. Its essence lies not only in a sense of the common or public good, but also in a set of distinctive values, relationships and ways of working. Its core is a common citizenship and a sense of mutual responsibility when we fall on hard times. Its distinctive ethos is one of public service – that furthering the common good is a worthy calling, deserving of the best talents. And its goal is a quality of service provision available equally to all whatever their background or level of resources. Against this the market promotes individual self-interest, aggressive competition and unchecked inequality, while also offering the illusion of unlimited choice to the consumer. Such features may indeed have their place in the provision of consumer goods and some kinds of service. Yet they need to be complemented by a strong and distinctive public realm if market values are not to end up destroying the fabric of civilised society.[11]

What we have been witnessing over the past 30 years has been the systematic erosion of this public realm as more and more of the public sector has been privatised, outsourced, or made subject to market principles. It is this process that has led to the long list of abuses catalogued at the outset of this chapter and by other contributors to this book. Is it any wonder that ministers, civil servants and military leaders should expect to use their office as a means of leveraging fat jobs in the private sector when those they rub shoulders with on a daily basis are doing the same in their own business sphere? Is it any wonder that those in the corporate sector should employ any means and connections they can to win lucrative contracts funded by our taxes, or work to promote further business opportunities when they are seconded to government service? Is it any wonder that politicians who look to the corporate sector to fund their electoral campaigns should be ready to return the favour with sympathetic policies and the offer of lordships?

Instead of the public sphere constituting a separate life domain, with its own values, relationships and ways of working, it has become an extension of the private market, permeated by the market's logic and interests. Instead of a common citizenship, we have subordination to an oligarchy of the wealthy and powerful. Instead of a public service ethos we have the well-oiled revolving door between government and business. And instead of governments controlling the excesses of the corporate sector in the public interest, they have increasingly become its chief promotional agent. Without a radical programme to restore the distinctiveness and integrity of the public sphere we shall have to learn to live with the recurrent abuses attendant upon its progressive dismemberment by market forces and their cheerleaders.

Notes

1   For the London Underground as a case study see the House of Lords Select Committee on Economic Affairs (2010) *Private Finance Projects and Off-Balance Sheet Debt*, London: The Stationery Office.

2   Ibid.

3   This process has been sharply criticised by both the National Audit Office and the Commons Select Committee on Business: see *Guardian*, 10 July 2014.

4   Florio, M. (2004) *The Great Divestiture: Evaluating the Welfare Impact of the British Privatizations 1979–1997*, Cambridge Mass. and London: MIT Press.

5   For the quadrupling of government expenditure on consultancies under the Blair government see the National Audit Office report, 15 December 2006.

6   See www.acoba.independent.gov.uk

7   Commons Public Administration Select Committee (2009) *Lobbying: Access and Influence in Whitehall*, London: The Stationery Office, pp. 3–5.

8   For detailed evidence see Beetham, D. (2011) *Unelected Oligarchy: Corporate and Financial Dominance in Britain's Democracy*, Liverpool: Democratic Audit.

9   Quoted in a Channel 4 *Dispatches* programme, 22 March 2010.

10   For examples of what this might involve see Meacher, M. (2013) *The State We Need*, London: Biteback; Mazzucato, M. (2013) *The Entrepreneurial State*, London: Anthem Press.

11   Marquand, D. (2004) *The Decline of the Public*, Cambridge: Polity.

2

The New Normal: Moral Economies in the 'Age of Fraud'

Jörg Wiegratz

Many countries around the world have been transformed since the late 1980s by a range of neoliberal policies and reforms: extensive privatisation, trade liberalisation, a lowering of protective regulatory standards concerning the economy, numerous public sector reforms, the promotion of a more commercialised and entrepreneurial society, and various measures to strengthen the power of the capitalist class and their economic allies. A closely connected strategy has been the weakening of the power of workers' organisations and other social movements capable of restraining capital's maximisation of profit-taking. These changes have deeply altered not only the economic and political structures of affected societies, but also their social and moral structures. Significantly, more than two decades into this period of neoliberal transformation, many countries in Europe and elsewhere have witnessed a string of both high- and low-profile cases of fraud and corruption. These cases have made it into local and national and sometimes global news. Journalists' reporting about economic fraud in the Global North for instance is particularly intensive – compared to the 1990s – since the late 2000s. Reporting about the financial crisis of 2007/08, and its causes and aftermath, gradually revealed the extent and routine character of trickery in the banking sector, and the role of the state institutions in condoning this trickery for years (see also Chapter 13).[1]

Since then, a series of fraud and corruption cases – including the famous years-long rigging of the LIBOR rate – has received coverage in the news, as have the latest settlements of multi-million pound fines that some banks and other firms have to pay for parts of their 'wrongdoing' in the recent past. Indeed, reports about fraud and corruption have become 'normal news' in various countries across the globe: from the United

Kingdom, the United States and Germany to South Africa, China and Brazil. There is now a long list of verbs regularly used in both media news and public debates that point to an element of deliberate dishonesty in business dealings: mis-selling; misleading, sharp, shady, dubious and predatory practice; unscrupulous and irresponsible practice; malpractice, and so on. The discussions about these practices also make reference to a so-called 'dark side', or 'under-belly' of capitalism and economic globalisation. The prevalence of the use of these words in our public (and private) debates, and the capitalist world of business they try to characterise and come to grips with, points to a key phenomenon that concerns us in this chapter: the normalisation of both political corruption and economic fraud across many business sectors in specific countries such as the United Kingdom and in the global economy more broadly (see the Introduction).[2] This development alone, this rise of what might be called 'the age of fraud' in our epoch, requires serious consideration.

In Britain, as elsewhere, concerns regarding the dubiousness, harmfulness, and (im-)morality of certain business operations, and suggestions about how to fix a problem that increasingly appears to be normalised are raised by almost all sections of the political spectrum: from left to liberal and conservative. Of course, each section offers a different analysis of the root of the problem and how to cure it. In the United Kingdom of the early 2010s for instance, in the face of the financial crisis, MPs' expenses scandal and the 'London riots', leaders of all the three major parties (including former Labour party leader Tony Blair) gave speeches or statements about issues of values and morality, moral decline, a broken society, greed, thuggery, criminality, problems of malpractice, short-termism and irresponsibility in today's business world, and the desirability and possibility of a better capitalism. The current leader of the UK Labour Party, Ed Miliband, for instance referred to 'true wealth creators' in contrast with 'asset strippers', 'predators', 'predatory behaviour', a 'fast-buck' culture, 'anything goes' culture, and suggested 'that the country is facing a "quiet crisis" caused by an economy and a society too often rewarding not the right people with the right values, but the wrong people with the wrong values'.[3] More specifically, Miliband said:

> For me, predatory behaviour is when a business does something which is in its own short-term interests but does significant damage to the long-term health of the economy .... The state sets rules in relation to our benefit system, social housing and the way our economy works. It is not like there is an option of not having rules, it's about what kind of rules they are – are they rules based on a set of values? ... [the idea] that as

long as people maximise their short-term interest, everything will be OK in business and elsewhere .... It was wrong ... it has caused problems for our society. ... We have got to choose as a society – do we change it or do we carry on as we are?[4]

In a different, but related way, Prime Minister David Cameron advanced notions of a 'slow-motion moral collapse', 'broken society', and 'demoralised' state and state agencies:

Do we have the determination to confront the slow-motion moral collapse that has taken place in parts of our country these past few generations ...? Do we have the determination to confront all this and turn it around?[5]

Cameron of course sees moral decline to be especially a problem among certain sections of society, predominantly low-status or subaltern classes.

The analyses of the British commentator Will Hutton illustrate the reasoning behind a wider acknowledgment that there is a moral problem with contemporary capitalism and capitalist society. Hutton noted that 'modern capitalism has arrived at a moral dead end, interested largely in feathering the nests of its leaders while imposing enormous costs on the rest of society and accepting no reciprocal obligations'.[6] Among academics, the US economist Jeffrey Sachs provides a good example of this line of analysis: for him, our economic crisis is the result of greed, and of individual freedom and self-interest gone too far:

When libertarians deride the idea of social fairness as just one more nuisance, they unleash greed. The kind of unconstrained greed that is now loose in America is leading ... to corporate criminality and deceit; ... to politics dominated by special interests; ... to income stagnation for much of the population and untold riches at the very top.[7]

Of course, neither Sachs nor many other analysts who refer to 'greed' as a causal factor of corporate criminality ever really define or conceptualise the term, let alone examine it via empirical study. His book's index does not have entries such as 'power', 'class', or 'corporate criminality', although it does include 'corporate dishonesty and lies'. The flatness in the analysis of corporate fraud is not only characteristic of Jeffrey Sachs' account[8] but of much our public debates about corruption and fraud in general.

Such debates reflect a certain moral unease and outrage about specific cases of fraud and corruption among at least part of the public, including the many victims, and a pressure to discuss the broader trends the cases might stand for. These exchanges of views about today's moral order, or moral disorder, are often expressed in discussions around the role of materialism, greed, selfishness and ruthlessness in our societies and economies on one hand, and solidarity, justice, decency and fairness on the other. Notably, debates about fraud, moral decline and moral crisis, out-of-touch captains of polity and industry, and the need for a moral revival are prevalent not only in today's Britain, but, again, in many other countries.

It seems a number of people across the world had to go through a steep learning curve in the past years in order to come to terms with the ever-changing dynamics of trickery, fraud and corruption in their neoliberalised societies: certain practices and norms that many people in the global North for instance considered 'shocking' and 'unthinkable' only a while ago have been gradually institutionalised as 'the new normal' (TNN).[9] This new state of affairs in the United Kingdom (and elsewhere) concerning what people (have to) do – and do to others – to make a profit or a living these days can be witnessed in a range of industries: not just in the notorious finance and insurance industry but also, as other contributors to this book show, in the supermarkets, food, media, private security, construction, health and care industries.

Notably, public debates about fraud and corruption tend to assert that something significant has changed in the past decades concerning people, their relationships with each other, their relationship with money, and their moral character or moral compass.[10] The remainder of the text briefly makes a few analytical points that allow us to deepen our analysis of moral economies of corruption in the neoliberal period.

Most debates that identify corruption and fraud as growing social problems offer the following explanations for the situation:

- the weakening of morals (for instance, because of the crowding out of non-market norms by market values)[11]
- the absence of morals (also described as the existence of immorality, as in 'bankers have lost their moral compass')
- the presence of specific morals.

The differences in the analysis have to do with, amongst other issues, different understandings of the term 'morality' that various commentators have or apply. I get back to that point at the end of the chapter.

In his book *Neo-liberal Africa*, Graham Harrison has argued explicitly that neoliberalism is not just about 'freeing' the economy from state intervention (as often argued by analysts) but is a political agenda that is about something much more all-encompassing and ambitious: the creation of fully fledged capitalist market societies across the globe.[12] This social engineering agenda broadly speaking advances the interests of capital, by which I mean 'bosses', investors, the rich, the 1 per cent – there are many ways of describing it. In simple terms, neoliberalism in this reading is about removing almost everything in society that is non-capitalist or anti-capitalist, and thus actually or potentially a problem, risk or hindrance for capital and its quest for absolute profit and social dominance.

Such an agenda is likely to include:

- the marketisation of the social relations in society
- the commercialisation of previously under-commercialised sectors such as health, education, housing and social care
- pushing people to see themselves and others as individuals, consumers and self-maximising economic players that aspire to individual material success and think, feel and act accordingly (like a business owner), instead of as members of a community.

Finally, and as a consequence of the above, the establishment of market society structures necessitated a shift in power between social classes and groups: away from workers, cooperatives, peasants and so on, and towards industrialists, investors and the like. In short, neoliberal reforms directly and indirectly seek to change not only the political and economic but also the *cultural* structure of a society. This process crucially includes reforming the moral order of society.[13]

Though this understanding of the profound social impact of neoliberalism is by now fairly well established in parts of the academic and public debate, relatively few social scientists have traced this process of cultural and moral engineering – and its drivers, characteristics and repercussions – via extensive empirical studies. In other words, the study of the cultural political economy dynamics of neoliberalism – by which I mean the explicit analysis of continuities and changes in the dominant values, norms and practices in specific communities, economic sectors and places of work that have been impacted by neoliberal reforms – is still in an early stage. Similarly, the analysis of the neoliberalism-induced moral change – and again, its drivers, characteristics and repercussions – remains understudied and is thus only superficially understood.[14]

In other words, the routinisation and normalisation of fraud and corruption can only be understood as part of changes in a wider *moral* economy.[15] The key here is to understand the point – missed in the public debates on corruption – that some set of values and norms underpins every social practice, including corrupt practices.

A moral economy analysis of corruption is useful because it brings to the fore the values and norms that underpin the actions of 'the corrupt'. This includes the analysis of the specific moral views and judgments of people who act fraudulently: for instance their moral reasoning about the world, themselves, others, the specific practice of concern, and generally, proper and acceptable behaviour (such as how others are to be treated) in the given situation. Data about the moral reasoning of the corrupt and fraudulent is hard to come by, also because only a very few social scientists do that sort of analysis. But documentaries such as *Inside Job*, published insider accounts written by former staff of key companies in global finance, various media reports and TV discussions about corruption and fraud, and findings from state investigations into specific cases, give some indication of the moral worldview of the actors and the moral climate in the organisations and industries they work(ed) in.

For instance, here are two of the statements that were circulated in the press in the late 2000s and became relatively famous. The first is an internal email from an unnamed analyst of the credit agency Standard & Poor's: 'Let's hope we are all wealthy and retired by the time this house of cards falters.'[16] The second is from Lloyd Craig Blankfein, CEO of Goldman Sachs, a company accused of fraud that settled the charges in 2010 with a fine of $550 million,[17] who claimed he was 'doing God's work'.[18] Without going into any analytical detail, we can detect in both statements an idea of doing something good, something that achieves a desirable goal (wealth, a religious plan), that is justifiable (in material and/or religious terms). The first statement is explicit regarding the moral dimension of treating others: someone's actions are likely to do harm to others, yet this is acceptable, necessary, normal, unavoidable in the given situation.[19] This moral mind-set that regards harming others as standard business practice to advance your own material and social interests – here, to make fast and significant money so as to retire soonest and enjoy the fruits of the fraud (while the tricked, victims, and general public pick up the fallout) – also comes out in a private email in 2007 from Fabrice Tourre, a former Goldman Sachs banker, convicted of securities fraud:[20]

> The summary of the US subprime mortgage business is that it is not too brilliant .... According to Sparks [a Goldman executive] that business is

totally dead and the poor little subprime borrowers will not last so long!!!
… I am now considered a 'dinosaur' in this business (at my firm the average
longevity of an employee is about 2–3 years!!!) people ask me about career
advice. I feel like I'm losing my mind and I'm only 28!!! OK, I've decided
two more years of work and I'm retiring …. When I think that I had some
input into the creation of this product (which by the way is a product of
pure intellectual masturbation, the type of thing which you invent telling
yourself: 'Well, what if we created a 'thing', which has no purpose, which
is absolutely conceptual and highly theoretical and which nobody knows
the price?) … It sickens the heart to see it shot down in mid-flight …. It's
a little like Frankenstein turning against his own inventor;) … Anyway I
don't want to bore you with my stories …. I believe that a soft and sensual
feminine intervention is necessary for Fab's survival.[21]

That said, some argue that fraudulent or corrupt people have neither
values nor morals because they break with norms of decency and harm
others. Some furthermore argue that banks (and by extension bankers)
in general are immoral: 'Let's face it, banks are instinctively immoral
institutions – necessary evils in a capitalist system', wrote a commentator
recently.[22] Another one writes:

> Banks love dictators, embezzlers, thieves, drug traffickers and monsters
> of every kind so long as they have money to bank. Banking is a world
> without moral compass ruled by moral cripples. …. [Al]l the banks need,
> in order to get their share [from criminal business], is to have in their
> employ bankers of a certain moral degeneracy and politicians ready to
> protect them.[23]

And finally, one of the most widely articulated positions in the debate
about cunning and defrauding bankers and other professions that a section
of the public regards as villains these days because of the various scandals
in their sectors is this one: they have lost their moral compass. This view
is for instance expressed in a letter to the head of the British Bankers'
Association, written by the chief executive of the consumer protection
agency Which?: 'As the head of an organisation that represents over 200
banks you are in a unique position to seize the opportunity to transform
a sector that ordinary people believe has lost its moral compass.'[24]

The public debate is dominated by this type of argument about
certain business and political practices and (im-)morality. The related
understanding of values and morals seems pretty common: values and
morals have always or necessarily something to do with pro-social, pro-
collective, good (that is, honest) practice. Further, the reference to values
or morals in public debates usually also suggests that there is no tension

or incompatibility between certain values or between certain moral attitudes, but rather, that the tension is between morality and selfishness or greed, for instance. This analytical take is limited and misleading, and of little help in understanding the sociocultural (including moral) dynamics that underpin corruption.

We can understand this point in a different way: values are desirable goals.[25] There are some values (such as achievement, enjoyment/pleasure and self-direction) that serve largely *individualistic* interests, and others (restrictive conformity to social expectations, concern for the welfare of others) rather *collectivist* interests.[26] In this sense, corrupt people (who harm others via their corrupt practice) may not have 'lost' their values or may not lack morals. Rather, 'the corrupt' may follow and aspire to a different set of values (such as achievement, wealth creation, entrepreneurialism and so on) that advance their self-interest. This understanding of the morality of corruption that sees competition and conflict between differing sets of values does not lead us to argue merely for a remoralisation of the worlds occupied by the corrupt. It would generate more fundamental questions such as, why are certain prevalent social values consistent with corrupt (and other-harming) practices? What promotes these values, and how are they translated into corrupt practice?

That said, how can we relate this understanding of moral economy to our concern with neoliberalism and corruption? There are two key insights. First, neoliberal reforms and transformations directly and indirectly advance certain values and norms: for instance, unrestrained self-interest, wealth accumulation and consumption; achievement, enjoyment, materialism, money availability, and individualism including individual choice, freedom and success. In other words, neoliberalism is value-based too; the issue however is that neoliberalism promotes values that can be conducive to corruption and fraud.[27] Importantly, the advocates of a neoliberal moral order have so far always argued that the individualistic moral core of the order – the maximisation of self-interest without the consideration of other moral imperatives – will serve (that is, it will maximise) our social welfare.[28] This view that self-interest is a good, necessary and economically and thus socially beneficial moral norm comes in various colours: from 'greed is good' (the phrase used by Gordon Gekko, the broker in the film *Wall Street*) to 'the social responsibility of business is to increase its profits' (as neoliberal economist Milton Freedman infamously argued). Those taking this stance claim that 'what is good for business is good for society', 'taxation is robbery' and so on. This view has considerable political and sociocultural support in today's capitalist social formations.

Second, neoliberal change not only advances certain values (those that generally serve individual interests), it does so at the expense of other values (those that generally serve collectivist interests), such as concern for the welfare of others. In short, neoliberalism is a 'cultural programme' that promotes pro-self-interest values and norms, and undermines pro-collective values and norms. Taking this argument a step further allows us to see that the issue might not be erosion or decline of morals (or norms generally) as such, but the transformation of (especially socially dominant) morals: that is, the shift from pro-social moral norms to pro-self-interest moral norms. This moral change – itself an outcome of political-economic change – seems to foster corruption and fraud.[29]

Importantly, we can now argue that 'the greedy' or 'the corrupt' actually aspire to and conform with rather than break with certain dominant social values, such as achievement and wealth.[30] Furthermore, the corrupt will have their own moral views and tales about society, life, money, success, survival, happiness, or supporting their family that allows them to justify what they do; in short, they have a moral compass too. These views and justifications (what we might call a moral compass position) are shaped by the social and the class context in which they live, the things they see around them, their experiences in life and reflections about them, and so on. In that sense, following the argument made in the Introduction to this book, they must be understood as part of a wider political economy of fraud. The morals of the corrupt politician and fraudulent banker – as much as general debate tends to individualise these phenomena and put the blame on particular individuals – are in fact an outcome of larger collective structures and processes, including the relationships of power that are supported by political and economic systems. In short, the moral economy of fraud is part of and interacts with the political economy of fraud.

We have arrived at an analytical position that allows us to speak about a moral norm, moral actor or moral economy without automatically referring to a pro-social, honest practice.[31] Instead, we can analyse a moral economy of corruption as a context-specific set of, amongst others, values, norms, practices, power relations, and benefit-harm structures, including specific views of dominant (and other, non-dominant) actors in them of what is good and bad, proper and improper behaviour. That is, we can consider the various views of concern regarding acceptable ways of treating others (read: victims) and their welfare in the process of making money, and gaining wealth and power in a corrupt way. Leaving aside debates concerning the moral philosophy of war, this position concerning the moral underpinning or moral economy of corrupt, deceitful and violent, and in any case other-harming practice, though fruitful in revealing key aspects of the phenomenon, seems a minority position in much of the social sciences, including in moral economy studies.

Neoliberalism's extensive transformation has advanced particular changes in various societies, including in Britain. Over a decades-long process it has promoted and made dominant a particular kind of moral economy that consists of a range of typical elements: self-interest as the core moral norm, low regard for others (especially in economic interactions), opportunism and so on. Further, it has attacked non-neoliberal elements of our moral economies: other-regard and self-restraint, for example. Understanding this process of neoliberal moral restructuring[32] – and the economic, political and cultural drivers and consequences of it – will help us understand better how and why neoliberal changes have created a society where fraud and corruption are so prevalent, common and routine, and constitute a key part of 'the new normal' that we (have to) operate in and have had to come to terms with in recent years. The question then is how the moral economies of corruption in a neoliberalised world can be identified, critiqued, denormalised and undermined. Keeping the eye on the ball in future requires not delinking but connecting issues of capitalism and morality in our analyses and in our politics.

Notes

1   Taibbi, M (2011) 'Why isn't Wall Street in jail?' *Rolling Stone*, 16 February, www.rollingstone.com/politics/news/why-isnt-wall-street-in-jail-20110216 (this and other URLs in this chapter were last accessed on 15 July 2014); Taibbi, M. (2011) *Griftopia: A Story of Bankers, Politicians and the Most Audacious Power Grab in American History,* New York: Spiegel & Grau.

2   United Nations Office on Drugs and Crime (2011) *Estimating Illicit Financial Flows Resulting from Drug Trafficking and Other Transnational Organized Crimes,* Vienna: UNODC.

3   *Independent,* 27 September 2011; *Guardian,* 28 September 2011.

4   *Guardian,* 28 September 2011.

5   *Telegraph,* 14 August 2011.

6   Hutton, W. (2010) 'Modern capitalism is at a moral dead end. And the bosses are to blame', *Observer,* 4 April 2010.

7   Sachs, J. (2012) *The Price of Civilization: Reawakening Virtue and Prosperity after the Economic Fall,* London: Vintage, p. 38.

8   Sachs (2012), pp. 23–5.

9   Wiegratz, J. (2014) 'The arrival of the New Normal', *Le Monde diplomatique*, 9 April, http://mondediplo.com/blogs/the-arrival-of-the-new-normal.

10 See for instance Sachs (2012); for online entries in the debate: www.marketwatch.com/story/4-reasons-capitalism-is-morally-bankrupt-dying-2013-07-31; http://standpointmag.co.uk/dialogue-november; www.jubilee-centre.org/is-capitalism-morally-bankrupt-five-moral-flaws-and-their-social-consequences-by-michael-schluter/; www.truthdig.com/report/item/20090323_america_is_in_need_of_a_moral_bailout; www.occupybristoluk.org/neo-liberal-capitalism-is-morally-intellectually-and-actually-bankrupt/

11 Sandel, M. (2012) *What Money Can't Buy: The Moral Limits of Markets*, London: Allen Lane.

12 Harrison, G. (2010) *Neoliberal Africa: The Impact of Global Social Engineering*, London: Zed. Harrison, G. (2005) 'Economic faith, social project, and a misreading of African society: the travails of neoliberalism in Africa', *Third World Quarterly*, vol. 26, no. 8, pp. 1303–20.

13 Wiegratz, J. (2010) 'Fake capitalism? The dynamics of neoliberal moral restructuring and pseudo-development: the case of Uganda', *Review of African Political Economy*, vol. 37, no. 124, pp. 123–37.

14 Wiegratz, J. (2012) 'The neoliberal harvest: the proliferation and normalisation of economic fraud in a market society', in Winlow, S. and Atkinson, R. (eds), *New directions in Crime and Deviancy*, London: Routledge.

15 De Sardan, J.-.P O. (1999) /A moral economy of corruption in Africa?' *Journal of Modern African Studies*, vol. 37, no. 1, pp. 25–52.

16 The analyst sent the email to a colleague in December 2006. See *New York Times*, 9 July 2008, www.nytimes.com/2008/07/09/business/09credit.html?adxnnl=1&adxnnlx=1303412194-BNurm1fBKXFVJ7cIwkXGVg

17 US Securities and Exchanges Commission (2010) 'Goldman Sachs to pay record $550 million to settle SEC charges related to subprime mortgage CDO', press release, 15 July, www.sec.gov/news/press/2010/2010-123.htm (17.07.2014). The firm is highly connected politically in the United States and the United Kingdom: see Rowell, A. (2011) *Doing God's Work: How Goldman Sachs Rigs the Game*, Spinwatch, www.spinwatch.org/index.php/issues/spying/item/214-exclusive-how-goldman-sachs-rigs-the-game

18 *Sunday Times*, 8 November 2009, www.timesonline.co.uk/tol/news/world/us_and_americas/article6907681.ece

19 Movies about corruption and fraud are also instructive: in a movie about the financial sector (*Margin Call*), a CEO of a Wall Street investment firm states. 'There are three ways to make a living in this business: be first, be smarter, or cheat' (*Rolling Stone*, 20 October 2011, www.rollingstone.com/movies/reviews/margin-call-20111020

20 'Former Goldman Sachs trader found guilty of mortgage fraud', *Guardian*, 1 August 2013, www.theguardian.com/business/2013/aug/01/fabulous-fab-tourre-guilty-fraud

21 *Telegraph*, 23 April 2010, www.telegraph.co.uk/finance/newsbysector/banksandfinance/7626096/Goldman-fraud-charges-emails-from-Fabrice-Tourre-to-girlfriend-Marine-Serres.html

22 www.irishexaminer.com/viewpoints/columnists/michael-clifford/politicians-bankers-lost-moral-compass-235418.html

23 www.golemxiv.co.uk/2011/04/money-laundering-and-the-moral-world-of-bankers/

24 www.telegraph.co.uk/news/uknews/9510087/Banks-have-lost-their-moral-compass-consumer-group-warns-new-industry-chief.html

25 Schwartz, S. H. and Bilsky, W. (1987) 'Toward a universal psychological structure of human values', *Journal of Personality and Social Psychology*, vol. 53, pp. 550–62.

26 Schwartz and Bilsky (1987).

27 Wiegratz (2010).

28 Beckert, J. (2005) 'The moral embeddedness of markets', discussion paper, Max Planck Institute for the Study of Societies (MPIfG), Cologne, Germany. Streeck, W. (2008) 'Social science and moral dialogue', in Discussion Forum: Amitai Etzioni – twenty years of The Moral Dimension: toward a New Economics, *Socio-Economic Review*, vol. 6, pp. 126–9.

29 Wiegratz (2010, 2012).

30 Merton, R. (1938) 'Social structure and anomie', *American Sociological Review*, vol. 3, no. 5.

31 Wrights Mill, C. (2000) *The Power Elite*, Oxford: Oxford University Press; de Sardan (1999).

32 Wiegratz (2010).

3

Neoliberalism, Politics and Institutional Corruption: Against the 'Institutional Malaise' Hypothesis

David Miller

What is behind the major ongoing wave of scandals and wrongdoing in British society? One public institution after another has been brought low as dishonesty, corruption, scandal and ethical and criminal misdemeanours have been exposed in the police, media, both Houses of Parliament, the banks and many other institutions. This chapter examines some of the answers given to that question, and focuses in particular on those given in a recent book by prominent British political scientists David Richards, Martin Smith and Colin Hay.[1]

My argument here is that many of the indications of scandal and corruption in the British landscape are the result of an institutionalised corruption in British public life which has arisen not by accident, as a consequence of technological developments, or unrealistic expectations amongst the public or the 'hyper-adversarialism' of the news media.[2] Nor is it the result of the well-known secrecy and unaccountability of the state. Instead it is to a significant extent the product of the neoliberal revolution. Of course, neoliberalism's advocates did not foresee all of the consequences, but it is also plain that much of what happened was done deliberately with eminently predictable consequences.

The term 'neoliberalism' is used here to refer to the 'doctrine that market exchange is an ethic in itself, capable of acting as a guide for all human action'.[3] It is important to stress that it is a doctrine and not a type of society. Neoliberalism affects societies unevenly and sometimes unpredictably. Often neoliberal reforms do not result in the claimed cuts to public spending or improvements in the 'efficiency' of public services. The gap between the claims of the doctrine and the results is perhaps produced in part because mistakes were made or the theory was inadequate, but most importantly it is because the doctrine is a means of pursuing – we might say masking – certain interests. It is, in other words, ideological.

The key result of the pursuit of neoliberal ideology in practice has been a society mired in institutional corruption, affecting both the public and private sectors. But institutional corruption did not just affect the private sector in the same way as public institutions, since it is itself one of the key vectors of this disorder. Institutional corruption should be distinguished from petty corruption such as the payment of bribes for political or other favours (see the Introduction to this book).

Although the explicit discussion of institutional corruption is an advance on those accounts that see corruption as individual failings, it can be problematic in that if there is a tendency to assume that institutions become corrupt as opposed to being corrupt from the beginning. In fact corruption is often embodied in the very purpose of the institution. This can be said to be the case where regulatory agencies are constrained against acting in the public interest and required to act in the market interest (see the Introduction and Chapters 12 and 13).

Public choice theory – which proposes that classical economic rationales of rational choice and self-interest can be used to determine the outcomes of politics and policy – is a key set of ideas that have given shape to the neoliberal project. In at least some versions of public choice theory the whole idea of public service is itself corrupt. A public sector that aims to serve the general interest and not the private interests of individuals is a problem for neoliberal theory. James Buchanan, one of the key theorists of public choice economics, has talked specifically about this:

> There's certainly no measurable concept that's meaningful that could be called the public interest, because how do you weigh different interest of different groups and what they can get out of it? The public interest as a politician thinks it does not mean it exists. It's what he thinks is good for the country. And if he'd come out say that that's one thing, but behind this hypocrisy of calling something the public interest as if it exists.[4]

Because of this radical inability to think about collective interests, says Buchanan:

> We're safer if we have politicians who are a bit self-interested and greedy
> than if we have these zealots. The greatest danger of course is the zealot
> who thinks that he knows best or she knows best for the rest of us. As
> opposed to being for sale, so to speak.[5]

According to this theory of public choice, bureaucrats are inevitably
self-interested, but if they adhere to an ideology of 'public service' they
are not self-interested enough. As a result, the market in 'politics as
exchange' can only work if everyone can be bought and sold without
the ideological 'fanaticism' of 'public service' getting in the way. In
other words public choice theory attempts to destroy all conceptions of
the public or general interest, and the central strategy is to introduce
mechanisms promoting institutional corruption. In some cases, in the
United States, including in the Department of Labor and the Securities
and Exchange Commission, those ideas were used to deliberately employ
incompetent public servants in order to bring discredit on governmental
institutions and undermine public interest regulation.[6]

Understanding corruption as pathology?

The predominant way in which corruption is treated in mainstream liter-
ature contains nothing on the specific approach of public choice theory
and neoliberal practice to corruption. Instead corruption is generally seen
as a kind of pathology. To take a recent example by the prominent British
political scientists Richards, Smith and Hay, the major question about
the malaise in public life is whether there is any 'connection' between
the various crises that they catalogue.[7] They rightly reject the thesis that
there is greater risk consciousness in the contemporary period – as in
the thesis of the 'risk society'[8] – and also the idea that this is a problem
caused by the public through its stupidity or ignorance or – alternatively
– its inflated expectations:

> That what we in fact see are not rising expectations for institutions to
> deliver (as the risk theorists suggest) but a continued defensiveness on the
> part of institutions threatened not by 'risk' but by more informed citizens
> and the demand for greater information… increased information makes it
> more difficult for organisations to control their policy domains.[9]

In their conclusion they alight on their explanation for the successions of
scandals in public life:

> A continual repetition of institutional failure or underperformance to the extent that it has undermined the faith of the citizen in those institutions.... The dilemma for our rulers is that ... closed decision making ... is losing legitimacy.[10]

There is little explanation for institutional failure or the quaintly technocratic term 'underperformance'. Either underperformance has increased, which would need explanation, or it has been relatively constant and only recently become visible in the scandals of recent years. The authors appear to opt for the latter, ascribing the change to 'the collapse in deference, the quantum change in available information and with it the demystification of how institutions have operated'.[11]

These changes have combined with the key factor – the 'main argument' – which 'focuses on ... a set of deeply embedded, pathological failings within the UK political settlement'. This sounds like an attempt to understand the institutional basis of the malaise we face. What are these failings? The authors claim that:

> the fault lies in the sustaining of the British political tradition (BPT) and with it the stoking up of a series of pathologies that have led to the present crisis.

But which pathologies? Crucial, they say, 'is the notion that the political class should operate within a self-regulating arena to protect against outside, potentially undemocratic, influence'.[12] This resulted in a closed and secretive system of government suffering from 'elitism, a lack of transparency and accountability and an aloof detachment' from the governed.[13] This way of doing things has a long history. They say that the 'crisis' of the UK state 'first became visible in the 1960s',[14] but that it can be 'traced back to the 19th Century'. This explanation for our contemporary malaise is almost entirely wrong. In key respects just the opposite has happened.

It can certainly be acknowledged that the kind of club government and knee-jerk secrecy exhibited by the UK state has an established history, but to suggest that this system of government has remained largely unchanged for 150 years and that it is the main reason for today's crises is a remarkable misdiagnosis, for the following reasons.

Their account is ahistorical. It neglects the changes to the system that came with universal suffrage and then with the social democracy of the period 1945–78, and then the changes post 1979. It can be argued that the elite fought the introduction of democracy tooth and nail, and were largely successful in retaining an elitist system in the postwar period, but it could and also should be recognised that certain things changed after 1945. The authors themselves quote data to the effect that the level of inequality in British society was not constant, nor was the direction of travel all one way, as might be expected from their static analysis. It declined markedly between 1945 and 1978, before widening again to outstrip the levels of 1945 by 2007.[15] Although they give these figures and quote one or two other sources they give no account of how these changes might relate to changes in governance structures or practice.

This critique of the 'BPT' fails to recognise that it is one of the things that the neoliberals fought so hard to change, at least when it interfered with 'market' mechanisms. This was, let us remember, the theme of Margaret Thatcher's favourite television drama *Yes, Minister*. As Sir Anthony Jay, one of the creators put it:

> we show that almost everything that the government has to decide is a conflict between two lots of private interest, that of the politicians and that of the civil service .... Public choice economics, which explains why all this was going on was at the root of almost every episode.[16]

More concretely, public choice economics also animated the market reforms to the British civil service and public institutions, giving us the internal market in the NHS and foundation hospitals, the Research Excellence Framework (REF) and student fees in higher education, and the deregulation and 'light touch' pro-market regulatory agencies of many other areas of public life, including of course the financial sector.

The most important problem with accounts like this is that they locate the explanation for institutional corruption entirely at the level of the state and political elite. No account is given of the relation between the political elite and wider forces – most obviously capital and labour. Indeed, there is no developed understanding of the changing role of business in the period after 1979. Left out of account is almost all of the evidence of the change in the political system that has occurred over the last 30 years. Neoliberalism is not part of the explanation – the term does not appear in the index of the book by Richards and his colleagues – and they pay scant attention to corruption (five index entries – only one of which is in the five chapters co-authored by the editors), preferring the term 'crisis' (nowhere clearly enough defined or used – 21 references). The problem with failing to understand the changing role of business in the neoliberal reforms of the past 30 years is that – as in public choice theory itself – the problem of corruption is located in the state itself.

The visible hand of the market ...

There has always been corruption in government, public institutions and indeed business in the United Kingdom.[17] Now the type, extent and effects of corruption appear to have intensified markedly. For some commentators, such as the sociologist Anthony Giddens, this is only a question of visibility. As he remarked back in 2001:

> I doubt that corruption is more common in democratic countries than it used to be – rather, in an information society it is more visible than it used to be. The emergence of a global information society is a powerful democratising force.[18]

However, we can point to the following elements of the changes of the period. The first was the transfer of wealth (and thus power – over at least investment decisions) to the rich via privatisation. There was a consequent reduction in the power of the electorate to decide (via 'liberal' democracy) which party should take such decisions. The private finance initiative (PFI) and public–private partnerships (PPP) were essentially a continuation of this, as they locked government into decisions under immense financial and corporate pressure (see Chapter 9).

Accompanying this was the assault on intermediary institutions capable of defending or protecting public interests – most notably the destruction, at great financial and human cost, of the trades union movement, symbolised and instantiated by the defeat of the miners in 1984–5 (see Chapter 5).[19] This was followed by the hollowing-out of the Labour Party, turning it into a vehicle for corporate interests,[20] a long-term process which had been in development before the 'reforms' initiated by former leader of the Labour Party Neil Kinnock and then was taken much further by one of his successors, Tony Blair.[21]

During the period of the Thatcher and Major governments there were major innovations in the marketisation of government itself.[22] This process is the most important direct consequence and facilitator of corruption. Neoliberal reforms can be seen as reforms which directly enable corruption and the pursuit of private, as opposed to general, interests. In other words corruption deliberately serves particular (class) interests (see the Introduction to this book). But we should also recognise that corruption had particular advantages for some of the individuals involved, allowing them to make considerable personal fortunes as a result of their employment in public service. In that neoliberalism encourages practices that resemble petty corruption, it is distinguished by its systemic character and by the fact that the new way of doing things means that the benefits secured are in the main legal and officially legitimate. Amongst the changes were internal reforms such as the introduction of performance-related pay, and the introduction of market mechanisms in the health service,[23] education[24] and other public services, including the BBC. These innovations in public policy were driven in a number of key cases by the appointment of neoliberal or public choice economists – most obviously the appointment of Alain Enthoven, the Stanford economist (and former employee of the Rand Corporation), who was brought to the United Kingdom in 1984 and was instrumental in the creation of the internal market in the NHS.

The process of opening the machinery of government to private interests required the influx of new ideas and practical ways of putting them into practice. As a result the neoliberal period saw the rise of a whole range of new policy intermediaries including management consultants, lobbyists, public relations advisers and think tanks.[25] The PR industry grew, initially on the back of privatisation contracts, by a factor of eleven in real terms.[26] Lobbying and PR firms and their principals (mostly corporate actors) aim to dominate civil society, science, the media, politics and policy.[27] There is a significant literature on how they have fared in relation to science[28] and other sectors. In the United Kingdom, the lobbying industry has – despite recurring controversy about its activities – been largely protected by government, which has refused to adequately require transparency from lobbyists and other influence peddlers.[29]

Although the earliest neoliberal think tank – the Institute of Economic Affairs – was created in the 1950s, it was the early 1970s that saw the creation of the Adam Smith Institute and the Centre for Policy Studies, important vehicles for the Thatcherite revolution. Since then think tanks have proliferated, and they are now central vehicles for enacting further neoliberal (or indeed neo-conservative[30]) reform.[31]

Governance reforms have resulted in a significant influx of private sector philosophy, money and indeed personnel into government service. The 'revolving door' is the phrase used to describe this process – encompassing several new risks to democracy (see Chapter 10). Taken together with the growing – and partly consequent – professionalisation of politicians, and the advent of market-friendly management and organisation in the public sector, this suggests marked changes in the way in which UK governance functions. As with lobbying, the revolving door as an issue is not properly regulated in the United Kingdom. The

Commons Select Committee report on the issue in 2012 recommended abolishing the advisory committee in charge of offering non-binding advice on particular appointments, although the government rejected the move.[32]

The financial crisis brought the inadequate – institutionally corrupt – regulation of the banking industry to public attention. Research using a sample of the 116 banks and other financial corporations in the *Fortune* Global 500 found that on average, the higher a company's ranking within the *Fortune* 500, the more revolving-door connections it had.[33] Neoliberal reform has involved not simply transferring wealth and property from the public sector to the private, but also transferring decision making from public to private hands. In other words the scope for business 'governance' markedly increases under neoliberalism, narrowing the scope for public sector decision making.

Neoliberalism fosters an ongoing process of transformation which disembeds policy networks from politics and reconfigures them – creating new relations between the state, the public and private interests. Power to take decisions is transferred to the market and secured from any interference from the citizenry via the democratic process. As the Austrian political economist Karl Polanyi put it, the rise of the market 'means no less than the running of society as an adjunct to the market. Instead of economy being embedded in social relations, social relations are embedded in the economic system.'[34] The argument here, then, is that the rise of new forms of policy intermediary, lobbyists, consultants and think tanks, is neither unremarkable, nor a neutral process of modernisation, professionalisation or specialisation, but specifically the mechanism by which politics is reconfigured to serve the market.

Conclusion

There is something particularly secretive and closed about the UK system of governance, compared with other systems such as that of the United States, Canada and Australia. To understand this it is important to understand the sinews of secrecy and the elitist history of the British system of government – a system which made very significant efforts to protect elite power in the face of the democratic reforms which gave all adults the vote, a reform only finally won in 1927.[35] But if we want to understand how 'institutional crisis' has engulfed all major political institutions in the United Kingdom, we cannot ignore the empirical record of the changes in governance over the last 30 years as neoliberal assumptions and ideas were progressively unleashed by the Thatcher, Major, Blair and Brown administrations. If the empirical record of the period teaches us one thing it should be that it is no longer enough, if it ever was, to study the political system by examining only its contents (Parliament, government, the civil service and public institutions) and refusing to ask about their relations with business, the trades unions and civil society.

This is (obviously) not to determine from the outset that 'fundamental forces' in the economy determine what happens in the 'superstructure' of politics. But it would be equally wrong to decide by omission that wider – perhaps fundamental – interests have no role in our theoretical conception or empirical strategy. If our aim is to understand how it is that we got to the widespread malaise and institutional corruption of contemporary Britain, an examination of the aims, strategy and practice of governmental reform must be put into a wider sociological context than a narrow internalist focus on the political system. Politics is determined not simply by politicians and civil servants but also by broader social forces.

We live in an advanced 'post democratic'[36] capitalist society in which corruption is endemic for perfectly understandable and not accidental reasons. The forces and people – most of whose names and addresses we either know or can find out – that brought us to this pass stand in need of forensic, focused and unrelenting analysis. David Richards writes that change can come from those in power – he calls for the political class to show 'willingness' to seek a 'smarter democracy' with 'much greater deliberation and participation'.[37] It is not adequate to think that the problem is some kind of mystery brought on by random processes such as new technology, inflated expectations or specifically British traditions of more than a century's duration. To hope piously for 'smarter' reforms is simply not enough.

The United Kingdom is institutionally corrupt, and that corruption was introduced with the aid of neoliberal theories of economics and politics, most notably public choice theory, which seeks to reform government by opening it up to the market in order that public officials might be more easily controlled via all sorts of monetary incentives. This is in itself a major reason for the endemic institutional corruption in public institutions in the United Kingdom. As a result, the United Kingdom stands in need of a very far-reaching democratic revolution. We can call on our leaders to reform the system all we want. If we want actual change, we will have to take matters into our own hands.

Notes

1   Richards, D., Smith, M. and Hay, C. (eds) (2014) *Institutional Crisis in 21st Century Britain*, Houndmills, Basingstoke: Palgrave Macmillan.

2   Miller, D. (2004) 'System failure: it's not just the media – the whole political system has failed', *Journal of Public Affairs*, vol. 4, no. 4, pp. 374–83.

3   Harvey, D. (2005) *A Brief History of Neoliberalism*, Oxford: Oxford University Press.

4   'The Trap (1/3): Fuck You Buddy! by Adam Curtis – Transcribed', Adam Curtis: the Transcripts. http://transcribecurtis.tumblr.com/

5   'The Trap (1/3)':

6   Frank, T. (2009) *The Wrecking Crew: How Conservatives Ruined Government, Enriched Themselves, and Beggared the Nation*, New York: Henry Holt.

7   Richards, D. and Smith, M. 'Introduction: a crisis in UK institutions?', in Richards et al. (2014), p. 7.

8   Beck, U. (1992) *The Risk Society*, London: Sage.

9   Beck (1992), pp. 6–7.

10 Richards, D., Smith, M. and Hay, C. (2014) 'Conclusion: apres le deluge? Crisis, continuity and change in UK institutions', in Richards et al. (2014), pp. 270–1.

11 Richards et al. (2014), p. 271.

12 Richards et al. (2014), p. 261.

13 Richards et al. (2014), p. 262

14 Richards et al. (2014), p. 260.

15 Richards et al. (2014), p. 265

16 'The Trap (1/3)' (see note 4).

17 Doig, A. (1984) *Corruption and Misconduct in Contemporary British Politics*, Harmondsworth: Penguin.

18 Giddens, A. (2001) 'Democracy and Third Way politics', *The Runaway World Debate*. https://web.archive.org/web/20010506010718/http://www.lse.ac.uk/Giddens/RWDdemocracyandthirdway.htm

19 Milne, S. (2004) *The Enemy Within: Thatcher's Secret War Against the Miners*, 4th edn, London: Verso.

20 Osler, D. (2002) *Labour Party Plc: The Truth Behind New Labour as a Party of Business*, Edinburgh: Mainstream.

21 Ramsay, R. (2012) 'How Labour embraced the City' *New Left Project*, 15 December. www.newleftproject.org/index.php/site/article_comments/how_labour_embraced_the_city

22 Leys, C. (2001) *Market-Driven Politics: Neoliberal Democracy and the Public Interest*, London: Verso.

23 Pollock, A. (2004) *NHS Plc: The Privatisation of Our Health Care*, London: Verso.

24 Ball, S. (2007) *Education plc: Understanding Private Sector Participation in Public Sector Education*, London: Routledge.

25 Cave, T. and Rowell, A. (2014) *A Quiet Word: Lobbying, Crony Capitalism and Broken Politics in Britain*, London: Bodley Head.

26   Miller, D. and Dinan, W. (2000) 'The rise of the PR industry in Britain 1979–1998', *European Journal of Communication*, vol. 15, no. 1, pp. 5–35.

27   Miller, D. and Harkins, C. (2010) 'Corporate strategy and corporate capture: food and alcohol industry lobbying and public health', *Critical Social Policy*, vol. 30, no. 4, pp. 564–89.

28   McGarrity, T. and Warner, W. (2008) *Bending Science*, Cambridge, Mass: Harvard University Press; Michaels, D. (2008) *Doubt is Their Product: How Industry's Assault on Science Threatens Your Health*, Oxford: Oxford University Press.; Wiist, W. (2010) *The Bottom Line or Public Health: Tactics Corporations Use to Influence Health and Health Policy, and What We Can Do to Counter Them*, New York: Oxford University Press.

29   Dinan, W. and Miller, D. (2012) 'Sledgehammers, nuts and rotten apples: reassessing the case for lobbying self-regulation in the United Kingdom', *Interest Groups and Advocacy*, vol. 1, no. 1.

30   Mills, T., Griffin, T. and Miller, D. (2011) *The Cold War on British Muslims: An Examination of Policy Exchange and the Centre for Social Cohesion*, September, Glasgow: Public Interest Investigations.

31   Mirowski, P. and Plehwe, D. (eds) (2009) *The Road from Mont Pelerin: The Making of the Neoliberal Thought Collective*, Cambridge, Mass: Harvard University Press.

32   Public Administration Select Committee (2012) *Business Appointment Rules*, Third Report, 17 July 2012. www.publications.parliament.uk/pa/cm201213/cmselect/cmpubadm/404/40402.htm

33   Miller, D. and Dinan, W. (2009) 'Revolving doors, accountability and transparency – emerging regulatory concerns and policy solutions in the financial crisis' (GOV-PGC-ETH-2009-2), paper for Global Forum on Public Governance 'Building a Cleaner World: Tools and Good Practices for Fostering a Culture of Integrity', OECD and Dutch National Integrity Office, Paris, 4–5 May.

34   Polanyi, K. (1944) *The Great Transformation*, New York: Farrar & Rinehart, p. 57.

35   Miller, D. and Dinan, W. (2008) *A Century of Spin*, London: Pluto.

36   Crouch, C. (2004) *Post-Democracy*, Cambridge, UK: Polity Press.

37   Richards, D. 'A crisis of expectation', in Richards et al. (2014), p. 37.

Part II

Corruption in Policing

4

Policed by Consent? The Myth and the Betrayal

Phil Scraton

'Plebgate'

On 19 September 2012 the UK Coalition government's chief whip, Andrew Mitchell MP, was involved in a brief but hostile altercation with Metropolitan Police officers on duty at the Downing Street security gates. Leaving his office, adjacent to the prime minister's residence, he was told to dismount his bicycle and leave via the pedestrian exit rather than the main gate. Mitchell's reaction was petulant and he admits to swearing at the duty officers. The official police log of the incident, however, records that Mitchell addressed the officers as 'fucking plebs'. Via email the following day this version, contested by Mitchell from the outset, was corroborated by an independent pedestrian who witnessed the confrontation from outside the gates. Within days the incident was widely reported, and immediately dubbed 'Plebgate'. Mitchell came under intense pressure, particularly from the Police Federation, to resign his government post.

Mitchell accepted that his language and his behaviour were inappropriate but he persisted in denying he had used the word 'plebs'. As demands for his resignation as chief whip intensified he bowed to pressure because, he claimed, the publicity jeopardised his capacity to 'fulfil my duties'. The Police Federation then considered the matter resolved. Three months later, however, it was disclosed that the 'independent' witness whose email had corroborated the police version of events was, in fact, a police officer who had not been in the vicinity at the time. CCTV footage also showed that the police claim that members of the public were present at the gates was untrue. Further, a recording of a meeting a month after the incident between Mitchell and Police Federation officials revealed their publicised account of the meeting to be false.

What began as an apparently innocuous, relatively minor interpersonal dispute soon was elevated to an issue of national importance concerning the integrity and accountability of the police and their representatives. By late December 2012, Operation Alice, led by a Metropolitan Police deputy chief commissioner who was also the force's head of professional standards, was established and staffed by 30 officers to investigate the incident and its aftermath. A further investigation was established by the Independent Police Complaints Commission (IPCC). These investigations led to the conviction of one police officer, his dismissal and that of three further officers for 'gross misconduct'. A further three officers were also disciplined for 'misconduct'. Three Police Federation officials remained under IPCC investigation, two of whom apologised for giving false evidence to the Home Affairs Select Committee. Addressing the House of Commons the prime minister, David Cameron, apologised to Mitchell. This came hard on the heels of his apology to the bereaved families and survivors of the 1989 Hillsborough disaster following publication of a scathing report by an independent panel of inquiry, discussed later in this chapter.

In May 2014 the home secretary, Theresa May, was invited to address the Police Federation. She demanded 'root and branch' change within the Federation, stating that the Mitchell incident had demonstrated, as had the Hillsborough Independent Panel's lengthy report, that 'platitudes about a few bad apples' constituted an insufficient response to deeply entrenched, institutionalised unprofessional conduct. Her strong words echoed the Home Affairs Committee's equally strident criticism that the Federation harboured a culture of bullying and intimidation that, alongside other high-profile cases of professional misconduct, had contributed to a crisis in public confidence in the police. In the year of Plebgate seven of the 39 chief constables or commissioners in England had been dismissed or suspended, were under investigation or impelled to resign, together with a further eight deputy or assistant chief constables. This trend continued into 2014, raising profound questions about the integrity and accountability of the police at all levels, from constables through to their senior managers. As the following brief excursion into the history of policing demonstrates, such questions are not new.

Contextualising the 'New Police'

During the early 19th century Home Secretary Robert Peel was determined to secure legislation to professionalise haphazard and inconsistent forms of policing in London while laying foundations for policing beyond its boundaries. His persistence resulted in the 1829 Metropolitan Police Act. According to the original circular instructions, it was intended that the police would be 'homogeneous and democratic', prioritising crime prevention, 'civil and obliging to all people of every rank and class', supported by civil society while retaining 'a perfect command of temper' and unmoved 'in the slightest degree by any language or threats that maybe used'.[1] Yet just four years after the 'new' police first entered London's communities two parliamentary committees of inquiry were established as a result of growing serious public concern about the conduct of police officers.

Opposition to the new police soon mounted focusing on the use of force against demonstrators campaigning for parliamentary reform, the in-house handling of complaints made by the public and police infiltration. While the 1833 inquiries found in favour of the police, their approval was rejected by those who considered that the new police favoured the moneyed classes, targeted the poor and were often brutal in their interventions, for which they were unaccountable. Further, the police were challenged consistently for abusing their powers of arrest. Quasi-official histories of the founding of the police assert that Peel's Act established and embedded the principle of policing by popular consent through safeguarding the interests of the law-abiding majority against the threat of crime and disorder emanating from the lawlessness and amorality of an 'underclass'. This notion that the police soon enjoyed universal acceptance as the guardians of consensus does not stand closer scrutiny.

As legislation signalled national policing via the 1835 Municipal Corporations Act and the 1839 County Police Act, the harsh policing of public demonstrations and working-class leisure pursuits led to popular, community-based resistance. Historian Robert Storch represents the intrusion of the police as 'domestic missionaries' civilising the masses; hence their portrayal as 'blue locusts' or 'blue idlers' doing the bidding of early industrialists who required compliant, obedient workers whose communities and activities were kept under surveillance, regulation and control.[2]

Drawn primarily from the working class, the constable was considered a pariah – the epitome of class betrayal. As industrialisation advanced and towns and cities expanded beyond recognition, the policing of social space included the regulation of the union movement, the reformist organisations and the alternative economy. The triptych of endemic poverty, physical disease and moral degeneracy was portrayed and regulated via a language of social contagion.

By the 1880s the socialist movement began to challenge casual work and structural unemployment, and expanding trades unions brought manual workers into their fold alongside craft workers. A less divided working class within an emerging rhetoric reflecting socialist conscious-ness established the revolutionary potential of organised labour. This first-generation 'enemy within', however, was not restricted to the containment of workers' conflict with their employers. It extended to policing incomers prepared to bring the struggle against colonial oppression to London. In 1883 the Fenian bombings led directly to the establishment within the Metropolitan Police of the Irish Special Branch, monitoring and containing Irish communities that had burgeoned four decades earlier as a consequence of the great starvation, falsely dubbed the 'Irish famine'. Within five years the new unit became the 'Special Branch', its brief extended to maintain close surveillance on all potential public order threats. Within 20 years the Special Branch was operating to monitor and subvert political activism that was considered a threat to the established order, using infiltration as a key strategy. Within provin-cial forces, surveillance, infiltration and informing were methods of 'proactive' policing adopted by detectives.

By the turn of the 19th century, less than 50 years after expansion throughout the regions, the focus of policing had become institution-alised across three fronts: 'crimes' and the street economy of the poor; industrial conflict and strikes; and political 'subversion' and protest. In working-class communities, hostility towards the police was profound, their presence 'grudgingly accepted'[3] rather than consensually welcomed. Trades unionism had expanded, the seeds of mass education had taken root, the franchise had been extended to include much of the male working class, and in this climate of change the struggle for women's suffrage gained ground. The state reacted strongly against women protesters, many of whom were from the 'respectable' upper-middle class. They were forcefully arrested and publicly humiliated. Their punitive incarceration, including force-feeding of those on hunger strike, was clear evidence that impartiality, neutrality and fairness as the watch-words of 'policing by consent' remained compromised.

As labour became organized, and a workers' movement gaining in influence was portrayed as harbouring the 'threat' of Bolshevism, the police were the frontline of strike breaking, from South Wales miners to the Liverpool general strike, to Clydeside shipbuilders. Despite the slight respite in industrial tension and political protest during the 1914–18 Great War, the exception being the 1916 Easter Rising in Ireland, in 1918 the police went on strike and Lloyd George anticipated a worker revolution. Reflecting his experience at the time, Allen Hutt stated that the 'revolutionary outburst that was threatening in 1914 now seemed likely to materialize in a far more acute form and in circumstances vastly more menacing to the existing social order'.[4] Maintaining a restless relationship with the military, the police were expected to contain the threat of unemployment marches, picket lines and growing civil disorder.

The early 1920s was a period of constant confrontation, with 2 million people out of work in 1921. When a General Strike was called in 1926 the police were identified as being firmly aligned with the interests of employers, in protecting a social order deeply divided by class and sanctioned by a partisan government. In the years preceding the Second World War the partisan role of the police consolidated in the minds and politics of working-class communities emboldened by new legislation, specifically the 1927 Trade Unions and Trade Disputes Act. Throughout the North of England forceful tactics were used by the police to contain political protest, extending to attacks on hunger marches. Poverty, exacerbated by the predominance of casual labour, declining housing stock and ill health, inspired political consciousness alongside criminality, ranging from 'hidden', street-based economies through to organised gang-related violence. While it originated in the destitution of marginalised communities and was often directly related to territory within towns and cities, much of this crime was predatory. Robbery, burglary, sex work, vice rings, protection rackets and gambling constituted the diet of professional gangs, whose members were 'career' criminals. Following the Second World War food rationing and scarce commodities were the foundation of a highly organised hidden market. At each level, low-level local street crime and well-organised 'gangland', the police operated with discretion.

Police surveillance, particularly through the employment of informants, brought officers – often of senior rank – into direct contact with what was dubbed the 'underworld' of organised crime. By the 1960s it was apparent that police proximity to gangs had resulted in large-scale corruption. Transferring money, buying information, inducing confessions and plea bargaining provided the means to manipulate evidence, thereby influencing the due process of the courts. Soon this became public knowledge, extending into popular discourse and leading to a crisis in credibility centring on the Metropolitan Police.[5]

Throughout the 1970s the controversies persisted, centring on targeting 'crime' and perceived 'criminal' areas, policing industrial disputes and political protest, and police incursions into Black, inner-city, communities. While the police continued to poll well in satisfaction ratings, the divisions of perception evident throughout the previous century remained as sharp as ever. Differential policing was woven into the fabric of policing urban populations.

In 1979 the deaths at the hands of the police of Jimmy Kelly in Huyton, Liverpool and Blair Peach in Southall, London once again brought the issue of police violence to the public's attention. Jimmy Kelly was a 54-year-old unemployed labourer arrested for being drunk and disorderly, carried on the floor of a minibus, dropped on his head outside the police station and laid on his back on a charge room floor where he died. Blair Peach was a young New Zealand teacher walking away from an anti-fascist demonstration when he was attacked from behind by a group of Metropolitan Police officers. His skull was shattered by a fierce blow to the head. While both cases received extensive media attention, and the death of Blair Peach was the focus of an unofficial full inquiry raising crucial questions regarding the circumstances of his death, the 'outcomes and conclusions' of internal police investigations were not disclosed.[6] These two prominent deaths, among others, were the prelude to the 1980–81 uprisings in the Black communities of Brixton, London; Handsworth, Birmingham; Toxteth, Liverpool and St Paul's, Bristol. A government inquiry headed by the eminent judge Lord Scarman unequivocally rejected allegations from Black communities that the police were 'institutionally racist'.[7]

As relations between Black/Asian communities and the police remained tense, conflict between white working-class mining communities and the police erupted following the use of close surveillance, infiltration and hardline responses throughout the 1984–85 coal dispute. Miners across the United Kingdom experienced unprecedented, centrally coordinated incursions into their communities, with over 5,000 police officers each day deployed across force boundaries in special police units. In November 1984 the prime minister, Margaret Thatcher, railed against a 'spectrum', from 'terrorist gangs within our borders and the terrorist states which arm them' to 'the hard Left, operating inside our system, conspiring to use union power and the apparatus of local government to break, defy and subvert the laws'. Democracy and the rule of law, she concluded, were under threat. As journalist Seamus Milne's book *The Enemy Within* subsequently revealed, covert and anti-democratic police strategies were the on-the-ground manifestation of policing the 'threat'.[8] Strategies included the use of the police and security services to infiltrate and undermine the National Union of Mineworkers, and the manipulation of the courts and media to discredit and tie the hands of its leaders.

The Institutionalisation of Differential Policing

In the wake of the coal dispute and the inner-city uprisings of the 1980s, it is difficult to assess accurately the extent to which public confidence and trust in the police had diminished. Opinion polls consistently delivered overall positive ratings. As was evident throughout the 20th century, however, depending on location, class, 'race', gender, sexuality and age, there were deep divisions and neighbourhoods in which the police were unwelcome and not trusted. Given that differential policing, in operational policies, strategies and practices, had remained institutionalised – in 'crime prevention' (particularly 'targeting' strategies in working-class and Black communities), in regulating public order, and on picket lines – the notion that communities were policed 'by consent' was as unsustainable in the 1980s as it had been a century earlier.

In 1993, twelve years after the publication of the Scarman Report, the murder of a young Black man in an unprovoked attack on a London street exposed the post-Scarman culture of denial and complacency in the politics of policing. The Metropolitan Police's handling the killing of Stephen Lawrence in April 1993, from first response through to the eventual investigation, failed to accept that the attack by five young white men was racially motivated. In not questioning known suspects immediately after the murder, while focusing their investigation on Stephen Lawrence and his friend Duwayne Brookes who had witnessed the murder, the police allowed essential incriminating evidence to be destroyed and created an opportunity for the attackers to establish alibis. In 1997, following demands by the Lawrence family for a full inquiry, Sir William Macpherson was appointed to consider Stephen Lawrence's death, and specifically 'to identify the lessons to be learned for the investigation and prosecution of racially motivated crimes'.[9]

Macpherson's 70 recommendations were considered a watershed in exposing the depth and breadth of racism in police forces nationally, and had consequences for all state agencies. Undoubtedly, and in marked contrast to the denials of Scarman, Macpherson endorsed what Black community-based organisations and critical research had evidenced since the 1980–81 uprisings: that racism in the police, like other forms of discrimination, not least misogyny and homophobia, was deeply ingrained. Macpherson, however, endorsed the view that discrimination was *institutional*; that racism and racist practices were tolerated as expressions of personal or individually held attitudes. A more critical perspective, in keeping with the wealth of evidence, argues that racism was – and has remained – *institutionalised*; a prevailing ideology initiating and reproducing policies, priorities and practices within institutions.

The Stephen Lawrence case not only revealed a reluctance by investigating officers at all levels to accept the clear and immediate context of his death – a racist attack. It failed at every subsequent stage, with the police eventually masking a flawed investigation by covering backs and corrupting the process. James Morton, lawyer and author of *Bent Coppers*, distinguishes between police officers who act corruptly for personal gain or out of personal prejudice and those who do so to protect 'the Job'.[10] Invariably, the latter category is characterised by shared or collective enterprise. A month before Labour Home Secretary Jack Straw announced the inquiry into the police response to the Stephen Lawrence killing, he had announced a judicial scrutiny of the evidence relating to the disaster at Hillsborough football stadium, Sheffield, in which 96 men, women and children were killed. The controversy regarding the deaths had been heightened by a Home Office inquiry conclusion that the main cause of the deaths had been overcrowding and the main reason had been police mismanagement of the crowd.[11] Seemingly inconsistent with these findings, the eventual inquests recorded verdicts of accidental death.[12]

The judicial scrutiny (chaired by a High Court judge, Lord Justice Stuart-Smith) among other issues considered evidence that police statements collected and presented to the initial Home Office inquiry, to the Director of Public Prosecutions and to the coroner's inquest had been changed by the South Yorkshire Police, the force responsible for policing Hillsborough, during the statement-gathering process. Stuart-Smith accepted that some changes had been made. Although in a few cases there had been 'an error of judgement' the process did not amount to 'unprofessional conduct', he concluded, and the evidence base had not been undermined.[13] A year later, once investigators had gained independent access to all police statements, the full extent of the process was revealed.[14] Whatever their rank, all South Yorkshire Police officers' statements had undergone an in-house process of 'review and alteration' in consultation with and on the advice of the force solicitors. The clear purpose of the institutionalised review and alteration process was to purge police officers' statements of any criticisms of the force's operational policies and senior officers' decision making on the day.

The Hillsborough Independent Panel (HIP) published its 395-page report in September 2013, detailing 153 significant findings.[15] One of its twelve comprehensive chapters presents 14 key findings on the significance and impact of the review and alteration process. From the research it was evident that those responsible for the conduct of all previous inquiries, investigations and inquests were aware that statements had been reviewed and altered. It was clear that the West Midlands Police team appointed to investigate the South Yorkshire Police and report to Lord Justice Taylor's initial inquiry, to the Director of Public Prosecutions and to the coroner, knew and approved of the process. The Panel's research revealed that 116 of the 164 significantly amended police statements had text removed that was unfavourable to the South Yorkshire Police. These issues were significant in what followed the publication of the HIP report: a prime ministerial 'double apology' to the bereaved families; a new full-scale criminal investigation; an investigation by the IPCC unprecedented in size and scope; and the quashing of the inquest verdicts and the holding of new inquests.[16]

The Hillsborough revelations, although first disclosed 13 years earlier, coincided with the unfolding story that was Plebgate. They came hard on the heels of another major controversy, this time caught on film. On 1 April 2009 Ian Tomlinson, a newspaper seller, was attempting to walk home through a cordon of officers in riot gear set up to police and disperse crowds involved in the G20 protest. Without objecting to his route being blocked, he turned away from the cordon, and was felled by a blow to the head from a police baton. Soon after he collapsed and died. Three days later, following examination by a Home Office pathologist, the City of London Police stated that he had died from 'natural causes' – a heart attack as a result of coronary heart disease. On 7 April film by a passer-by of the assault by an officer of the Metropolitan Police's Territorial Support Unit was published.

Two subsequent post mortems challenged the first pathologist's findings, and established that Ian Tomlinson had died from internal bleeding. Initially suspended, the first pathologist was eventually struck off. The Director of Public Prosecutions decided not to prosecute the police officer responsible for the assault. In May 2011 an inquest jury returned a verdict of unlawful killing, concluding that the officer had use 'unreasonable and excessive' force. Following the inquest verdict the DPP reversed his original decision and the officer was charged with manslaughter. After lengthy deliberation, he was found not guilty by the jury. Subsequently a Metropolitan Police disciplinary panel judged that the officer's actions amounted to 'gross misconduct'. He was dismissed from the force, which paid significant out-of-court compensation to the family while apologising for the use of 'excessive' and 'unlawful' force.

These cases have had a defining impact not only on public confidence in how cities and towns are policed, but equally significantly, on the withholding and fabrication of evidence in contested cases (see also

Chapter 6). They informed a growing public concern regarding police powers and accountability. While this concern has focused on institutionalised racism, particularly deaths of Black people at the hands of the police, it also has extended to systemic failures in policing and the corruption of evidence, including after Hillsborough. Simultaneously there has emerged a question of accountability about police surveillance operations, particularly the infiltration and monitoring of environmental campaign groups. The sizeable extent of infiltration, harking back to late 19th-century policing of the 'Fenian threat', and the potential for entrapment has been a feature of policing animal rights activists and others. It soon emerged that male undercover police officers were not only immersed in surveillance but had initiated and established sexual relationships with those on whom they were spying. In October 2014 the Metropolitan Police agreed to pay a woman £425,000 as an out-of-court settlement in recognition of the trauma she had endured as a consequence of discovering that her son's father, who had abandoned her 24 years previously, was an undercover officer. She and her fellow activists had been under surveillance. In their investigation of undercover surveillance, journalists Paul Lewis and Rob Evans demonstrate how the process was institutionalised in a unit – the Special Demonstration Squad – within the Special Branch. Its covert activities extended to include Stephen Lawrence's family.[18]

This brief excursion into the historical context and contemporary manifestations of operational policing demonstrates that 'corruption' is not reducible to direct transactions for financial gain (see also the Introduction to this book). The notion, of being corrupt for self-gain has been well established over many years, as James Morton noted, not least in the transactional arrangements between the CID and organised crime.[19] However, entrapment, infiltration, surveillance, intimidation, manufacturing evidence, and the review and alteration of police statements, whether to secure convictions or to deflect culpability, collectively represent institutionalised corruption. It was in this context that 'Plebgate' captured public attention.

Holding the police accountable for systemic abuses of power is a challenge in a political climate where any attempt to be proactive is met with resistance by senior officers arguing that 'their' autonomy in prioritising operational policies and practices is being undermined. Corruption is often represented as being for financial gain or in securing dubious convictions. Yet the corruption of evidence ranges from the regular practice of officers 'getting their story straight' to the more profoundly institutionalised purposeful reconstruction of events. In the public's consciousness the former is well established, while the latter challenges the very foundations of 'policing by consent'. It is instructive that while the review and alteration of police statements after Hillsborough was closely researched, identified and widely publicised ten years after the disaster, political recognition, accompanied by outraged media coverage and public response, took a further 13 years to achieve.

Notes

1   Critchley, T. A. (1978) *A History of the Police in England and Wales*, London: Constable, pp. 52–3.
2   Storch, R. (1975) 'The plague of blue locusts: police reform and popular resistance in Northern England, 1840–57', *International Journal of Social History*, vol. 20, no. 1, pp. 62–90.
3   Cohen, P. (1978) 'Policing the working-class city' in B. Fine et al. (eds), *Capitalism and the Rule of Law*, London: Hutchinson, p. 23.
4   Hutt, A. (1936) *The Post-War History of the British Working Class*, London: Gollancz, p.16.
5   See Cox, B. et al. (1977) *The Fall of Scotland Yard*, Harmondsworth: Penguin.
6   See NCCL (1980) *The Death of Blair Peach*, London: National Council for Civil Liberties; Scraton, P. (2007) *Power, Conflict and Criminalisation*, London: Routledge, ch 2.
7   Scarman, Lord (1981) *The Scarman Report*, CMND 8427, London: HMSO, p. 64.
8   Milne, S. (2014) *The Enemy Within: The Secret War Against the Miners*, 2nd edn, London: Verso.
9   Macpherson, Sir W. (1999) *The Stephen Lawrence Inquiry Report* ,CMND 4262-I, London: The Stationery Office
10   Morton, J. (1993) *Bent Coppers: Survey of Police Corruption*, London: Little, Brown.
11   Taylor, Rt. Hon L. J. (1989) *The Hillsborough Stadium Disaster, 15th April 1989; Interim Report. Cmnd 962*, London: HMSO.
12   See Scraton, P. et al. (1995) *No Last Rights: The Denial of Justice and the Promotion of Myth in the Aftermath of the Hillsborough Disaster*, Liverpool: LCC/Alden Press.
13   Stuart-Smith, Rt Hon. L. J. (1998) *Scrutiny of Evidence relating to the Hillsborough Football Stadium Disaster*, CMND 3878m, London: The Stationery Office, p. 80.
14. Scraton, P. (1999) *Hillsborough: The Truth*, Edinburgh: Mainstream (3rd edn 2009).
15   Hillsborough Independent Panel (2012) *The Report of the Hillsborough Independent Panel*, London: The Stationery Office. The author was a Panel member, headed the Panel's research and was primary author of the Report.
16   See Scraton, P. (2013) 'The legacy of Hillsborough: liberating truth, challenging power', *Race and Class*, vol. 52, no. 2, pp. 1–27.

17   Scraton (1999).
18   Evans, R. and Lewis, P. (2013) *Undercover: The True Story of Britain's Secret Police*, London: Faber and Faber.
19   Morton (1993).

5

Hillsborough: The Long Struggle to Expose Police Corruption[1]

Sheila Coleman

It is no longer controversial to say that the aftermath of the Hillsborough disaster is marred by police corruption and the manipulation of evidence of mammoth proportions. It has been a long struggle to get to where we are today, and it has been a struggle that has involved the smearing, bullying and intimidation of those who dared say these things. But now they are accepted, and Prime Minister David Cameron was eventually forced to apologise for them.

But there is a bigger picture than the prime minister's apology – and any other apologies for that matter. That bigger picture has never been adequately recognised. In order to fully understand the corruption and cover-up by the police following the Hillsborough disaster it is necessary to recognise and understand the context in which the disaster occurred.

By 1989 the country had experienced the miners' strike, growing unemployment and increasing civil unrest. Liverpool, as a city, had a negative reputation closely linked to its alleged militancy. Football fans in general were defined within the context of hooliganism, and the government was aiming to introduce a system of mandatory ID cards. Supporters going to a football match were treated very much like cattle, and the terminology in police operational orders was that of animal traders. Fans 'corralled' from the train station to the football ground would be 'herded' into 'pens'.

Increasingly oppressive policing throughout the 1980s gave rise to the police being viewed as political agents of the government rather than as public servants. It has been argued that in this period the police were empowered to act with impunity. Prior to the Hillsborough disaster nowhere was this more evident than in the policing of the miners' strike. Indeed the policing of the striking miners and their supporters came to symbolise the worst aspects of the Tory government under the leadership of Margaret Thatcher. Strikers and protesters were systematically brutalised by a police force overtly acting as an arm of government. Nothing typifies this more than the battle of Orgreave in June 1984. Police forces from across the country swelled South Yorkshire Police ranks. The ferocity of the police action will long be remembered for its brutality, false imprisonment and lies. This was 'war not law'.[2] The now iconic image of a police officer on horseback wielding a truncheon against a diminutive woman protester illustrates the reality of what people were up against.

Five years separate the battle of Orgreave and the Hillsborough disaster. At first sight they appear to be two distinct issues. However these two events are inextricably linked by the involvement of South Yorkshire Police.

On 15 April 1989, Liverpool football club played Nottingham Forest in the FA Cup semi-final (a repeat of the previous year's semi-final which was also held at the Hillsborough Stadium in Sheffield). Ninety-six Liverpool fans who had gone to watch their team never came home. They were killed at Hillsborough (the 96th victim was in a persistent vegetative state for several years before he died). Hundreds of fellow fans were physically injured, and an inestimable number were traumatised by their experience of that day. A public inquiry by Lord Justice Taylor in 1989 concluded that the main reason for the disaster was the failure of police control.[3]

In spite of Lord Justice Taylor's findings in respect of South Yorkshire Police, to the present day no police officer has ever been publicly charged in relation to the deaths (although there was a failed private prosecution case brought in the 1990s by some of the families against two senior officers). Aside from the fact that it was the loss of control by the South Yorkshire force that led to the deaths, what the police went on to do first in the immediate aftermath, and subsequently in the longer term, led to a cover-up of the greatest magnitude. This cover-up which began on the day of the disaster would only be acknowledged by the state in 2012, some 23 years later, when the prime minister publicly apologised in the House of Commons, following the publication of the Hillsborough Independent Panel (HIP) Report.[4] The government acknowledged that what occurred in the intervening years between 1989 and 2012 was a systematic and sustained cover-up, and highlighted the police collusion involved.

While the 1989 semi-final was a re-run of the previous year, there was one major exception: the police chief in charge of the 1988 game, Brian Mole had been removed from his usual post which gave him overall command. The man who was to replace him, David Duckenfield, was considered less experienced than Mole, and it has been argued that this inexperience provoked the resentment of other officers in attendance on the day of the disaster. Collectively the South Yorkshire officers present at Hillsborough on the 15 April 1989 failed to respond to visible signs of distress in the overcrowded pens 3 and 4 on the Leppings Lane terraces. Moreover, when Duckenfield agreed to a request from Superintendent Marshall to open Gate C (which led onto the concourse area and the fateful tunnel) the police effectively lost control of the crowd. Their immediate response to the emerging disaster was to treat it as a hooligan issue, and indeed officers were ordered to form a cordon across the centre of the pitch to keep 'rival' fans apart. It was left to Liverpool fans to take control and lead the emergency response by tearing down advertising hoardings to use as makeshift stretchers to ferry the dead and injured.

It can be argued that the police cover-up began at the stadium, in the midst of the disaster, when David Duckenfield chose to lie to FA chief executive Graham Kelly by saying that fans had pushed Gate C open. This lie was repeated to the waiting media, and although Mr Duckenfield would later say that he had lied in panic, nevertheless this lie formed the basis of the narrative of explaining the Hillsborough disaster for many years to come.

In the days that followed the disaster, the cover-up continued. The notorious *Sun* newspaper headline 'The Truth'[5] caused outrage on Merseyside and led to mass burning of the paper and to a boycott that continues to the present day. Far from being 'The Truth', this fiction of a story proved to be the outcome of a planned police strategy.

In the days that followed it is obvious that South Yorkshire Police needed to maintain control of the narrative relating to the cause of the disaster. Although the West Midlands Police assumed control of the investigations on 20 April 1989, on 26 April a group of South Yorkshire Police officers met to decide how they would take statements from the officers involved. Chief Superintendent Terry Wain was in charge of what was effectively an internal inquiry running parallel to the West Midlands investigation. A small team of five officers led by Wain had the task of establishing the case for the police. Chief Inspector Norman Bettison acted as deputy for Wain and was also a point of contact.

It is important to note in respect of this information gathering by South Yorkshire Police that officers were told not to use their pocket notebooks but rather to make notes on paper. The relevance of this is that pocket notebooks could be called in by the inquiry but separate notes would remain confidential to the South Yorkshire Police. The information gathered loosely became known as the 'Wain Report' when it was submitted to the Taylor Inquiry. It was agreed that senior officers and those officers present at the Leppings Lane end of the ground could write their own statements ('self-taken'). Unusually, it would appear that this process was conducted with the approval of Assistant Chief Constable Mervyn Jones of the West Midlands Police, who headed up the investigation for Lord Justice Taylor.

Given this highly irregular system of recording police evidence, we are left to speculate if it is any wonder that Lord Justice Taylor in his Interim Report considered most senior officers to be evasive and defensive in their testimonies:

> It is a matter of regret that at the hearing, and in their submissions, the SYP were not prepared to concede they were in any respect at fault in what occurred.[6]

By the time South Yorkshire Police officers gave evidence to the Taylor Inquiry it is hardly surprising that they had the confidence to be 'defensive and evasive'. By that time the cover-up was well established. The scene had been set through the media. That scene was that drunken, ticketless hooligans from Liverpool had killed their fellow fans by arriving late and pushing in. This gross distortion of the truth has its origins in the propaganda disseminated by the elite team of police that included Norman Bettison. It took many years to discover where the *Sun* headline came from. It is now believed that it emerged from a process which included this elite team, the Conservative MP Irvine Patnick and Whites News Agency in Sheffield, which released it to the press. Maria Eagle MP raised the question as far back as 1998 of the role of what she termed to be a 'black propaganda unit',[7] and argued that there was an orchestrated campaign to shift the blame from South Yorkshire Police. In recent evidence to the new Hillsborough inquests, one of the officers involved, Gordon Sykes, clearly stated that at a Police Federation Meeting of 19 April 1989, the then chief constable of South Yorkshire, Peter Wright, had said, 'If anybody should be blamed it should be the drunken, ticketless individuals.'[8] Sykes also stated in evidence that he did indeed meet with Irvine Patnick MP and offered to tell him 'the truth'.[9]

Eagle also said she had requested the names of those in the 'black propaganda unit', and had asked who had changed police statements and who supervised the process. The unit, she noted, was headed up by Norman Bettison.[10] Although she asked these questions in 1998, the answers would remain unconfirmed till 2012, when the Hillsborough Independent Panel report validated her revelations. To the present day, exact details of the team are not known. It is also worth pointing out that following on from Maria Eagle raising these questions in May 1998, in November of that same year

Norman Bettison was appointed chief constable of Merseyside, the region from which most Hillsborough victims came.

Aside from the MP's questions being known, the Hillsborough Justice Campaign collected 15,000 names on a petition to Merseyside Police Authority (MPA) calling on them not to appoint Bettison as the new chief constable. In spite of this public opinion and the fact that the group staged a sit-in at the headquarters of the MPA when the decision was to be made, Bettison was nevertheless appointed. When later he was questioned by the BBC he rejected the suggestion that there was a special unit and said his role was 'peripheral'. He went on to state, 'Around anything as emotionally and politically charged as Hillsborough, there is a danger of myths starting to be created.'[11]

The then home secretary, Jack Straw MP, had previously been quoted as saying that he had 'full confidence' in Bettison.[12] The MPA would later go on to appoint another former South Yorkshire Police officer to the post of chief constable: Bernard Hogan-Howe, who had been assistant chief constable on Merseyside since 1997. So between 1998 and 2009, two chief constables who had come directly from South Yorkshire Police policed the people of Merseyside.

The appointment of two officers to head the Merseyside force, both of whom had played such a significant role in the South Yorkshire Police at the time of Hillsborough, and especially of one known to be operating 'a black propaganda unit', is astonishing. Of course there are many people in Merseyside who suspect that there were reasons for those appointments. If nothing else, those appointments indicate both the singular power and arrogance of the police establishment, and its wholesale lack of concern for 'consensus' policing. It was an arrogance that was politically supported. Certainly in the case of Norman Bettison this was an appointment approved and (in the opinion of some) influenced by the then home secretary, Jack Straw.

The West Midlands Police were appointed as the 'independent force' charged with investigating the disaster. In fact they controlled all three investigations emanating from the disaster: the investigation into the immediate aftermath for South Yorkshire Police, the investigation for the Taylor Inquiry, and the investigation for the coroner. The evidence they gathered subsequently went to the Director of Public Prosecutions (DPP), who would later go on to state that there was insufficient evidence to prosecute any police officers.

Up until the Hillsborough disaster, the West Midlands Police was noted for being the force that had interrogated and charged six Irishmen for two pub bombings in Birmingham in 1974. The men, who collectively became known as the 'Birmingham Six', would go on to spend 16 years in prison before their innocence was accepted and they were released. Amnesty International argued forcefully that the Birmingham Six had been ill-treated while in custody and had been subject to inhumane interrogation methods.[13]

The notorious West Midlands Serious Crime Squad had been disbanded by the time of the Hillsborough disaster. A former head of that squad, Detective Superintendent Stanley Beechey, was transferred to 'non-operational duties' investigating 'technical aspects of the Hillsborough Disaster'. In fact his role was quite the contrary of non-operational, as he played a key part in the investigations, especially the inquests. He was also charged with re-interviewing survivors who had criticised the conduct of South Yorkshire Police. Given that fabricating confessions was a common problem within the West Midlands Serious Crime Squad, Beechey seems a strange choice of investigator. Moreover, from 1989–90 he was himself under investigation over malpractice in the Serious Crime Squad. In January 1989 (three months before the disaster), Clare Short MP had called for an inquiry into the alleged malpractices of the West Midlands Police. Beechey was singled out as someone who had played a pivotal role in framing a Liverpool man, George Tomkins, on an armed robbery charge. Tomkins would go on to spend 18 months in Winson Green Prison before being acquitted and released. Tomkins subsequently received a settlement, having taken out a private prosecution against the West Midlands Police for malicious prosecution. He named Beechey as the person who had framed him.

The HIP findings in respect of Stanley Beechey bore out what families of victims and survivors of the disaster had suspected for many years: that the role Beechey played was central to the investigation. Bizarrely, this meant that he liaised directly with both the DPP and the Police Complaints Authority (PCA) in respect of Hillsborough at the same time as both those agencies were investigating him.

When the first part of the original inquests (the 'mini inquests') was concluded in May 1990, Stefan Popper, the coroner, singled out certain West Midlands Police officers for particular thanks. In respect of Stanley Beechey and his colleague Chief Inspector Tope, he said that they 'had an awful lot to do' and:

> they have been making sure that things were going smoothly, doing the back-up, watching, and undertaking anything that needed checking. Thank you very much indeed. We could not have managed without you.[14]

Was the coroner unaware that Beechey was himself under investigation?

Certainly the office of the DPP would have known this, yet Beechey freely communicated with the office in respect of Hillsborough.

It is equally pertinent to ask why such a notorious force as the West Midlands Police should have been chosen in the first place to investigate the disaster. It has been argued that it was chosen specifically because of its reputation. The fact it led all three investigations into the disaster did not inspire confidence in either bereaved families or survivors. Witnesses interviewed by the force spoke of feeling pressured and coerced into altering statements.

The well-documented case of Kevin Williams, a 15-year-old boy who died at Hillsborough, is a case in point. Two witnesses, ironically both police officers, one an off-duty Merseyside officer and the other a South Yorkshire special WPC, spoke of agreeing to sign second statements following visits by West Midlands officers. Both witnesses indicated that they had been pressured to sign. While both their first statements included evidence that Kevin was alive after 3.15 pm, the second statements did not.[15] The relevance of these changes of statements in respect of signs of life was crucial to maintaining the coroner's declaration that all victims would have been dead by 3.15pm on the day of the disaster, or at least would have been beyond saving. It is an example of how the inquest was itself used a vehicle for the cover-up.

The West Midlands role throughout the course of the inquests was crucial. The South Yorkshire Police were able to use the inquests as a means of counteracting criticism made of them by Lord Justice Taylor. In this sense it would seem that rather than investigating the South Yorkshire Police, the West Midlands Police were investigating for them.

As far back as August 1989, when the then home secretary, Douglas Hurd, proposed a statement welcoming the broad thrust of the [Taylor] report, Prime Minister Margaret Thatcher argued, 'What do we mean by "welcoming the broad thrust of the report"? The broad thrust is a devastating criticism of the police. Is that for us to welcome?'[16]

This sums up the context in which the Hillsborough disaster was investigated from the beginning. The 'enemy within', a phrase popularised by Thatcher, covered a wide spectrum of the population, as notes of the final draft of what was to be her conference speech in 1984 indicate (the Brighton bombing led her to tone down her language in this speech): 'Enemy within – Miners' leaders ... Liverpool and some local authorities – just as dangerous ... in a way more difficult to fight ... just as dangerous to liberty'.[17]

This quote illustrates how those who challenged the government of the day were judged as a homogenous group. This linking of the miners and Liverpool would again emerge after the Hillsborough disaster. This very same view of 'the enemy within' was what motivated the cover-up by the South Yorkshire and the West Midlands Police, and fuelled a culture of uncontrolled corruption in the policing of football fans, the miners and the Irish communities in Britain. The police could act in the confidence that at the very heart of the British establishment their impunity would be protected.

There is a murkiness to the entire Hillsborough disaster that is defined by the political climate; the lies and myths that have been documented here served to sustain the decision makers over more than two decades. In spite of the initial conclusion of Lord Justice Taylor that the police were responsible, no prosecutions followed. Moreover, the chief constable of South Yorkshire Police at the time of the disaster, Peter Wright, never resigned. The limited evidence presented to the inquest jury led to accidental death verdicts being recorded against all the deceased. A judicial review of the inquest verdicts in respect of six of the victims was rejected in the Divisional Court in London in November 1993. It would take until 19 December 2012 for the verdicts of accidental death to be quashed in the same courts. On the latter occasion, the attorney general turned up in person (which was highly unusual) to argue the case for quashing the verdicts. In stating the case he used many of the facts that campaigners had presented to the court in 1993. It can be argued that this is a telling example of how the legal system operates within the prevailing political climate.

The policing of the Hillsborough disaster and subsequent police investigations highlight the fact that such corruption was politically supported at the highest level. One indication that this politics of policing is now being more widely recognized is provided by the decision to request an Independent Police Complaints Commission (IPCC) investigation into whether there is a case to answer in respect of South Yorkshire Police behaviour at the 'battle of Orgreave'. Moreover, in respect of West Midlands Police, some of the families of victims of the Birmingham bombings and one of the Birmingham Six (Paddy Hill) have called for an inquiry to ascertain who really carried out the bombings, arguing that the West Midlands Police knew from the very beginning who was responsible.

Numerous other examples of police corruption and cover-ups lead us to conclude that very little has changed over the intervening years. However, it can also be argued that (certainly in the case of Hillsborough), the state and its agents repeatedly underestimate the drive and commitment of decent people when they are criminalised, maligned and demonised. The fact that more than a quarter of a century since the Hillsborough disaster, there are now fresh inquests being held and investigations into criminal behaviour, offers a message of hope to all who have suffered at the hands of the state. We know that the establishment will always reorganise to protect vested interests. However, it can never be disputed that the strength and tenacity of innocent people and those who campaign with them will at the very least leave a legacy for a better, fairer future. We hope it will inspire future generations to question, challenge and above all else, treat their fellow human beings with a respect that was denied to victims of landmark miscarriage of justices in the north of England in the 1980s.

Notes

1   The coroner in the ongoing Hillsborough inquest has issued strict instructions on refraining from publishing statements that might prejudice the outcome of proceedings. For this reason, this chapter has been obliged to omit some details and arguments that would have been included under other circumstances.

2   The phrase used by Gareth Peirce, the solicitor who acted for some of the miners arrested, in her speech to the Marxism Today conference in 2013.

3   Rt Hon. Lord Justice Taylor (1989) *The Hillsborough Stadium Disaster, 15th April 1989; Interim Report*, CMND 765, London: Home Office: p. 49, para. 278.

4   Hillsborough Independent Panel (2012) *The Report of the Hillsborough Independent Panel*, London: The Stationery Office.

5   *Sun*, 19 April 1989.

6   Taylor (1989), p. 3, para. 19.

7   *Hansard*, 8 May 1998.

8   *Guardian*, 10 October 2014.

9   *Guardian*, 9 October 2014.

10   *Guardian*, 13 April 2009.

11   *BBC News*, 16 November 1998.

12   *BBC News*, 9 November 1998.

13   Amnesty International Report. 1989.

14   Conn, D. (2005) *The Beautiful Game: Searching the Soul of Football*, London: Yellow Jersey, p. 315.

15   See the website of the Hillsborough Justice Campaign, Kevin Williams, www.contrast.org/hillsborough

16   Hillsborough Independent Panel (2012), p. 199.

17   Travis, A. (2014) 'Thatcher was to call Labour and miners "enemy within" in abandoned speech', *Guardian*, 3 October.

6

Justice Denied: Police Accountability and the Killing of Mark Duggan

Joanna Gilmore and Waqas Tufail

Introduction

On 4 August 2011, Mark Duggan, a young black man from Tottenham, North London, was shot dead by a police officer from London's Metropolitan Police Service (MPS). This killing followed a period of surveillance from MPS officers, eventually resulting in a 'hard stop' of the taxi cab Mark Duggan was riding in. Shortly after exiting the taxi cab, Mark Duggan was shot twice and died at the scene. In the immediate aftermath of the killing, which took place in broad daylight on a busy Tottenham street, it was reported by mainstream media institutions that a 'shootout' had taken place resulting in a police officer being shot and a man being shot dead.[1] The source was a spokesperson for the Independent Police Complaints Commission (IPCC). Despite the information being patently false, the image of Mark Duggan as a violent 'gangster' soon came to characterise the media framing of the events leading to his death.[2] In January 2014 an inquest jury delivered their verdict on the legality of the police shooting.[3] The jury found that contrary to the testimony of the police officer responsible, Mark did not have a gun in his hand at the time he was shot. To the dismay of Mark's family, the jury nonetheless found that he had been 'lawfully killed'.[4] This chapter explores some of the key failures of the police complaints system exposed in the Mark Duggan case, and considers the possibility of radical, community-based alternatives.

A Crisis of Accountability

The death of Mark Duggan is one of a series of high-profile cases involving police violence and corruption that have raised important questions about the extent to which the IPCC – the main body responsible for overseeing the system of police complaints in England and Wales – operates in the interest of the victims of police wrongdoing. In December 2013 the IPCC was forced to reopen its investigation into the death in police custody of Sean Rigg in August 2008 after an independent report concluded that the Commission 'committed blunder after blunder' in the initial investigation. Shortcomings identified in the report included a failure to secure the crime scene, lengthy delays in interviewing police officers and a failure to examine crucial CCTV evidence.[5] Just three months later, an independent report led by Mark Ellison QC concluded that the IPCC had failed to properly investigate allegations that the MPS withheld information on police corruption from the Macpherson Inquiry into the murder of black teenager Stephen Lawrence.[6] The report triggered an apology from IPCC Chair Dame Ann Owers for the IPCC's role in prolonging the family's search for truth.[7] Lengthy delays in the publication of reports into police collusion following violent confrontations with striking miners at the Orgreave coking plant in 1984,[8] and the fatal shooting in 2012 of Anthony Grainger – an unarmed man shot dead by a Greater Manchester Police officer – have further eroded public confidence in the IPCC's ability to hold police officers to account.

As noted in the Introduction to this book, the recent crisis in police accountability has arisen in the context of a wider institutional crisis of legitimacy in policing. The institutional corruption exposed in these cases has challenged traditional conceptions of police corruption as an abuse of power and authority by individual officers. As the criminologist Maurice Punch[9] puts it, the problem is not simply one of 'bad apples', but of 'bad orchards'.

Scandals of this kind are not new. Indeed, police corruption is as old as the institution of the modern police itself. In stark contrast to nostalgic portrayals of the 'Great British Bobby', during the last 50 years the public image of the police has been tarnished by periodic scandals of financial corruption, arbitrary violence and miscarriages of justice.[10] In common with earlier periods of crisis, these latest revelations have called into question the legitimacy of official state organisations that ostensibly exist to hold the police to account. With corruption a seemingly pervasive feature of police work in Britain, it is essential to ask – who polices the police?

The Independent Police Complaints Commission

The IPCC was established under New Labour in the aftermath of the Macpherson Inquiry, which found existing investigative procedures to be wholly inadequate. Established by the Police Reform Act 2002, the IPCC is tasked with investigating the most serious complaints and allegations of misconduct against the police, as well as handling appeals from people who are dissatisfied with the way the police have dealt with their complaint. While the statutory purpose of the IPCC is to increase public confidence in the police complaints system, the organisation has, since its inception, failed to secure public legitimacy. Much of this scepticism reflects doubts that the IPCC constitutes a genuinely 'independent' investigative body. According to the IPCC's latest annual report, seven out of eight senior investigators are former police officers, as are nine out of twenty deputy senior investigators and over a quarter of investigators.[11]

Moreover, the IPCC only investigates a small proportion of complaints against the police – the overwhelming majority are investigated by each police force's own professional standards department. Some 130 independent investigations were completed by the IPCC between 2011 and 2012.[12] In contrast, 27,157 complaints were finalised by local investigation during the same period, of which only 12 per cent were upheld.[13] The IPCC's record of dealing with corruption complaints is particularly discouraging. Of the 837 corruption cases referred to the IPCC between 2008 and 2011, only 3 per cent were independently investigated by the Commission, and 12 per cent subject to a 'managed' investigation.[14] The majority of complaints concerned allegations of perverting the course of justice and dishonesty offences. In 2008, members of the Police Action Lawyers Group, a national organisation of lawyers representing complainants against the police, resigned from the IPCC's advisory board, citing 'increasing dismay and disillusionment' at what they described as 'the consistently poor quality of decision-making at all levels of the IPCC'.[15]

In the rare occasions that the IPCC conducts a full investigation, its powers to do so are limited. Although regulations introduced under the Police (Complaints and Conduct) Act 2012 enable the IPCC to require a serving police officer to attend an interview as a witness, the powers carry no sanction for refusal to answer questions, nor do they prevent a police officer from reading from a pre-prepared statement. Moreover, the IPCC has no authority to compel a former police officer to attend an interview as a witness, regardless of the seriousness of the complaint investigation.

It is perhaps no surprise, therefore, that the IPCC has in recent years reported a significant reduction in the number of people making complaints against the police.[16] Figures collected by the Crime Survey for England and Wales show that only 10 per cent of those who recall being 'really annoyed' with the actions of a police officer in the last five years went on to make a complaint. The main reason for not complaining was that there was seen to be no benefit or point in doing so.[17] Of those who did, three-quarters reported being dissatisfied with the way their complaint was handled.

Significantly, research commissioned by the IPCC found that those most likely to bear the brunt of corrupt policing practices – young people, ethnic minority groups and those from a low socio-economic background – are also those that are most sceptical of the system and least inclined to complain, with a significant proportion (some 40 per cent of individuals from ethnic minority groups) fearing police harassment if they do.[18]

Unanswered Questions: the Killing of Mark Duggan

The multiple flaws in the police complaints system were brought into sharp focus in the aftermath of the killing of Mark Duggan and the subsequent investigation and inquest into his death. In August 2011 long-term community campaigner and Tottenham resident Stafford Scott left his role as a member of the IPCC's Community Reference Group in protest at the IPCC's handling of the fatal shooting. Writing in the *Guardian* newspaper, Scott alleged that the IPCC investigation was flawed from the very outset, with misleading and inaccurate information being released to the public, and obvious opportunities for evidence collection not pursued.[19] Although the IPCC released a defensive statement in response to this article, attempting to challenge what they regarded as inaccuracies that may undermine the investigation,[20] these questions remained unanswered for Scott, who repeated them after the inquest verdict in January 2014.[21] Specifically, Scott questioned why the IPCC authorised the removal of the taxi cab from the scene prior to forensic examination, and furthermore, why evidence from two independent witnesses who reported seeing police officers remove a gun from the cab was not pursued.

The IPCC investigation was also strongly condemned by coroner Keith Cutler who, in an official report into the killing, described a failure by the IPCC to prevent police officers from conferring when writing statements as creating 'a perception of collusion' in the eyes of the public.[22] In response to these concerns, the IPCC issued an apology to the Duggan family and in March 2014 published draft statutory guidelines suggesting that police witnesses should be kept separate after incidents and stating that conferring has the potential to undermine public confidence.[23] However, these guidelines provide no specific sanctions or penalties for police officers failing to cooperate, with only a warning that the IPCC would make a note of their lack of cooperation in its investigation reports. The plans were condemned by police chiefs including Neil Basu, Scotland Yard's head of armed policing, who argued that half of all armed officers would stop carrying firearms if this amendment to current protocol was forced through.[24]

As Adam Elliot-Cooper noted in *Ceasefire Magazine*,[25] sitting together for hours in an office writing statements did not prevent police officers from delivering contradictory evidence at the Mark Duggan inquest. Indeed, police officers contradicted one another over the most contested elements of the case, such as where the gun was found, how it got there and who secured it. It is no surprise, therefore, that Mark Duggan's family have rejected the inquest verdict. Appearing at the High Court in July 2014, the family argued that the coroner should have directed the jury to reach a different conclusion on the basis that they reached a majority decision that he was unarmed. In October 2014, the challenge by the Duggan family to have the inquest verdict overturned was rejected by the High Court. Later in the same month, it emerged through an article in *The Times* that IPCC officials had actively taken steps to hide the true circumstances of the shooting of Mark Duggan. It was reported that a senior IPCC official had, in the aftermath of the shooting, 'suppressed a ballistics report for several days that indicated that Mark Duggan had not shot at officers when he was stopped by police'.[26] *The Times* established through a freedom of information (FOI) request that the IPCC possessed the findings of the ballistics report a day after Mark Duggan was killed and the then Commissioner, Rachel Cerfontyne, decided that this information was not to be released when 'anti-police feelings will be high' (ibid.). An IPCC report into the investigation of Mark Duggan's death, initially due in early 2012, is expected to be available by the time this book is published.

Radical Alternatives

The renewed crisis of legitimacy in policing has highlighted the need to look beyond official state mechanisms for holding corrupt police officers to account. Rather than providing a much-needed service to the victims of police wrongdoing, the IPCC has at critical times served as a barrier to achieving justice. More recently, following the 'plebgate' scandal that resulted in the criminal conviction of one police officer and allegations of misconduct upheld against others, home secretary Theresa May vowed to strengthen the IPCC.[27] However, the promise of additional resources does little to address the deep-rooted institutional failures exposed in the Mark Duggan case, and thus gives little ground for optimism.

A radical alternative is the establishment of independent police monitoring groups to investigate instances of police deviance and hold corrupt police forces to account. The recent creation of the Northern Police Monitoring Project (NPMP) suggests that such spaces of resistance can be found. Launched following a vibrant meeting in Moss Side, Manchester in October 2012, the NPMP acts as a forum from which individuals, groups and communities can collectively challenge corrupt policing practices and monitor instances of police violence and harassment.

Inspired by similar initiatives that arose out of the anti-racism struggles of the 1970s and 1980s, the NPMP works in communities experiencing some of the most repressive styles of policing, providing advice, advocacy and access to specialist legal assistance, and supporting emerging campaigns as and when they are established. The NPMP aims to provide a genuine challenge to the official narrative on crime and policing. It therefore operates entirely independently from the police and other official state agencies.

The NPMP emerged from the successes of 'Justice4Bolton' – a defence campaign launched in response to the arrest of 55 anti-fascist protesters at a demonstration against the far-right English Defence League in Bolton in March 2010. Following a high-profile public campaign and the systematic gathering of footage and witness testimony, charges were dropped or not pursued against 54 of the arrested protesters. Two police officers were subsequently charged with perverting the course of justice after footage emerged of an officer assaulting a 63-year-old man, who himself went on to be arrested on suspicion of a public order offence.

As numerous campaigns have demonstrated, justice for the victims of police corruption is not something that will be handed down from above, but must be fought for from below. These examples, from the family of Stephen Lawrence, to the families of the victims of the Hillsborough disaster (see Chapter 5), serve as a powerful reminder of the dangers of relying on institutions of the state to self-regulate. The campaigns for justice by the families of those killed or wronged by the police receive little if any media attention, and many struggle for decades searching for answers, seeking to hold corrupt police officers and police practices to account. What unites these campaigns is a deep and ingrained sense of injustice that the state and its institutions have failed to offer accountability and the opportunity for justice. In the absence of effective official mechanisms of holding police officers to account, vibrant community-led campaigns and radical independent police monitoring groups continue to play an essential role in seeking justice.

Notes

1   *Mirror*, 4 August 2011, www.mirror.co.uk/news/uk-news/cops-shoot-dead-gunman-in-north-184278 (accessed 22 August 2014).

2   *Daily Mail*, 9 August 2011, www.dailymail.co.uk/news/article-2024094/Mark-Duggan-Gangster-shot-dead-police-sparking-riots-did-NOT-officers.html (accessed 22 August 2014).

3   See *Inquest into the Death of Mark Duggan*, http://dugganinquest.independent.gov.uk (accessed 7 October 2014).

4   Inquest (2014) 'Jury in Mark Duggan inquest concludes he did not have a gun in his hand when he was shot', press release, 8 January, London: Inquest, www.inquest.org.uk/media/pr/jury-in-mark-duggan-inquest-concludes-he-did-not-have-a-gun-in-his-hand-whe (accessed 7 October 2014).

5   IPCC (2013) 'Report of the independent external review of the IPCC investigation into the death of Sean Rigg' London: IPCC, www.ipcc.gov.uk/sites/default/files/Documents/investigation_commissioner_reports/Review_Report_Sean_Rigg.PDF (accessed 7 October 2014).

6   Ellison, M. (2014) *The Stephen Lawrence Independent Review*, HC 1038-I, London: HMSO.

7   IPCC(2014) 'Statement from IPCC chair following publication of the Ellison Review', London: IPCC, www.ipcc.gov.uk/news/statement-ipcc-chair-following-publication-ellison-review (accessed 7 October 2014).

8   Townsend, M. (2014) 'Police are accused of foot-dragging over miners' strike inquiry', *Guardian* ,15 June, www.theguardian.com/uk-news/2014/jun/15/orgreave-police-inquiry-foot-dragging-clashes (accessed 7 October 2014).

9   Punch, M. (2009), *Police Corruption: Deviance, Accountability and Reform in Policing*, Cullompton: Willan.

10 Reiner, R. (2010) *The Politics of the Police*, 4th edn, Oxford: Oxford University Press.

11 IPCC (2013) *Annual Report and Statements of Accounts 2012/2013*, London: IPCC.

12 IPCC (2013).

13 IPCC (2012a) *Police Complaints: Statistics for England and Wales 2011/2012*, London: IPCC.

14 IPCC (2012b) *Corruption in the Police Service in England and Wales, Second Report*, London: IPCC.

15 Davies, N. (2008) 'Crisis at police watchdog as lawyers resign', *Guardian*, 25 February, p. 1.

16 IPCC (2013).

17 Office for National Statistics (ONS) (2012) *Crime Statistics for England and Wales 2011/12*, London: ONS.

18 IPCC (2012a).

19 Scott, S. (2011) 'The investigation of Mark Duggan's death is tainted. I want no part in it', *Guardian*, 20 November, www.theguardian.com/commentis-free/2011/nov/20/investigation-mark-duggan-tainted (accessed 22 August 2014)

20 IPCC (2011) 'Clarification of recent reports regarding investigation in to shooting of Mark Duggan', statement made by IPCC chair Len Jackson, 24 November, www.ipcc.gov.uk/news/clarification-recent-reports-regarding-investigation-shooting-mark-duggan#sthash.Zs5WHHi5.dpuf (accessed 22 August 2014).

21 Scott, S. (2014) 'This perverse Mark Duggan verdict will ruin our relations with the police', *Guardian*, 9 January, www.theguardian.com/commentis-free/2014/jan/09/mark-duggan-verdict-relations-police (accessed 22 August 2014).

22 Dodd, V. (2014) 'Mark Duggan coroner: police created perception of collusion', *Guardian*, 4 June, www.theguardian.com/uk-news/2014/jun/04/mark-duggan-coroner-police-perception-collusion (accessed 22 August 2014).

23 See Consultation on draft amendments to IPCC statutory guidance to the police service on the handling of complaints, www.ipcc.gov.uk/news/consultation-draft-statutory-guidance-police-post-incident-management-launched (accessed 22 August 2014).

24 Dodd, V. (2014) 'Police chief condemns IPCC plan to keep officers apart after shootings', *Guardian*, 18 May, www.theguardian.com/uk-news/2014/may/18/police-ipcc-armed-officers-conferring (accessed 22 August 2014).

25 Elliot-Cooper, A. (2014) 'Mark Duggan, state violence and the long history of British propaganda', *Ceasefire*, 10 January, http://ceasefiremagazine.co.uk/mark-duggan-state-violence-long-history-british-propaganda/ (accessed 22 August 2014).

26 Mattson, J, and Hamilton, F. (2014) 'Police watchdog hid truth about Duggan shooting', *Times*, 28 October, www.thetimes.co.uk/tto/news/uk/crime/article4249930.ece (accessed 27 November 2014).

27 Travis, A. (2013) 'Theresa May to expand IPCC in crackdown on police corruption', *Guardian*, 12 February, www.theguardian.com/politics/2013/feb/12/theresa-may-ipcc-police-corruption (accessed 7 October 2014).

Part III

Corruption in Government and Public Institutions

7

British State Torture: From 'Search and Try' to 'Hide and Lie'

Paul O'Connor

In June 1975 an eminent Harley Street doctor flew to Dublin. The purpose of the trip was to carry out a medical examination of a patient in the St John of God Hospital in the Irish capital. The patient was suffering from severe angina, a condition which is 'always associated with the risk of sudden death' according to the doctor.[1] The doctor was Dr Denis Leigh, a leading consultant psychiatrist at the Bethlem Royal and the Maudsley Hospitals in London, and more importantly, medical consultant to the British Army.

The patient, Sean McKenna, was a former member of the IRA who had been subjected to so-called 'in-depth interrogation' following the introduction of internment without trial in August 1971. He was one of the 14 'hooded men' whose infamous treatment forced the Irish state to launch a case alleging torture against the UK government at the European Court of Human Rights in Strasbourg. Leigh's medical examination was being carried out on behalf of the Crown to bolster the UK defence that the men had not suffered long-term physical or psychiatric damage as a result of their interrogation.

The 'in-depth interrogation' that McKenna and the others were subjected to consisted of five techniques that had been widely used by the British army in counter-insurgency campaigns in Aden, Cyprus, Malaya, Palestine and elsewhere – hooding, white noise, deprivation of sleep and food, and finally, wall standing in a stress position. There was a sixth technique not alluded to in the training manual, regular physical beatings of the men. Codenamed 'Operation Calaba', the in-depth interrogations took place at a former military airbase at Ballykelly outside Derry which had been specially modified for interrogation. Until 2013 the men and the general public believed that the torture had in fact occurred at a different military base.

Dr Leigh reached some alarming conclusions. He found that McKenna's angina was known to British army doctors before the interrogation went ahead, and 'it would be hard to show ... that it was wise to proceed with the interrogation, and that the interrogation did not have the effect of worsening his angina'.[2]

McKenna complained of a number of psychiatric symptoms 'mainly of an anxious and fearful nature'[3] according to Leigh, who concluded, 'with regard to his other psychiatric symptoms I think that one will probably have to regard them as being the result of the so-called "deep interrogation" procedures'.[4]

In fact McKenna's psychiatric condition was such that he had been released from Long Kesh internment camp in May 1972 directly into the care of a psychiatric unit. Within one week of his arrest his shock of black hair had turned white. His daughter described 'a very broken man, sitting crying, very shaky'.[5]

Four days after the June 1975 medical examination Sean McKenna died. He had suffered a massive heart attack. The notes of this medical examination, discovered almost 40 years later in the British National Archives, may yet come to haunt the British state.

In 1976 the European Human Rights Commission (EHRC) upheld a complaint by Ireland that the treatment of the 'hooded men' constituted torture, and referred the case to the European Court of Human Rights for judgement. The Commission had condemned the five techniques as a 'modern system of torture' with 'a clear resemblance to those systematic methods of torture that have been known over the ages'.[6]

The stakes could not have been higher in terms of the legal and political fallout if the United Kingdom, one of the original signatories to the European Convention on Human Rights, had been found to have sanctioned torture. One memo warned that 'the security forces will be on international trial and we must do everything possible to minimise the risk of losing this battle'.[7] This was until recently one of the few inter-state cases taken to the court that ran its full term. As this chapter will show, the case and the subject matter dealt with in the case would also have major international implications many years later in Iraq, Afghanistan and at Guantanamo.

The United Kingdom successfully used the pretext of 'security' to ensure that British witnesses gave their evidence to the EHRC at a secret NATO airbase in Norway. In these hearings the United Kingdom argued that the use of the five techniques did not constitute 'administrative practice' and had not been sanctioned down a chain of command. It was further argued that the men had not suffered any long-term physical or psychiatric effects.

In his evidence to the Commission Dr Leigh testified that the psychiatric effects of the interrogations were minor and their persistence was due to the conditions of everyday life in Northern Ireland. His confidential report on Sean McKenna cited above painted a very different and alarming picture.

The Irish government had enlisted the help of two expert witnesses, Professor Robert Daly who had worked with the RAF and Professor Jan Bastiaans who had treated Nazi concentration camp survivors. Both men were adamant that the 'hooded men' had been tortured and were suffering serious after-effects on both their physical and psychiatric health. Dr Leigh weighed in on the side of the UK government. He failed to mention his own medical assessment of Sean McKenna. This was not the only evidence being withheld from the Commission and the court.

The Irish attorney general, Declan Costello, had no access to military or police witnesses, no ability to cross-examine, and crucially, had been denied sight of hundreds of documents which were extremely damaging to the British case. By this stage the tortured men had also initiated civil cases against the British government alleging torture. The legal advice within the Ministry of Defence was blunt: the cases should be settled out of court to avoid embarrassment or worse. Officials feared that the minister for defence at the time of the interrogations, Lord Carrington, could face conspiracy charges if evidence were heard in open court.[8] So anxious was the government to settle out of court at all costs that a recommendation was made to pay compensation to one of the men despite the fact that he was believed to be active in the IRA at the time the recommendation was made. Both the prime minister and the attorney general were advised of this at the time in a letter which warned, 'Given the interrogation procedures themselves were unlawful, it would constitute a conspiracy to arrange for these procedures to be put in place.'[9]

Some of the documents that the European Court did not see have now emerged from the archives. These include memos between ministerial aides and a Lt Col. Richard Nicholson. He led the interrogation team that had been brought in from the Joint Services Interrogation Wing in Ashford, Kent to train the Royal Ulster Constabulary special branch officers who carried out the interrogations. Nicholson admitted that some of the men had spent 36, 45 and even 49 hours in stress positions against a wall, but 'never more than 6 hours at a stretch'.[10] The ministerial aide reported that Nicholson had assured him that if a detainee collapsed he was allowed to get a 'second wind'. The memo continues, 'In our own interests we did not want detainees to be in such a state of collapse that they could not talk to us.'[11]

A detainee who was not cooperating also faced deprivation of sleep and a bread and water diet: 'once a prisoner was cooperating he was allowed to sleep ... in some cases an interrogatee (*sic*) could go for a couple of days without sleep'. Nicholson reported that a diet of bread and water was provided every six hours 'until they began to talk'. This led to an average weight loss of between 6 and 7 lbs in less than a week, although the official record notes that one prisoner 'who had not provided much useful information lost over a stone'.[12] In addition the 'hooded men' had to endure ongoing sensory deprivation in the form of white noise, which was described by one of the victims as 'absolutely ear piercing'.[13]

Needless to say the records make no mention of the ongoing brutal assaults on the men. Nicholson, who was later awarded an OBE, made the astonishing Kafkaesque claim that the hooding of the men was a voluntary process, and offered to provide statistics on voluntary versus mandatory hooding. His statistics claim, with no trace of irony, that two of the men spent 120 per cent more time 'voluntarily hooded than mandatorily hooded'.[14]

The circulation list on these documents show that ministers, their permanent under-secretaries, and even the director-general of intelligence (DGI) were being copied in on these exchanges and were well aware of the situation.[15] In one letter the DGI explained to a minister of state that some of the men volunteered to keep their hoods on because there were 'windows in the cells'.[16]

By 1974 the Labour minister for defence, Roy Mason, was aware of 'substantial medical evidence of lasting psychiatric damage' to one of the other men, Pat Shivers, who had lost 16 lb in interrogation and developed a facial tic.[17]

From 1971 to 1978 both Conservative and Labour governments conspired to withhold evidence and mislead the EHRC, the European Court of Human Rights and Ireland, a member state of the European Community. In 1978 the European Court ruled that the treatment of the men constituted 'inhuman and degrading treatment' but not torture. The judgement thus overruled the earlier finding of the Commission. Four of the 17 judges disagreed, and the Irish judge argued in a dissenting opinion that a site visit should have taken place to properly establish the facts. Had such a visit taken place (as occurred in another contemporaneous investigation involving allegations of torture during the military dictatorship of Greece)[18] we can only speculate which of the interrogation centres would have been shown to the learned judges, since Lt Col Nicholson had warned Whitehall that it was vital to keep the existence of Ballykelly secure. It was 'not known that it existed', he added ominously.[19]

In its judgement the Court found that 'the five techniques, as applied in combination ... were used systematically, they did not occasion suffering of the particular intensity and cruelty implied by the word torture as so understood'.

A 'special stigma' was attached to the word torture, the Court opined.[20] In 1977 the British attorney general, Sam Silkin QC, solemnly promised in Strasbourg that the five techniques, which no longer carried the 'special stigma' of torture, would never again be used as an aid to interrogation in Northern Ireland or elsewhere. That appeared to be the end of the matter.

In 2013 the Pat Finucane Centre,[21] an independent non-governmental organisation (NGO), discovered hundreds of documents about the Ireland *v* UK case that contradicted the judgement. It approached Ireland's national broadcaster, RTE, whose investigative journalists then began their own research in the National Archives in London. They made a dramatic discovery. Buried among the thousands of documents was a 1977 memo from the then secretary of state for Northern Ireland, Merlyn Rees, to his Labour prime minister, James Callaghan, about the ongoing case. Rees wrote, 'It is my view, (confirmed by Brian Faulkner[22] before his death) that the decision to use methods of torture in Northern Ireland in 1971/72 was taken by ministers – in particular Lord Carrington, then Secretary of State for Defence.' In a hand-written note on the margin, a senior civil servant commented, 'this could grow into something awkward if pursued'.[23]

The allegation that a minister of the Crown had sanctioned the use of torture would indeed have been awkward, had it been pursued. The special stigma attached to the word torture is reflected in international law, which allows for no departure under any circumstances from the strict prohibition of torture. There is no statute of limitations in respect of possible criminal charges, so seriously is this violation regarded.

In *Combating Torture: A Manual for Judges and Prosecutors*, academic Conor Foley refers to the Search and Try obligation on states:

> The four Geneva Conventions ... require states parties to search for people alleged to have committed or ordered grave breaches of the Conventions, such as torture and inhuman treatment, or who have failed in their duties as commanding officers to prevent such grave breaches occurring. The 'search and try' obligation is without frontiers under the Geneva Conventions.[24]

Successive UK governments, rather than comply with their legal obligation to 'search and try' allegations of torture, adopted a policy more akin to 'hide and lie'. This was to have consequences many years later.

The inquiry into the 2003 murder of an Iraqi civilian, Baha Mousa, by British soldiers was told that the five techniques had again been used in Iraq by every single battle group in the field.[25] The failure by the ECHR to attach the special stigma of torture to a member state in 1978 had fatal consequences for Baha Mousa. Others took note.

In 1999 the High Court of Israel ruled that certain interrogation practices used by the General Security Service against Palestinian prisoners, while illegal, did not constitute torture, and specifically referenced the Ireland *v* UK judgement in doing so.[26] The US attorney general also took note when seeking to justify torture in Iraq, Afghanistan and at Guantanamo Bay. The infamous 'torture memos' prepared for President Bush made direct reference to the Ireland *v* UK judgment. On page 31 the memo reads:

> The European Court of Human Rights ... recognised a wide array of acts that constitute cruel, inhuman, or degrading treatment or punishment, but do not amount to torture. Thus they appear to permit, under international law, an aggressive interpretation as to what amounts to torture, leaving that label to be applied only where extreme circumstances exist.[27]

In *Cruel Britannia: A Secret History of Torture, Guardian* journalist Ian Cobain provides damning evidence that the UK government did in fact 'do' torture, and had been doing so for decades in counter-insurgency wars from Brunei to Aden, and from Ireland to Iraq. In June 2013 UK foreign secretary William Hague apologised in Parliament for the torture of Mau Mau suspects in Kenya during the 1950s. Over £50 million was paid out in compensation to some 5,000 Kenyan victims. In 1972 prime minister Edward Heath had promised Parliament that the Ballykelly torture techniques would never be used again.

As the declassified documents make clear, both he and his cabinet colleagues actually went to great lengths to ensure that those responsible for torture would not face any sanction. The international legal obligation to 'search and try' those involved in sanctioning and carrying out torture was ignored. Successive governments adopted the motto 'hide' (the evidence) and 'lie' (to the court). The process was corrupted from beginning to end, from the interrogations at an isolated airfield on the banks of Lough Foyle to the office of the prime minister in Whitehall.

Notes

1   The National Archives CJ4 967, 'Settlements out of court civil actions: medi-
     cal report authored by Dr Denis Leigh RE: Sean Mc Kenna addressed to Noel
     Rea ESQ', Chief Crown Solicitors Office, 30 June 1975, p. 4.
2   National Archives CJ4 967, p. 4.
3   National Archives CJ4 967, p. 4.
4   National Archives CJ4 967, p. 4.
5   Interview on RTE documentary *The Torture Files*, broadcast 4 June 2014.
6   ECHR, Ser. B, vol. 23-1, pp. 377–90 (1976–78).
7   TNA DEFE 24 / 1151, John M Parkin, C2 (AD) MoD to Brig. Tickell, Chief of
     Staff, HQNI, 31 January 1972.
8   TNA CJ4 2202 Memo marked: *Confidential The DEEP INTERROGATION
     CASES.*
9   TNA DEFE 13 / 1044, memo for the prime minister marked 'Confidential
     deep interrogation : the case of Francis McGuigan', 1 April 1976.
10   TNA DEFE 13 917, *Interrogation: The follow up to the report on the Compton
     Committee*, p. 2.
11   TNA DEFE 13 917, p. 2.
12   TNA DEFE 13 917, p. 2.
13   Interview with Pat Shivers on *The Torture Files*.
14   TNA DEFE 13/ 917, 'Note of a telephone conversation between PS/PUS
     (private secretary to the permanent under-secretary) and Lt Col Nicholson',
     25SU, 28 October 1971.
15   For instance the circulation list on the 'Note of the Telephone Conversation'
     referred to in Note 14 included the APS/SofS (assistant private secretary/
     secretary of state) PS/Minister of State (private secretary/ minister of
     state), MA/CGS (military assistant/chief of the General Staff) and DGI
     (director-general of intelligence) .
16   TNA DEFE 13 / 917, 'Memo – Secret – UK EYES ONLY' (No date).
17   *The Torture Files.*
18   www.bailii.org/eu/ECHR/1978/1.html (accessed 10 September 2014). Sepa-
     rate Opinion of Judge O'Donoghue, p. 59. O'Donoghue had himself taken
     part in a site visit to Greece in the case involving allegations of torture during
     the military dictatorship. See *Yearbook of the European Convention on Human
     Rights: The Greek Case* (1969).
19   TNA DEFE 13 917, p. 2.
20   www.bailii.org/eu/ECHR/1978/1.html (accessed 10 September 2014).
21   www.patfinucanecentre.org
22   Brian Faulkner had been the Unionist prime minister of the devolved local
     government in Northern Ireland in 1971 when internment was introduced.
23   TNA DEFE 68/152, memo from SoS NI Merlyn Rees to prime minister James
     Callaghan titled 'Meeting between the Attorneys General of the Republic
     of Ireland and the United Kingdom', 31 March 1977. In this memo Rees
     discusses the insistence of the Irish attorney general that policemen and/
     or soldiers should be prosecuted for torture. In his opinion they should not

because 'in the particular circumstances of 1971/72 a political decision was taken'.

24 Foley, C. (2003) *Combating Torture: A Manual for Judges and Prosecutors*, Colchester: Human Rights Centre, University of Essex, available for free download at: www.essex.ac.uk/combatingtorturehandbook/

25 webarchive.nationalarchives.gov.uk/20120215203912/http://www.bahamousainquiry.org/

26 See Koenig, A., Stover, E. and Fletcher, L. (2009) 'The cumulative effect: medico-legal approach to United States torture law and policy', *Essex Human Rights Review*, vol. 6, no. 1, p. 155, fn 55.

27 Memorandum for Alberto R. Gonzales, counsel to the president, re. standards of conduct for interrogation under 18 U.S.C., p. 31, www2.gwu.edu/~nsarchiv/NSAEBB/NSAEBB127/02.08.01.pdf (accessed 10 September 2014).

8

The Return of The Repressed: Secrets, Lies, Denial and 'Historical' Institutional Child Sexual Abuse Scandals

Chris Greer and Eugene McLaughlin

Introduction

This chapter may seem like an awkward fit for a book on the causes, extent and consequences of institutional corruption, which is conventionally defined and understood as financial and political malfeasance: that is, fraud, bribery, fraud, extortion, embezzlement, insider dealing, market manipulation, nepotism, buying influence and so on. However we would argue that there is a need to widen the frame of institutional corruption to include moral touchstone issues such as institutional child sexual abuse. This is a classic case of institutional corruption because it involves exploitation of the most basic kind, namely the sexual abuse of the vulnerable, powerless and dependent in institutions that are entrusted with the power to care, protect, help and/or educate.

It is important to realise that in these institutions, like the others discussed in this book, we find concentrations of status hierarchies and networks, privilege, power relations, vested interests and ideological agendas. They are also places where secrets and lies are monitored and policed, and because of the nature of the crime, where various forms of blackmail take place. Child sexual abuse morally corrupts any institution in which it takes place because it is a criminal violation of the stated purpose and expectations of the institution. The corruption is deepened if it is established either in public perception or legal fact that the institution had/has knowledge of the criminality and through inaction, incompetence or concealment, had/has protected perpetrators and disregarded or undermined victims and/or silenced whistleblowers. When unveiled, the resultant scandal about the criminality, the institutional knowledge and the decision to place institutional reputation before the interests of victims corrodes the legitimacy of that institution, particularly if it is a culturally venerated institution. The public revulsion damages the reputation of anyone associated with the institution, and undermines public trust in institutions.

Institutional Child Sexual Abuse: From Denial to Recognition

The long-standing cultural taboos that had kept the sexual abuse of children marginalised from UK public debate were finally challenged in the 1980s by feminist campaigning, media coverage and public testimony from individual survivors.[1] Media studies expert Jenny Kitzinger notes that news media exposure 'fundamentally transformed private and public discourse' about child sexual abuse.[2] Because coverage of abuse continued to be shaped by the dominant news frames of 'predatory paedophiles' , little attention was paid to more prevalent problems of institutional and familial abuse (other than 'problem families').[3] However, a succession of scandals since the 1980s has exposed the 'historical' sexual abuse of children in residential care homes, schools, young offender institutions and religious institutions, and forced the problem of institutionally facilitated abuse onto the UK political agenda.[4]

Institutional scandals resulting from silence, stonewalling, denial and deception led to the establishment of official inquiries which raised further public awareness of this hidden crime.[5] As a result, it was no longer possible for British society to deny knowledge of child sexual abuse in institutional settings. However, doing something about it was a very different matter. It was not until 2012 and the scandal that resulted from the naming of Sir Jimmy Savile as a prolific sexual offender who had allegedly offended for decades, that the issue of 'historical' institutional child sexual abuse was forced to the front of public consciousness in the United Kingdom in an unprecedented manner.

We would argue that the sociologist Stan Cohen's understanding of denial can provide us with a framework to investigate the institutional response to allegations of child sexual abuse. Cohen set out three distinct, though at times intersecting. primary techniques of denial: literal denial, interpretive denial and implicatory denial. These forms of denial are deployed in the attempt to protect the reputation of the institution.[6] With **literal denial**, the facts or knowledge of the facts about the alleged crimes are rejected by the institution. Literal denial may be genuine, it may be a means of disregarding a 'truth' too traumatic to acknowledge, or it may be a form of deliberate lying. With **interpretive denial**, the facts of the child sexual abuse are not denied, but they are given a different institutional meaning from that which seems evident to others: the crime is 'cognitively reframed and then reallocated to a different, less pejorative class of event'.[7] Finally, **implicatory denial** accepts the facts of the crime and their conventional interpretation, but rejects or transfers their institutional significance or consequences. Powerful institutions can deploy significant public relations resources to deny and/or suppress allegations of individual and institutional criminality and question the credibility and motives of those making the allegations.

Whichever of these is used, public denial is the main force that drives and animates an activated institutional child sexual abuse scandal. Since public naming requires editorial assurance that there is enough evidence to substantiate the allegations, the default news media position at the point of scandal activation is that the accused is guilty. Institutional denial, therefore, is perceived and interpreted as a form of calculated lying, and those accused of lying about or concealing child sexual abuse will be plunged into a volatile 'trial by media' in which claims and counter-claims are publicly scrutinised for validity.[8]

The Sir Jimmy Savile Scandal

After Sir Jimmy Savile's death on 29 October 2011, at the age of 84, he was memorialised in news features and obituaries as a 'national treasure' who had lived a truly eccentric and exceptional life in the full glare of publicity.[9] Savile was acclaimed as the United Kingdom's first celebrity disc jockey, the instantly recognisable face and voice of *Top of the Pops*, and the presenter of *Jim'll Fix It*, one of the most successful BBC television shows, which ran from 1975 to 1994. At the height of the show's popularity, approximately 20,000 children a week would write to Savile asking him to 'fix it' for them. Savile presented each lucky child who appeared on the show with a medal engraved with the words 'Jim Fixed It For Me'.

A friend of the famous and powerful, Savile, a northern working-class boy made good, was appointed OBE in 1971. He received a knighthood from the Vatican in 1982 and from Buckingham Palace in 1990 for his phenomenal charity work, which raised tens of millions of pounds for his good causes.[10] Following his death, there were tributes from Buckingham Palace, politicians, fellow celebrities and representatives of the charities, hospitals and children's homes for which he had worked. The then director general of the BBC, Mark Thompson, made a public statement eulogising the veteran broadcaster's unique place in post-war British popular culture and his untiring charitable deeds. The symbiotic relationship between the BBC and Savile was commemorated in a series of tribute programmes. Savile's 'national treasure' status was reinforced with a fittingly unconventional funeral that spanned three days between 8 and 10 November 2011.

From Latent to Activated Scandal

On 8 January 2012 the *Sunday Mirror* claimed that *Newsnight*, the BBC's flagship current affairs programme, had abandoned an investigation into allegations that Savile had sexually assaulted under-age girls in the 1970s. It was alleged that the news story, which included victim testimony, was 'killed' because it would have undermined the BBC's tribute programmes. For a brief period, the framing of Savile as 'national treasure' was challenged publicly across mainstream news outlets and blogs. Although Savile was not alive to deny the allegations, or to threaten legal action, the scandal remained latent. What is most striking is that the following period of news coverage, from March to July 2012, reaffirmed the default 'national treasure' framing by focusing on the 'fortune' that that Savile had bequeathed to his charities.

The Savile allegations resurfaced in August 2012, with the *Sunday Mirror* and *Mail on Sunday* reporting that an ITV documentary team had unearthed enough evidence to name Savile not just as a prolific sexual predator but as a paedophile. Once again, however, the latent scandal failed to initiate any form of subsequent newspaper investigation, and did not progress to the activated phase.

On 3 October 2012 ITV broadcast *Exposure: The Other Side of Jimmy Savile*, naming Savile as a prolific sexual predator who for decades had offended with impunity inside UK public institutions. The heavily trailed ITV documentary contained three potentially incendiary claims. The first was that for decades Savile's prime-time BBC programmes and celebrity status had enabled him to sexually assault or sexually exploit star-struck, naïve teenage girls. Many of the assaults took place on BBC premises.

The second accusation was that, within the BBC and across the entertainment industry, Savile's sexual predilections were 'common knowledge' but no one had challenged him. As a powerful, high-profile and well-connected BBC celebrity and acclaimed charity worker, Savile was described as being untouchable. His 'eccentricities' were tolerated, and as a consequence nothing was done by the corporation to protect teenage girls from Savile and his acquaintances.

The third allegation was that a BBC *Newsnight* investigation had been blocked from broadcasting the allegations in order to protect the reputation of the BBC.

The retrofitting of Savile as a 'prolific sexual predator' whose offending had been known about and possibly concealed by the BBC consolidated over the next two days. No national news outlet deviated from this characterisation, and no one came forward to defend Savile's reputation. It was the turn of the national newspapers to demand answers to four mutually reinforcing questions that would drive the next phase in the Savile scandal's development.

- How many people had Savile sexually assaulted, when and where?
- Who at the BBC shared the guilt for Savile's sexual assaults, and what was their role in the cover-up?
- Did the BBC drop its own investigation because of plans to screen tribute programmes to Savile and to protect the corporation's reputation?
- Could those who colluded with Savile at the BBC and were still alive be brought to justice?'

Institutional Denial by the BBC

Prior to the broadcast of the ITV documentary Savile's family, friends and institutional supporters reacted to the allegations with literal denial. The BBC's denial was comprehensive, and its self-exoneration absolute. The corporation insisted that it could not find any evidence of complaints about Savile in the BBC archives. Because the allegations were from another era, the past was the past and nothing more could be known or done about Savile. *Newsnight* released an aggressive statement, deploying both literal and interpretive techniques of denial, to reject the ITV allegations, absolve itself of responsibility and shift attention onto those whom it accused of ulterior motives in circulating a 'false' and 'malicious rumour'.

On the day of the ITV documentary, with newspapers carrying corroborating accounts of sexual assault by Savile and other BBC celebrities, literal, interpretive and implicatory techniques of denial were evident in the BBC's attempt to neutralise the activated scandal. Despite the now widespread understanding that rumours and allegations against Savile had been circulating for years, there was literal denial of historical knowledge in the corporation's horror at discovering that an employee could have perpetrated sexual assaults on BBC premises. This literal denial of historical knowledge facilitated an interpretive denial of institutional culpability: there was no acknowledgement of the widespread criticism that the BBC had failed to take seriously and investigate rumours and allegations of sexual abuse in the past. Rather, the focus was placed on the present and future, through pledging to cooperate fully with a criminal investigation. Finally, there was implicatory denial: even if historical sexual abuse had taken place that did not mean that it incriminated the BBC or it was the BBC's responsibility to investigate. Only the police could do that.

Newsnight published another outright rejection of the accusations surrounding the cancelled investigation. Newspapers expressed incredulity, given the focus of *Newsnight*'s aborted investigation, at what were deemed to be the BBC's disingenuous denials of any knowledge of Savile's offending, its repudiation of the corporation's symbiotic links with Savile and its perceived indignant stance towards a rapidly escalating scandal.

The chaotic fall-out from the Savile scandal and what we define as the retrofitting of Savile as not just a prolific sex offender but a paedophile created an unprecedented crisis for the BBC. Thrown into disarray by its perceived failures in the Savile investigation, *Newsnight* proceeded to broadcast allegations of an alleged sexual abuse cover-up involving an unnamed Conservative politician. The politician was not named, but Lord McAlpine was immediately identified on the internet as the subject of what turned out to be groundless allegations. The outcome was the resignation of the director general, after just 54 days in post, the redeployment of staff, question marks over the journalistic credibility of *Newsnight*, the reorganisation of BBC news reporting, and inquiries into the corporation's failings both before and after the scandal broke. Under intense news media and political pressure, and now operating with a rearview image of Savile, senior BBC personnel offered abject public apologies to his victims, conceding liability for the need to compensate anyone whom he had assaulted on BBC premises. The corporation also admitted that it was a mistake to have cancelled the *Newsnight* investigation into Savile's alleged sexual offences.

Looking Back and Looking Forward: Institutional
Child Sexual Abuse Scandal without End

The BBC's extraordinary shift from public denial to public acceptance that Sir Jimmy Savile had been able to offend with impunity inside the corporation for decades had serious consequences for the other institutions and charities connected to Savile. The BBC revelations triggered numerous allegations which created a possible six-decade-long history of sexual abuse by Savile and others. An amplifying institutional child sexual abuse without end is being driven in England and Wales by four networked dynamics.

First, the police are conducting at least six publicly known investigations. **Operation YewTree** is investigating historical allegations of child sex abuse by Savile, people who knew Savile and others with no connection to Savile. According to Scotland Yard, approximately 600 people came forward to provide information, of whom 450 alleged sexual abuse mainly involving Savile, and 214 criminal offences were formally recorded across 28 police forces.[11] This police operation has resulted in the questioning, and in some cases high-profile arrest and successful prosecution, of other ageing celebrities on charges of historical sexual assaults.

Operation Fernbridge is looking into claims that a paedophile network linked to Parliament had operated with impunity in the 1970s and 1980s. This investigation has centred on Elm Guest House in southwest London. Greater Manchester Police is examining allegations that police and politicians conspired to hush up the sexual abuse of children by Cyril Smith, the now deceased MP for Rochdale.

Operation Cayacos is re-examining allegations of a paedophile ring linked to Peter Righton, a founding member of the Paedophile Information Exchange, a group that campaigned to make sex between adults and children legal.

Operation Pallial is examining allegations of historical abuse from1953 to 1995 at children's homes in North Wales, while a review is also taking place into the previous inquiry into North Wales abuse dating back to the 1970s.

Operation Garford is investigating historical abuse allegations centred on Kesgrave Hall School, Suffolk from the 1970s to the 1990s, and a separate inquiry is assessing historical abuse claims in Jersey's care system from 1960 to the present day.

For those researching institutional corruption, what is being alleged here is that powerful men at the heart of the British establishment who sexually exploited children and under-age teenagers were protected from prosecution and/or set up and blackmailed by the authorities.[12] This has resurrected memories of the still unanswered questions surrounding the investigations into the Kincora boys home scandal in Northern Ireland in the 1980s.[13]

Second, and equally significantly, the Independent Police Complaints Commission is investigating claims that officers in the Surrey, North Yorkshire and West Yorkshire police forces ignored or covered up allegations against Savile.

Third, the Savile scandal has activated official inquiries into a flood of complaints that Savile sexually abused patients in NHS hospitals, including Broadmoor, Leeds General Infirmary and Stoke Mandeville, where he worked as a volunteer and charity worker. To date 28 hospitals have published reports on the allegations. And local authorities have been instructed to investigate claims that Savile abused children at 21 children's homes and schools in England in between the 1960s and 1980s.

Finally, in July 2014 the government was forced to establish an independent inquiry looking at how all public bodies dealt with allegations of child sexual abuse, while another will look at how the Home Office handled sexual abuse claims dating from the 1980s.

The investigations and prosecutions, the publication of inquiry reports into the amplifying Savile scandal, and the naming of individuals on the internet as paedophiles, are generating further revelations and new allegations. The floodgates have opened regarding further allegations of sexual abuse, historical and otherwise, in residential care homes, state and private schools, young offender institutions and religious institutions. Equally significantly are testimonies explaining how victims were mocked, belittled and condemned when they reported the abuse.

To illustrate this point, a report published in September 2014 by Professor Alexis Jay, the former chief inspector of social work in Scotland, declared that at least 1,400 teenage girls had been sexually exploited in Rotherham by gangs of men who were predominantly of Asian origin between 1997 and 2013. The report detailed the collective, systemic failures by politicians, the police, social care workers and the Home Office, who allowed the sexual exploitation of girls and young women to carry on despite three previous reports which had identified the problem. Rotherham will not be the last local authority in England to have to account for the sexual abuse crimes that its staff knew about but ignored.

What we are witnessing is nothing less than a rewriting of significant aspects of postwar social history. For example, two of the BBC's iconic programmes, *Top of the Pops* and *Jim'll Fix It*, are now automatically associated in the public imagination not with more innocent times but with providing an opportunity structure and front for a serial sex offender. However, there is still much more to know. Savile is now regarded as guilty of being 'a prolific, predatory sex offender' who exploited virtually every institution he came into contact with, and in the words of Metropolitan Police Commander Peter Spindler, 'groomed the nation'. However, what is still to be researched is how institutional priorities and cultures, and the moral milieu of the 1960s and 1970s, empowered and permitted Savile and other celebrities to carry out sexual assaults with institutional protection and impunity.

There are limitations to the current investigations and prosecutions. For example, for the most part the chains of historic responsibility are difficult to establish, because those with knowledge are dead and/ or records are missing. We also need to be conscious of the fact that institutions are deploying a new technique of denial – public apology for historical wrongdoing. Carefully choreographed public apologies are becoming a routinised way of attempting to deflect criticism and draw a line between then and now. However, a key 'historical' lesson of the still amplifying Savile scandal is that the past can no longer be conveniently bracketed as the past, nor is it 'another time and place' – it is the ever-present future.

Notes

1   Angelides, S. (2005) 'The emergence of the paedophile in the late twentieth century', *Australian Historical Studies*, vol. 36, no. 126, pp. 272–95; Campbell, B. (1988) *Unofficial Secrets: Child Sexual Abuse, the Cleveland Case*, London: Virago; Department of Health (1991) *Child Abuse: A Study of Inquiry Reports 1980–89*, London: Department of Health; Department of Health and Social Services (1982) *Child Abuse: A Study of inquiry Reports 1973–8*, London: Department of Health and Social Services; Greer, C. (2012) *Sex Crime and the Media: Sex Offending and the Press in a Divided Society*, London: Routledge; Kitzinger, J. (2001) 'Transformations of public and private knowledge: audience research, feminism and the experience of childhood sexual abuse', *Feminist Media Studies*, vol. 1, no.1, pp. 91–104; Kitzinger, J. (2004) *Framing Abuse: Media Influence and Public Understanding of Sexual Violence Against Children*, London: Pluto; La Fontaine, J. S. (1990) *Child Sexual Abuse*, Cambridge: Polity in association with Basil Blackwell.

2   Kitzinger (2001), p. 91. See also Radford, L., Corral, S., Bradley, S., Fisher, H., Bassett, C., Howat, N. and Collishaw, S. (2011) *Child Abuse and Neglect in the UK Today*, London: NSPCC.

3   Critcher, C. (2002) 'Media, government and moral panic: the politics of paedophilia in Britain 2000–1', *Journalism Studies*, vol. 3, no. 4, pp. 521–35; Silverman, J. and Wilson, D. (2002) *Innocence Betrayed : Paedophilia, the Media and Society*, Cambridge: Polity.

4   Davidson, J. C. (2008) *Child Sexual Abuse: Media Representations and Government Reactions*, Abingdon/New York: Routledge-Cavendish; Franklin, B. and Parton, N. (1990) *Social Work, the Media and Public Relations*, London: Routledge; Jenkins, P. (1992) *Intimate Enemies: Moral Panics in Contemporary Great Britain*, New York: Aldine de Gruyter; Kitzinger, J. (1996) 'Media constructions of sexual abuse risks', *Child Abuse Review*, vol. 5, no. 5, pp. 319–33; Moore, C. (1996) *The Kincora Scandal : Political Cover-up and Intrigue in Northern Ireland*, Dublin: Marino Press; Silverman, J. and Wilson, D. (2002) *Innocence Betrayed : Paedophilia, the Media and Society*, Cambridge: Polity.

5   Barter, C. (1998) *Investigating Institutional Abuse of Children: An Exploration of the NSPCC Experience*, NSPCC Policy Practice Research Series, London: NSPCC; Corby, B., Doig, A. and Roberts, V. (1998) 'Inquiries into child abuse', *Journal of Social Welfare and Family Law*, vol. 20, no. 4, pp. 377–95; Department of Health (1991) *Child Abuse: A Study of Inquiry Reports 1980–89*, London: Department of Health; Waterhouse, S. R. (2012) *Lost in Care: Report of the Tribunal of Inquiry into the Abuse of Children in the former County Council areas of Gwynedd and Clwyd since 1974*, London: The Stationery Office for Department of Health.

6   Cohen, S. (2001) *States of Denial: Knowing about Atrocities and Suffering*, Cambridge: Polity; Sykes, G. and Matza, D. (1957) 'Techniques of neutralization: a theory of delinquency', *American Sociological Review*, vol. 22, no. 6, pp. 664–70; Zerubavel, E. (2006) *The Elephant in the Room: Silence and Denial in Everyday Life*, Oxford/New York: Oxford University Press; Gardner, F. (2012) 'Defensive processes and deception: an analysis of the response of the institutional church to disclosures of child sexual abuse', *British Journal of Psychotherapy*, vol. 28, no. 1, pp. 98–109.

7   Cohen (2001), p. 106.

8   Greer, C. and McLaughlin (2011) '"Trial by media": policing, the 24-7 news mediasphere and the "politics of outrage"', *Theoretical Criminology*, vol. 15, no. 1, pp. 23–46.

9   For an extended discussion of the initial phases of the Savile scandal see Greer, C. and McLaughlin, E. (2013) 'The Sir Jimmy Savile scandal: child sexual abuse and institutional denial at the BBC', *Crime, Media Culture*, vol. 9, no. 3, pp. 243–64.

10 Bellamy, A. (2012) *How's About That Then? The Authorised Biography of Jimmy Savile*, Leeds: Great Northern Books; Davies, D. (2014) *In Plain Sight: The Life and Lies of Jimmy Savile*, London: Quercus; Savile, J. (1974) *As It Happens*, London: Barrie & Jenkins.

11 Metropolitan Police Service/NSPCC (2013) 'Giving victims a voice: a joint MPS and NSPCC Report into allegations of sexual abuse, made against Jimmy Savile under Operation Yewtree', www.nspcc.org.uk/globalassets/documents/research-reports/yewtree-report-giving-victims-a-voice

12   Danczuk, S. and Baker, M. (2014) *Smile For The Camera: The Double Life of Cyril Smith*, London: Biteback.

13   Moore, C. (1996) *The Kincora Scandal: Political Cover-up and Intrigue in Northern Ireland*, Dublin: Marino Press; Greer, C. (2012) *Sex Crime and the Media: Sex Offending and the Press in a Divided Society*, London: Routledge; Dillon, M. (1991) *The Dirty War*, London: Arrow.

9

Politics, Government and Corruption: The Case of the Private Finance Initiative

Michael Mair and Paul Jones

Introduction

In this chapter we trace some of the ways in which the United Kingdom's private finance initiative (PFI) – a species of 'public private partnership' (PPP) whose operations and effects we explore in what follows – can be treated as an example of 'corruption'.[1] Through an examination of associations between practice, process and context in the implementation of PFI, we focus on the role of the state and new forms of governmental arrangement in establishing contexts in which corruption, understood in different ways, can flourish.

As David Whyte points out in his Introduction to this book, corruption is too often cast in either/or binaries predicated on the formal separation of private and public spheres. This invites analyses in which state and market are pitted against one another. As we shall show, such analyses can be misleading. The rise of new governmental arrangements like PFI significantly destabilise such distinctions. Arrangements like PFI work to incorporate market actors within the circuits of government, making them public authorities by proxy which undertake the functions of the state at the behest of the state but on the basis of restricted, one-sided and corrupt/ible contractual agreements established on commercial terms and shielded from public view.[2] These arrangements exhibit a particular kind of logic, which Lynch calls the 'logic of sleaze' – opening up room for 'transgressive' and 'scandalous' activities while simultaneously working to close down and undermine attempts to bring those transgressions and scandals to light.[3] We argue, therefore, that if we are to analyse corruption, we must understand those aspects of government which make it possible. The example of PFI – just one of the many state-market hybrids which are increasingly coming to define the governmental landscape in the United Kingdom and elsewhere – will help us to arrive at a clearer view of this 'logic of sleaze' at work.

After providing some background on PFI, sketching its scale and scope, we outline three senses in which PFI can be thought of as 'corrupt'. First, we look at the PFI commissioning process as a site of corrupt activity. Second, we look at PFI as a corruption of equity – that is, as a site where relations of equity are inverted through the flow of funds from the public to private and from poor to rich. And, third, we look at PFI as a corruption of practices of accountability – that is, a site where political responsibility can be obscured and therefore denied, and where even minimal democratic controls and oversight mechanisms are being eroded (see also Chapter 1). The connecting thread is how PFI works to displace and dislocate accountability, itself a deliberate, sought-for outcome of the policy and the wider political strategies which inform it as well as many other recent governmental innovations. If, then, PFI is corrupt, it is a form of corruption that has been nurtured and allowed to spread for political purposes.

PFI: Background, Scale and Scope

> We do not believe that politicians and officials should take key [public] investment decisions.[4]
>
> (Kenneth Clarke, chancellor of the exchequer, 1994)

PFI is a species of public–private partnership that has become the primary mechanism for capital investment – that is, infrastructure projects – in the public sector in the United Kingdom. PFI has its origins in the Thatcher and Major governments of the late 1980s, but was extended and amplified under the Blair–Brown administrations, where it became a cornerstone of public policy.[5] A way of leveraging funding for infrastructure projects, PFI takes capital investment off the public sector balance sheet via private sector financing. Under PFI, capital investment no longer counts as borrowing, and therefore does not count as public debt, but as current expenditure (that is, payments) instead. This (artificially) improves public sector borrowing figures and allows government to build new roads, schools, hospitals and so on while maintaining a reputation for fiscal constraint. A nebulous, suspect accounting device, PFI has proven enduringly controversial, but despite sustained attacks by the Liberal Democrats and Conservatives as well as the Scottish National Party when in opposition, all three parties have continued the policy when in office, signing off new Private Finance 2 (PF2) deals it is claimed will not repeat the mistakes of those past 'PF1' initiatives they once so vehemently decried. PFI, in political terms, has thus been reaffirmed as 'the only game in town'[6] when it comes to public infrastructure investment.

In her analysis of PFI, Professor Jean Shaoul of Manchester University summarises the broad rules of the 'game' as follows:

> Under PFI [and now PF2], the private sector designs, builds and finances much needed new hospitals, schools, roads, prisons and other social and public infrastructure and provides the ancillary, but not the 'core' professional, services for 20–35 years, in return for an annual fee that covers both the capital cost of the asset and service delivery. In effect, the public authorities lease the infrastructure required for the delivery of public services from the private sector.[7]

PFI is thus akin to a multi-billion-pound hire-purchase scheme with servicing arrangements thrown in, one that comes with all the drawbacks of raised costs but multiplied by its massive scale. Concentrated in health, education and transport but employed in all areas of government local and national, the decades-long lifespans and ring-fenced funding status of these contractual commitments means they will remain an enduring feature of the policy and indeed physical landscape for some time to come.

Based on figures released to the *Guardian*,[8] by 2012, 719 major infrastructure projects had been delivered via PFI, a large number partly attributable to the fact that, at its peak in 2009, PFI projects accounted for an estimated 70 per cent of new builds in health and 60 per cent in education. These 719 projects had a stated capital value of £55 billion. While total repayment costs are difficult to quantify, the limited public domain data available showed these would result in direct repayments alone of £301 billion over 50 years – six times the capital value. Existing direct repayment costs will peak in 2017–18 at £10.1 billion, with a further 39 projects, with a capital value of £5.6 billion, in the pipeline at the time these figures were released.

As an illustration of the cost inflations associated with many PFI schemes, the proposed Calderdale Royal Hospital PFI in Yorkshire, for instance, has a capital value of £65 million but will result in direct repayments of £773 million over the lifetime of project. The recent Mersey Gateway Bridge project, to take another example, which will result in a second bridge across the Mersey at Runcorn, has a capital value of £600 million but associated long-term costs of £2 billion.[9] Operating with additional financing from Halton Council, much of the cost is to be recovered from bridge users – that is, the same taxpayers footing the bill – through tolls. Originally projected to be comparable to the tolls on the Mersey Tunnels (currently £1.70), it is now thought the tolls could cost £3 or more.[10] Furthermore, road users seeking to cross the Mersey from this direction have no choice but to pay, as the existing bridge will also be tolled. As Professor Shaoul notes, this is 'the first known instance of tolling a hitherto free public bridge in order to make a private scheme viable'.[11]

PFI deals also leave plenty of scope for companies to inflate costs after contracts reach 'financial close'. In terms of hospital PFIs, for example: 'actual payments to the private sector turned out to be 20 per cent higher on average than originally estimated', rising to 71 per cent higher in some cases.[12] In terms of roads:

> [the Highways Agency's] payments ... are £300m a year, or 20 per cent of . its budget for 8 per cent of its roads. The contract for the M25 will add a further £300m a year, meaning that 40 per cent of the budget will be committed for a very small proportion of the network.[13]

PFIs also incur significant pre-contract costs, with the price for facilitating contracts £2.7 billion in the first half of 2010 alone, a substantial proportion of which was allocated via Partnerships UK (PUK), a semi-public body incorporating industry representations which oversees the tendering process on the UK government's behalf. As PFI contracts are deemed 'commercially sensitive', and fall outside the scope of freedom of information requests, information about its workings is highly limited. It is thus difficult to be clear about the true costs involved.

But PFI looks like a bad deal no matter what angle we come at it from. PFI projects would not be commercially viable without substantial commitments of resources on the part of the state, and PFI is therefore best seen as a 'political, not a market, construct'.[14] As private debt is more expensive than public debt, private sector companies have little incentive to become involved in infrastructure projects unless the terms are loaded in their favour: PFI deals are simply not attractive without substantial 'sweeteners' before, during and afterwards. This sets the context for our first substantive point.

PFI as Corrupt/Corruptible Practice

Concerns have been raised about the anti-competitive character of the PFI tendering and bidding process, as well as the conflicts of interest involved since its introduction. There has been considerable concentration in the PFI 'industry', with the numbers of companies bidding to win contracts falling over time. By 2009, 'one in three PFI projects ... attracted only two bidders'.[15] The problems that industrial concentration can create were underscored in 2009 when the Office for Fair Trading (OFT) brought cases against over 100 companies, many of which were and are key PF1/2 contractors, accusing them of 'collusive practices' such as cover pricing and bid rigging.[16] The OFT's investigation had begun in 2004 when allegations regarding PFI contracts were reported to it.[17] The charge was that, prior to submitting bids, 'competitors' had been in contact with one another regarding the contracts. Informal agreements were reached that one company would submit an unrealistically inflated bid which the other would then undercut with a slightly less inflated one. The favour would be returned as part of the bidding on other contracts, when the roles would reverse.

As regulation consultants Europe Economics put it in their report on a survey of the impact of the OFT's investigation on business practices (itself commissioned by the OFT):

> In September 2009, the OFT announced its decision to fine 103 construction companies a total of £129.2 million for infringing UK competition law by engaging in bid rigging activities, largely in the form of cover pricing, on 199 tenders between 2000 and 2006. Prior to this, the OFT had issued a Statement of Objections in April 2008 against 112 construction companies for alleged bid rigging. The OFT's decision followed a four year investigation into the sector, and constituted one of the OFT's largest investigations under the Competition Act. Cover pricing is an illegal form of bid rigging, where a firm submits an artificially high bid after discussion with another bidder. These types of bids are not priced to win the contract but clients are not aware of this or of the discussion between the bidders, giving them a misleading impression with regards to the real extent of competition.[18]

Specifics have been hard to prove, but the general conclusion has been that overpricing has led to substantially higher costs to the taxpayer for services that could have been secured at a much lower cost via the public sector. As Ballieu put it, a 'procurement system meant to be more competitive appears to have engendered a whole new level of corruption' and raised questions as to whether 'bid-rigging [is] intrinsic to PFI'.[19] The potential for illegal activities such as bid rigging, as well as legal but morally dubious practices connected with pre- and post-contract cost inflation, are problems that arise in a system claimed to be operating in the public's interest but which is shrouded in secrecy. PFI, put simply, lacks moral, legal, political and financial integrity, and it is because of this that it is haunted by the spectre of corrupt practice, real and potential.

PFI as a Corruption of Equity

PFI is far more expensive than conventional financing, as it generates substantial 'transaction costs' which are typically borne by the public, either directly (through charges) or indirectly (through taxation). As a result, the outcome of implementing these schemes is redistribution from public to private and from poor to rich in a subversion of notions of equity. Despite the costs of servicing the contracts to the public, once outside public ownership, some PFI deals have produced returns on capital of over 60 per cent, a return on which the public has no claim.[20]

However, PFI is not simply an accountancy device weighted in favour of the financial interests and balance sheets of contractors; it also involves the transfer of staff from the public to private sector into more precarious and insecure forms of employment. According to the National Audit Office, by 2004 an estimated 35,000 ancillary employees (janitors, porters, cleaners, catering staff and the like) had been transferred from the public sector to the private sector workforce.[21] While the first generation of PFI workers were protected to a degree, those who now work in what would have been public sector employment before PFI are not. With poorer terms and conditions and lower wages than their (dwindling) public sector counterparts, PFI contracts have thus been key drivers in the creation of a differentiated workforce involved in the supply of public services, with a publicly employed 'core' and a cheaper, casualised, privately employed and disposable 'maintenance' workforce now in place alongside it.

Working on the public's behalf, the track records of PFI companies as employers also deserve greater attention than they normally receive. For instance, companies like Carillion, the company awarded the contract for the £429 million new Royal Liverpool Hospital, alongside many other established PFI contractors, have been charged with systematic anti-union activities. As Keep Our NHS Public Merseyside pointed out in its official objections to the scheme:

> Carillion, the construction company now selected as Preferred Bidder for the Royal, is deeply implicated in the national construction 'blacklist',[22] racist bullying and victimisation of healthcare staff at a PFI hospital in Swindon, ... deaths at a surgical centre in Hertfordshire ... [and] has been involved in several PFI schemes with financial problems.[23]

While PFI acts as a mechanism for reconfiguring labour markets, under-cutting the labour market position of the most vulnerable in structural terms, the issues around inequity extend further. PFI schemes are political priorities reified as features of the built environment. And in terms of their location, they have tended to be built in areas where new infrastructure has been most needed: that is, in the poorest communities. As PFI has expanded, buildings delivered under its auspices are now the places where people pay their rent, access healthcare, visit their libraries, and possibly work in the delivery of public services. The introduction of PFI schemes has actually led to a contraction in the provision of those services. A fixed item on public sector budgets, PFI commitments have to be paid before any other obligations are met. When public sector budgets are cut, as they have been systematically in the United Kingdom since 2008, core provision has to be sacrificed to maintain buildings. As Jean Shaoul puts it, 'PFI comes at the expense of both capacity and access [to public services]' (2009: 10), a loss of capacity and restrictions on access that affect those most reliant on services the most.[24]

PFI as a Corruption of (Democratic) Accountability

> Finding out which PFI deals the UK is involved is notoriously hard because to figure out what is going on you need to know: the name of the project, which is often not used consistently over time; the contract for the project, which is not public; the name of intermediary private company where the money is exchanged, then their accounts can be purchased from Companies House; the name of the private companies involved in the package and their annual reports; the public spending on the project, but this often doesn't show up in annual accounts because the rules for which PFI agreements to include are varied greatly over time. The obvious question to ask of a PFI is, is it value for money? The answer is almost impossible to find out at the moment, for the public.[25]

The socially harmful repercussions of PFI encourage reflection on a political context in which it is able to function and grow. PFI does not operate in a vacuum, nor did it fall from the sky: setting up and sustaining a policy of this kind requires very particular forms of political action and ongoing commitment over time. In many respects, PFI is one of the most clear-cut examples we have of the extension of 'political authority beyond the state'.[26] That is, the promotion and implementation of PFI involves a reconstitution of the state's fields of activity, with private sector actors becoming directly involved in the work of the state but without any formal responsibility beyond their (unknown) contractual obligations.

At least two dimensions of this are worth noting: first, the displacement of politics, and second, the reconfiguration of lines of public accountability. The two are intimately linked because it is the reconfiguration of government in ways that include private sector actors that mandates changes in practices of accountability. If the workings of PFI were transparent and publicly accountable, it couldn't function. Notions of public accountability have therefore had to be suspended. The effect of such displacements is to make it much more difficult to identify who is responsible when things go wrong, as they often do. When complaints are registered, they are short-circuited by the confidentiality clauses inserted into PFI contracts. The public does not even have a statutory right to information on whether or not a contractor is actually delivering on its side of the contract.

These reconfigurations of political and governmental practice have repercussions beyond decision-making centres in Whitehall and Downing Street, playing out across the locales and sectors in which PFI has been implemented. Centre/local and before/after distinctions are critical here. While there is often quite high-level political and bureaucratic involvement prior to PFI contracts being agreed, with departments and ministers working together to deliver projects, ensuring contractors meet their obligations afterwards becomes the problem of the local authority or trust on whose behalf the contract was signed. However, these agencies have limited capacity to exercise oversight, let alone control the running of these key elements of public infrastructure. Projective interventions that involve predetermined commitments and the tying of hands, PFI contracts therefore do not so much displace as evacuate politics, with the emphasis shifting from decision making to managing the fall-out of the problems they create. In this way, PFI represents a corruption of democratic practice and the erosion of control over the workings of the state through the creation of arrangements which asymmetrically lock in the public sector on terms favourable to their private sector 'partners', based on contracts which are almost impossible in practice to renegotiate.[27]

Conclusion

We have suggested three senses in which PFI arrangements can be thought of as 'corrupting': encouraging corrupt practices, inverting relations of equity, and undermining democratic accountability. However, we can only make sense of these forms of corruption by setting them in context. It is tempting to conclude that PFI and its equivalents are indexes of the capture of the state by corporate capital. But we think that is an overly simplistic interpretation. PFI is just one of a series of practical attempts to reconfigure state–society–market relations in ways that benefit the state as much as the market, and in which politics has been a central driver. (Again, as we noted above, without significant political intervention infrastructure projects are not a 'natural' home for private investment.) One of the most politically attractive features of PFI, as in related though differently organised schemes focused on the local, is that the work of the state continues while central government is divested of the responsibility and the associated costs of actually performing and being held accountable for it. It is the establishment of arrangements of this kind, and the political strategies that inform them, that give shape and momentum to contemporary corruption within government.

Notes

1   As is indicated in the Introduction and in Chapter 1 of this book, the term has a range of meanings. For us, the important point is that 'the corrupt act' can be thought of as emerging against a background web of legal, political, administrative and bureaucratic practices which have themselves lost structural 'integrity', which have been remoulded in specific ways and have become something other than they were or might be thought to be.

2   Shaoul, J. (2011) 'Sharing' political authority with finance capital: the case of Britain's public private partnerships', *Policy and Society*, vol. 30, no. 3, pp. 209–20; Shaoul, J. (2009) 'The political economy of the Private Finance Initiative', in P. Arestis and M. Sawyer (eds), *Critical Essays on the Privatisation Experience*, Basingstoke: Palgrave Macmillan, pp. 1–38.

3   Lynch, M. (2011) 'The logic of sleaze', paper presented to the International Institute of Ethnomethodology and Conversation Analysis, Freiburg, Switzerland, August; Lynch, M. and Bogen, D. (1996) *The Spectacle of History: Speech, Text and Memory at the Iran-Contra Hearings*, Durham, N.C.: Duke University Press.

4   Kenneth Clarke was addressing the Confederation of British Industry in 1994 as chancellor of the exchequer; cited in Hellowell, M. (2009) 'Right thinking on PFI', *Public Finance*, 5 August.

5   For an account of the origins of the term, see House of Commons Library (2001) 'The Private Finance Initiative', House of Commons Library Research Paper 01/117.

6   Hellowell, M. (2011) 'Payback time for the PFI?', *Public Finance*, 28 March.

7   Shaoul, J. (2009) 'The political economy of the Private Finance Initiative', in P. Arestis and M. Sawyer (eds.) *Critical Essays on the Privatisation Experience*, Basingstoke, Hampshire: Palgrave Macmillan, pp. 1–38 (p. 2).

8   Campbell, D., Ball, J. and Rogers, S. (2012) 'PFI will ultimately cost £300bn', *Guardian*, 5 July; Rogers, S. and Ball, J. (2012) 'PFI contracts: the full list', *Guardian* Datablog, 5 July.

9   *BBC News Online* (2014) 'Mersey Gateway bridge project underway next month', 29 March.

10 *Liverpool Echo* (2012) 'Tolls on the planned Mersey Gateway bridge could be as high as £3', 29 November.

11 Shaoul, J. (2011) '"Sharing" political authority with finance capital: the case of Britain's Public Private Partnerships', *Policy and Society*, vol. 30, no.3, p. 214.

12 Shaoul (2009), p. 18–19.

13 Shaoul (2009), p. 21.

14 Shaoul (2011), p. 214.

15 Shaoul (2009), p. 6.

16 OFT (2012) *Response to the Scottish Government's Consultation on the Procurement Reform Bill*, London: Office of Fair Trading, www.scotland.gov.uk/Resource/0040/00409810.pdf

17 Omonirs-Oyekanmi, R. (2008) 'OFT finds bid rigging rife in PFI projects', *Partnerships Bulletin*, 6 May; Pollock, A. (2009) 'Uncovering the true costs of PFI', *Guardian*, 23 September.

18 Europe Economics (2010) *Evaluation of the Impact of the OFT's Investigation into Bid Rigging in the Construction Industry*, London: OFT, p. 4.

19 Ballieu, A. (2008) 'Is bid-rigging intrinsic to PFI?', *Building Design Online*, 25 April.

20 Heller, R. (2012) 'A private scourge on public finances', *Yorkshire Post*, 20 March.

21 National Audit Office (2008) *Protecting Staff in PFI/PPP Deals*, London: National Audit Office, p. 2.

22 As they explain: 'In 2009 the Information Commissioner seized a database of 3,213 construction workers used by 44 companies to vet new recruits and block employment of trade union and health and safety activists, almost none of whom knew they were on this list. In June 2012 the GMB estimated that from Oct 1999 to Apr 2004 Carillion checked at least 14,724 names with the Consulting Association "blacklist". The Commissioner confirmed that 224 UK construction workers were blacklisted by Carillion.' Keep Our NHS Public Merseyside (2013) 'Royal Liverpool PFI: a threat to our future', information leaflet, pp. 7–8, www.labournet.net/ukunion/1308/RoyalPFI.pdf

23 Keep Our NHS Public Merseyside (2013).

24 Shaoul (2009), p. 10.

25 Evans, L. (2010) 'The Datablog guide to PFI', *Guardian Datablog*, 19 November.

26 Rose, N. and Miller, P. (1992) 'Political power beyond the state: problematics of government', *British Journal of Sociology*, vol. 43, no. 2, pp. 173–205.

27 Shaoul (2009), p. 26; Shaoul (2011), pp. 209–20.

10

Revolving-Door Politics and Corruption

Stuart Wilks-Heeg

Introduction

The term 'revolving door' has long been used in US politics to describe the process through which senior figures move from the public to private (or private to public) sectors. It is closely associated with concerns that collusive relationships have developed between the US government and business in policy areas such as defence contracting and food regulation. Until recently, there was little research into such personnel movements in the United Kingdom, and doubts were expressed about whether the notion of the revolving door was applicable to British politics. However, in the last few years, a distinct body of research has emerged on revolving door relationships in British government and politics, often with reference to wider concerns about growing corporate influence over public policy. Drawing on these studies, this chapter suggests there can be little doubt about the existence of revolving door connections in Britain. It also argues for a broader conceptualisation of the revolving door in light of evidence that private sector interests are able to use a wide range of mechanisms to 'revolve in' to government and influence public policy.

Revolving Door Connections in UK Politics

The revolving door is not unique to US politics. In France, *pantou-flage* (literally 'putting on slippers'), describes the tendency for retiring senior public officials to take up lucrative business positions. In Japan, *amakundari* ('descent from heaven') refers to a similar pattern of former civil servants acquiring leading business or political roles. However, until recently, there was little research into such tendencies in UK politics. Some authors even doubted whether such concepts applied to the United Kingdom. Writing in 1992 on British industrial policy, Philip Daniels suggested that 'there is little career movement between industry and the civil service'.[1] Political scientist Peter Calvert suggested a decade later, that in contrast to the United States or France, the UK civil service 'is seen as a career to be followed till retirement, followed by receipt of an inflation-proofed pension'.[2]

In fact, there is longstanding evidence of the British equivalent of *pantouflage*. Alan Doig has noted that 'civil servants moving to well-paid jobs in the City was first the subject of rules from the 1920s as well as a major (and ignored) parliamentary inquiry in 1984'.[3] He also suggests that the 'unregulated one-way traffic to well-paid seats in City boardrooms' remained in evidence in the mid-1990s.[4] Similarly, the public administration expert, Professor Christopher Hood found that '"revolving door" appointments of civil servants in the private sector after resignation or retirement [were] a prominent feature in the senior civil service over the 1980s and early 1990s'.[5]

Significantly, these conclusions are reinforced by more recent evidence on 'revolving out' provided by studies which have examined the data contained in the annual reports of ACOBA, the Advisory Committee on Business Appointments.[6] Since 1975, ACOBA has reviewed applications from senior civil servants to take up outside appointments. The remit of the committee remains ostensibly the same as it did when set up (although the guidelines it works to, the Business Appointment Rules contained in the Civil Service Management Code, have been subject to change). Since 1996, ACOBA has also played an advisory role with respect to applications from former ministers to take up business appointments, as governed by the Ministerial Code. The committee is able to impose conditions on Crown servants taking up outside appointments, but has no such powers with respect to ministerial applications.[7] ACOBA's annual reports provide a statistical summary of 1) the total number of applications submitted from across the civil service; 2) the number of these applications which were considered by ACOBA (mostly senior civil servants); and 3) a breakdown of the number of applications approved a) unconditionally and b) subject to conditions. Separate statistical information is also provided about applications from former ministers.

Analysis of applications submitted by Crown servants and former ministers from 1998/99 to 2008/09 reveals that between 400 and 800 applications were submitted annually by civil servants seeking permission to take up external appointments. The data shows no obvious trend in the overall number of applications submitted over time. However, during the 2000s there was a clear rise in the proportion of cases where conditions were imposed, up from 20 per cent in 2001/02 to 34 per cent in 2008-09.[8] Researcher Liz David-Barrett notes in a report for Transparency International that the proportion of applications from senior Crown servants resulting in conditions being imposed was higher still, at 60 per cent. Of the 216 applications from senior Crown servants in this period, 36 (17 per cent) resulted in a waiting period being specified while 94 (43 per cent) were subject to other conditions, such as restrictions on the activities the individual would be engaged in. Only 86 (40 per cent) were approved without conditions.[9]

With respect to former ministers, there are three significant patterns in the ACOBA data. First, while between 5 and 30 ministers typically seek advice from ACOBA annually about appointments, there is clear evidence of ministerial applications fluctuating in step with the electoral cycle. Applications peak in the year after a general election, then fall to their nadir the year before the next election. This effect was particularly clear in the year following the 2010 General Election, when 52 former ministers took up a total of 107 appointments between them. Second, there is a tendency for some ministers to take up positions without seeking the advice of ACOBA. Six of the 52 former ministers taking up external roles in 2010/11 failed to provide the committee with advance notification of at least one appointment.

This observation is particularly significant given that ACOBA has very limited powers with respect to ex-ministers. ACOBA expressed its concern about four of these failures to notify, although it also clarified it would have approved all the appointments concerned. ACOBA's 'retrospective' assessment of these cases must, however, be considered in the context of the third tendency, which is that the ACOBA process prompts some applicants to make the decision to decline appointments. Just short of 30 appointments were not taken up by former ministers from 2005/06 to 2008/09 once they had received advice from ACOBA, including details of any proposed conditions.[10]

Until recently, the Ministry of Defence (MoD) was by far the largest source of applications to take up outside appointments. Prior to the 1990s, over half of applications typically originated from the MoD, with only a small number of other departments accounting for more than 10 per cent of the total. By the late 2000s, the proportion of applications originating from the MoD had fallen to about a third.[11] Two key factors explain this trend. First, defence-related applications fell in absolute terms, almost certainly reflecting the relative contraction of defence spending following the end of the cold war. Second, the close relationships between the state and specific corporations which have long typified defence contracting became increasingly evident in other policy areas. During the 1990s, privatisation and contracting-out 'made civil servants in areas such as prison policy more valuable to the private sector'.[12] Similarly, energy, transport and healthcare have joined defence 'as frequent destinations for former Ministers, civil servants and MPs'.[13] The common feature of all of these sectors, as Liz David-Barrett notes, is that they 'are all areas where government is a key buyer, or indeed, the only buyer'.[14] The figures contained in ACOBA's most recent reports suggest there may be signs of a rise in revolving door departures in areas where the coalition has been keen to encourage private sector service delivery, notably education and welfare reform. As the Introduction to this book notes, the apparent erosion of boundaries between the public and private sectors has therefore served to diversity the nature of revolving door connections.

As opportunities for generously remunerated private sector employ-ment or consultancy have grown, the tendency for former public servants to take up company directorships now appears less pronounced. Research by sociologist Sandra González-Bailón and her colleagues found that only a small minority of former civil servants, ministers and parliamentarians take up places on corporate boards. Moreover, they show that company directors with past government experience do not receive higher remu-neration than board members from other backgrounds.[15] However, the same authors provide further evidence that 'revolving out' is particularly pronounced among those who have previous senior-level engagement at particular government departments or agencies. It is service at the Treasury, Foreign Office and Ministry of Defence that 'provide the greatest opportunities for access to the corporate world'.[16] It seems likely that the chances which arise for such individuals stem from both the specialist knowledge they gained while working in these fields and the value of their personal contacts with senior figures in the departments in question.

Although the extent of 'revolving out' has been relatively well docu-mented, less attention has been paid to 'revolving in'. Based on figures reported in the annual reports of the Civil Service Commission, Ivan Horrocks, a researcher at the Open University, notes an increase in the share of senior civil service appointments from the private sector from less than 20 per cent to over 40 per cent during the 2000s.[17] My analysis shows that while around a third of all appointments to senior civil service posts from 2004 to 2008 were external recruits, the proportion rises to one half for appointments at the most senior ('Top 200') level.[18] This evidence also suggests external appointees are more likely to then 'revolve out' than senior civil servants promoted internally. Among those appointed to senior civil service positions in April 2004, 68 per cent of internal recruits were still in place four years later, compared with just 49 per cent of external recruits. This contrast was almost certainly due to differential rates of departure to employment outside the civil service. The majority of internal recruits no longer in the civil service had retired, whereas for external recruits, resignations accounted for the bulk of departures.[19]

This growing circulation of senior personnel between the senior civil service and the private sector is highlighted by David Marquand, author of the book *Mammon's Kingdom*, as a core factor explaining why 'civil servants are now, willy-nilly, agents of a market state'.[20] Similarly, 'revolving in' is identified by Professor Stephen Wilks of the University of Exeter as being central to the process of creating 'a civil service that became partially absorbed into the corporate elite', through which:

> The leadership of the British civil service is now predominately composed of private sector appointees. They can be expected to deploy corporate management strategies, to be aware of business interests, and to base their leadership on corporate management norms.[21]

However, as a number of commentators underline, David Marquand and Stephen Wilks included, external recruitment to the civil service is part of a wider dynamic. There are a variety of additional routes through which corporate influence on public policy has grown. It is to these other forms of 'revolving in' that we now turn.

Revolving (In) Without Moving

While the existence of revolving doors in UK politics is beyond doubt, it is also evident from recent studies that revolving door connections involve more than the mobility of senior personnel between the public and private sectors. In particular, the wider set of arrangements through which commercial interests have been drawn into policy making merit closer attention. 'Revolving in' takes various forms beyond the recruitment of senior civil servants from the private sector, including the appointments of leading private sector players to advisory groups, commissions of inquiry, task forces and the management boards of government depart-ments.[22] To this list we should also add the tendency for the civil service to resort 'on a grand scale to the employment of management consultants for advice, project management and policy implementation'.[23] As a result, private corporations have gained an unprecedented level of 'insider' access to government. As one recent account puts it:

> Private actors (and some others) are invited into the state to make policy. It is no longer enough to think about corporations only as attempting to influence policy. In reality much decision-making power has been directly devolved to them while corporations are increasingly 'internal' to the state.[24]

Pursuing this theme, David Miller and Claire Harkins argue in an article in *Critical Social Policy* that many areas of contemporary policy making are characterised by a form of 'institutional corruption'. They suggest that lobbyists are effectively invited to 'revolve in' via the various mechanisms of market-led politics. Using the fast food and alcoholic drink sectors as case studies, Miller and Harkins point to evidence of 'policy capture', through which private corporations are able to exert a dominating influence over government decision making. The extent of corporate power implied by 'policy capture' extends further than the concerns with 'lobbying capture' and 'regulatory capture' highlighted in the US liter-ature.[25] Moreover, achieving policy capture requires corporate interests to go beyond the opportunities to 'revolve in' to government directly. Of equal importance are the indirect means of capturing policy through corporate support for a variety of lobby groups, research institutes and think-tanks, and via an associated capacity to shape media reporting.[26]

This value of this perspective is highlighted by recent case studies of financial services regulation.[27] In a report for the OECD, David Miller and Will Dinan highlight how revolving door connections were a central facet of the confused regulatory mission of the UK Financial Services Authority (FSA), which conflated public interest with the interests of the financial sector.[28] Established in 2000 as an independent regulator with statutory powers, the FSA was funded by the financial sector itself. Regarded as a paradigmatic example of the failure of self-regulation to prevent the financial crash of 2008–09, the FSA was replaced by alternative regulatory arrangements in 2011. The FSA's shortcomings as a regulator arose in part from the manner in which revolving-door relationships brought about policy capture. Miller and Dinan note that 26 of the 36 people who served on the FSA board from

2000 to 2009 'had connections at board or senior level with the banking and finance industry either before or after their term or office, whilst nine continued to hold appointments in financial corporations while they were at the FSA'.[29] Indeed, so extensive was the interplay between the FSA and the banks that from 2004 to 2006 the chief executive of HBOS, James Crosby, was simultaneously a FSA board member, meaning that 'the head of a regulated institution was overseeing the regulator'.[30]

Two other recent studies highlight how major 'cross-cutting' policy initiatives with dubious track records were shaped by 'invited' corporate interests which stood to gain substantially from them. Private finance initiative (PFI) expert Sally Ruane examines the role of Partnerships UK (PUK), a joint venture between the Treasury and the private sector, in the growth of the PFI (see Chaper 9).[31] From 2000 to 2011, PUK advised the government on PFI issues while also assisting government departments, agencies and local authorities to forge public–private partnership deals. (It was involved in over 900 PFI projects, worth in excess of £70 billion.) Ruane notes that PUK board members, including the chair and chief executive, came overwhelmingly from the financial sector, with several also serving as board members on investment and infrastructure bodies such as the Northern Ireland Strategic Investment Board and Transport for London.[32]

Elsewhere, Ivan Horrocks documents the 'power loop' through which private sector consultants were able to push for the adoption of e-government 'solutions' while simultaneously promising the expertise needed to deliver them. At the heart of this process was the formation of what he describes as a 'consultocracy' which helped drive up government spending on IT projects, many of which were doomed to fail. Again, 'revolving in' is key to understanding how policy was captured by commercial interests. Horrocks identifies seven senior civil servants who were recruited directly from the private sector consultancies during the mid-2000s. These included the chief executive of the Identity and Passport Service, who had previously been a managing director of Accenture, and the director general of NHS IT, previously a partner at Deloitte.[33]

Conclusion

The evidence summarised in this chapter confirms the existence of a revolving door, in both directions, between government and business in the United Kingdom. That such movement takes place, and appears to have increased, is unsurprising. For several decades, UK governments have encouraged senior-level movement between the public and private sectors. The factors promoting revolving door movements are equally easy to identify. As the traditional boundaries between state and market have dissolved, the opportunities for individuals to switch between government and business have grown, as have the potential rewards. Yet, the revolving door is not merely a manifestation of the wider process of the blurring of the boundaries between the public and private sectors. It is also a driver of this process, serving to blur how public officials and private corporations understand their roles.

As with any area where corruption and misconduct are a concern, it is difficult to quantify the extent to which revolving door connections translate into undue influence or policy capture. The mere fact of senior-level movements between the public and private sectors clearly cannot, and should not, be interpreted as evidence of wrongdoing. However, given that ACOBA represents a 'light-touch' approach to regulating the revolving door, evidence that the committee imposes conditions in a significant, and growing, proportion of cases underlines the potential for conflicts of interest to occur. Regular calls for ACOBA to be replaced with a more robust set of regulatory arrangements also indicate a lack of confidence that existing safeguards are sufficient. But tinkering with ACOBA misses the point. ACOBA was set up to address concerns about the scope for individual corruption. Its limitations are all the more obvious if the spinning of the revolving door is understood as a symptom of a deeper corruption of public life arising from the process of policy capture.

While more effective regulation of the process through which senior civil servants and politicians 'revolve out' to corporate roles would be welcome, such measures will therefore do little to mitigate growing corporate influence in public policy circles. Reforms must focus on the need to regulate, and in many cases roll back, the full range of mechanisms through which corporate interests are being 'invited in' to shape public policy.

Notes

1   Daniels, P. (1992) 'Industrial policy', in Harrop, M. (ed.), *Power and Policy in Liberal Democracies*, Cambridge: Cambridge University Press, p. 140.

2   Calvert, P. (2002) *Comparative Politics: An Introduction*, Harlow: Pearson/ Longman, p. 222.

3   Doig, A. (1996) 'From Lynskey to Nolan: the corruption of British politics and public service', *Journal of Law and Society*, vol. 23, no. 1, p.53.

4   Doig (1996).

5   Hood, C. (1995) '"Deprivileging" the UK civil service in the 1980s: dream or reality?' in Pierre, J. (ed.), *Bureaucracy in the Modern State: An Introduction to Comparative Public Administration*, Cheltenham: Edward Elgar, p. 111.

6   David-Barrett, L. (2011) *Cabs for Hire? Fixing the Revolving Door between Government and Business*, London: Transparency International; Wilks-Heeg, S., Blick, A. and Crone, S. (2012) *How Democratic is the UK? The 2012 Audit*, Liverpool: Democratic Audit.

7   For an overview of the procedures governing outside appointments, see David-Barrett (2011).

8   Wilks-Heeg et al. (2012).

9   David-Barrett (2011), p. 21.

10   Wilks-Heeg et al. (2012).

11   Wilks-Heeg et al. (2012).

12   Hood (1995), p. 111.

13   David-Barrett (2011).

14   David-Barrett (2011).

15   González-Bailón, S., Jennings, W. and Lodge, M. (2012) 'Politics in the boardroom: corporate pay, networks and recruitment of former parliamentarians, ministers and civil servants in Britain', *Political Studies*, vol. 61, no. 4, pp. 850–73.

16   González-Bailón et al (2012), p. 869.

17   Horrocks, I. (2009) '"Experts' and e-government: power, influence and the capture of a policy domain in the UK', *Information, Communication and Society*, vol. 12, no. 1, pp. 110–27.

18   Wilks-Heeg et al. (2012).

19   Wilks-Heeg et al. (2012).

20   Marquand, D. (2014) *Mammon's Kingdom: An Essay on Britain, Now*, London: Allen Lane.

21   Wilks, S. (2013) *The Political Power of the Business Corporation*, Cheltenham: Edward Elgar, pp. 77–8.

22   Beetham, D. (2011) *Unelected Oligarchy: Corporate and Financial Dominance in Britain's Democracy*, Liverpool: Democratic Audit.

23   Wilks (2013), p. 78.

24   Miller, D. and Harkins, C. (2010) 'Corporate strategy, corporate capture: food and alcohol industry lobbying and public health', *Critical Social Policy*, vol. 30, no. 4, pp. 564–89.

25   See for example Meghani, Z. and Kuzma, J. (2011) 'The "revolving door" between regulatory agencies and industry: a problem that requires reconceptualizing objectivity', *Journal of Agricultural and Environmental Ethics*, vol. 24, pp. 575–99; Vidal, J., Blanes, I., Draca, M. and Fons-Rosen, C. (2012) 'Revolving door lobbyists', *American Economic Review*, vol. 102, no.7, pp. 3731–48.

26   Miller and Harkins (2010); see also Beetham (2011) on how corporations 'buy influence'.

27 Baker, A. (2010) 'Restraining regulatory capture? Anglo-America, crisis poli-
    tics and trajectories of change in global financial governance', *International
    Affairs*, vol. 86, no. 3, pp. 647–63; Miller, D. and Dinan, W. (2009) *Revolving
    Doors, Accountability and Transparency: Emerging Regulatory Concerns and
    Policy Solutions in the Financial Crisis*, Paris: OECD.

28 Miller and Dinan (2009).

29 Miller and Dinan (2009).

30 Baker (2010), p. 653.

31 Ruane, S. (2010) 'Corporate and political strategy in relation to the private
    finance initiative in the UK', *Critical Social Policy*, vol. 30, no. 4, pp. 519–40.

32 Ruane (2010).

33 Horrocks (2009).

Part IV

Corruption in Finance and the Corporate Sector

11

On Her Majesty's Secrecy Service

John Christensen

Introduction

This chapter explores Britain's role as the world's leading purveyor of financial secrecy. In conjunction with its overseas territories (OTs) and crown dependencies (CDs), the City of London controls around a quarter of the global market for offshore financial services. Importantly, British OTs and CDs rank among the world's most opaque secrecy jurisdictions: in the Tax Justice Network's 2013 Financial Secrecy Index, for instance, Bermuda, Gibraltar and the Turks and Caicos Islands were assigned secrecy scores of 80, 79 and 78 respectively, among the highest scores in the world. Jersey, where this author grew up and worked as government economic adviser for eleven years, scored 75. The Cayman Islands is one of the world's biggest banking centres, while the British Virgin Islands is the world's biggest supplier of secretive offshore companies. All the above territories are British.

Secrecy enables concealment of a wide variety of corrupt practices, including fraud, embezzlement, non-disclosure of conflicts of interest, illicit political funding, insider dealing, market rigging, bribery, tax evasion and tax avoidance. Legalised secrecy creates a criminogenic environment which encourages and enables corrupt practices by blocking investigation, prosecution and recovery of stolen assets.[1] There is a lucrative market in providing financial secrecy, and a large private-sector 'pinstripe infrastructure' of enablers and intermediaries – banks, accountancy firms, boutique law practices, and trust and company administrators – has embedded itself in secrecy jurisdictions to facilitate individual and corporate tax abuses.

Secrecy comes in many flavours. One of the commonest is the lack of transparency of corporate ownership. As the satirical magazine *Private Eye* has revealed *ad nauseam*, the ease and low cost with which companies can be incorporated in the United Kingdom and in its OTs or CDs without being required to disclose any details about genuine ownership attracts corrupt activities from around the world.[2] Few experts were surprised when, following the ousting of Ukrainian president Viktor Yanukovych in February 2014, investigators discovered that his extravagant palace was part-owned by a British-registered company. Wealthy elites from former Soviet Union (FSU) countries have shifted ownership and control of their assets, however obtained, into offshore companies registered in either the United Kingdom or in British secrecy jurisdictions, earning the United Kingdom's capital city the moniker 'Londongrad'.[3] We cannot estimate how much of the estimated £480 billion[4] that flowed illicitly out of the FSU region between the 1970s and 2010 is now managed and controlled in London, but nobody would dispute that the United Kingdom is a destination of choice for Russian and Ukrainian oligarchs.

The UK financial services industry, popularly known as the City of London, lies at the epicentre of what investigative journalist Nicholas Shaxson calls a 'spider's web' of secrecy jurisdictions dotted across many time zones, including the OTs and CDs, along with several British Commonwealth countries and former Crown colonies like Hong Kong, Mauritius and Singapore.[5] Collectively, these secrecy jurisdictions act as hidden conduits for dirty money originating from countries across the world, much of it destined for the City. By the time the money has reached London the origins can be untraceable, hidden behind a complex of secretive offshore bank accounts, companies and trusts.[6]

Detailed official data on the scale of illicit financial flows is scarce, but one report by a New York-based economic investigation agency in 2011 estimated that between £13–20 trillion (one trillion equates to one million million) of privately owned wealth is held offshore, escaping domestic taxes in the high net worth individuals' (Hen-Wees') countries of residence.[7] A pile of pound coins to this value would stretch three times the distance between the Earth and the Sun. These kinds of sums do not fit in suitcases: facilitating illicit flows of this scale necessarily involves the world's biggest banks. The income tax losses as a result of tax evasion from these sums are estimated at up to £170 billion annually; that sum would go a long way to plugging the budget deficits of many countries. Imposing wealth taxes on this vast hoard, as proposed by French economist Thomas Piketty,[8] would significantly reduce the extremes of inequality that have built up over the past 35 years, not least in the United Kingdom, where Oxfam has revealed that the wealth owned by the five richest families exceeds that of the poorest 20 per cent of the population.[9]

Contrary to popular conception, these offshore asset holdings are not managed and controlled mostly from tiny islands in the Caribbean or Alpine principalities. According to International Monetary Fund (IMF) data, the principal offshore financial centres are the United States (led by New York), the United Kingdom (London) and Luxembourg, which have 23 per cent, 19 per cent and 12 per cent respectively of the global market share of offshore financial services. Add the United Kingdom's market share with those of its OTs and CDs, however, and it advances to first position, controlling approximately 24 per cent of the global market in 2012.

The United Kingdom did not achieve market dominance in offshore financial secrecy by accident. For decades it has covertly supported and, in some cases actively encouraged its OTs and CDs to become secrecy jurisdictions.[10] After the collapse of the formal empire in 1956, and facing chronic trade deficits and long-term underinvestment in productive capacity, successive UK governments, especially after Margaret Thatcher took power, pursued a development strategy of giving primacy to London's offshore financial centre. But the Big Bang of 1986 was merely another waymark along a journey that started in the mid-1950s with the creation of the unregulated Euromarkets which placed London at the epicentre of the unregulated offshore global capital markets. Historians Peter Cain and Anthony Hopkins observed in their landmark study of British imperialism, 'As the imperial basis of its strength disappeared, the City survived by transforming itself into an "offshore island" servicing the business created by the industrial and commercial growth of much more dynamic partners.'[11]

It is already widely recognised that tax havens have contributed to the impoverishment of countries, rich and poor, by enabling capital flight, kleptocracy, tax evasion and avoidance on an industrial scale. Tax havenry has significantly contributed to rising wealth and income inequalities and to increased corruption.[12] For example, researchers at Washington-based Global Financial Integrity have estimated the scale of illicit financial flows out of developing countries at US$5.9 trillion during the ten-year period ending in 2011. Alarmingly, the scale of these outflows is increasing by about 10 per cent annually.[13]

Less recognised is the possibility that an oversized offshore financial centre might actually harm the country that hosts it, undermining growth and corrupting political processes.

Has the growth of an offshore financial services centre been an overall net benefit to the United Kingdom, beyond the special interests of the City and those selling London real estate to foreign oligarchs? This is debatable. The 2008 financial crisis exposed the extent to which the

United Kingdom has fallen victim to a political economic phenomenon that has recently been called the finance curse.[14] This phenomenon involves an over-sized financial services sector actively harming its host economy and society through 'Dutch disease' effects (overvaluing the exchange rate)[15]; crowding out other industrial sectors; volatile financial cycles; overdependence on the dominant industry; and in due course, state capture.[16] The overall net effect of oversized finance may be negative. Students of the widely recognised resource curse that afflicts mineral-dependent economies will find much that is familiar in finance-dependent economies like the United Kingdom's, not just in the causes, but in the impacts too: lower rates of long-term economic growth, higher levels of inequality, widespread cronyism and rampant corruption.[17]

How the United Kingdom's Tax Haven Empire Came to Rule the World

Tax haven secrecy is a long-established phenomenon; bankers in Geneva and Zurich were already catering to wealthy European élites long before the creation of the Swiss federal state in 1848. Caribbean islands have served as 'offshore' pirate coves for centuries.

But a new, more hyperactive phase of the offshore financial economy began in the mid-1950s with the creation of the London-based Euromarkets, and the accumulation of large sums of footloose financial capital outside the owners' countries of residence, providing a basis for the emergence of financial transnationalism.[18] Decisions relating to the management of this capital are largely taken in major financial centres like London, New York, Luxembourg, Zurich, Frankfurt, Tokyo, but – mainly to avoid taxes or financial regulations – transactions are booked through a variety of offshore jurisdictions including British OTs and CDs which have purposefully set themselves up as tax havens.

Tax havens in this context are defined as autonomous or semi-autonomous jurisdictions offering lax regulation, low or zero taxation on non-resident income and capital, secrecy facilities for banking or corporate or trust ownership, and nonexistent or weak effective infor-mation exchange treaties and processes with other countries. Opacity is typically a key attraction, and the term 'secrecy jurisdiction' (which originated in the United States) often better describes the activities of these places; this term is frequently used as a substitute for 'tax haven', depending on the context.

Several factors might explain the emergence of British OTs and CDs among the leading secrecy jurisdictions. First, the United Kingdom's imperial pre-eminence was partly due to the City's dominance in finance, insurance and shipping services. English common law is used for business purposes worldwide, and allows for the creation of offshore trusts and non-resident companies with minimal requirements to report or disclose the identity of their real, warm-blooded ultimate owners, controllers and beneficiaries. The constitutional links with the United Kingdom and access to the Supreme Court in London also provide a reassuring bedrock of solidity and stability not available to independent jurisdictions.

Second, faced with the prospect of having to financially support its post-imperial territories, the Foreign and Commonwealth Office encouraged some British OTs to develop as secrecy jurisdictions, especially if they became conduits for capital flows into the City of London.

Third, many of these colonial territories comprised small islands and microstates where financial and commercial elites, working with local leaders, could easily shape the island polities to suit financial interests, with little or no local democratic oversight or accountability.[19]

Archival research suggests that Whitehall paid scant attention to nefarious activities happening on its overseas territories, even when its own officials raised the alarm. A Bank of England letter, dated 11 April 1969 and prominently marked SECRET, addressed an anxious request by Her Majesty's Inland Revenue for help with cracking down on British residents using offshore facilities in the Caribbean to evade taxes. The bank showed no willingness to support the Revenue's requests, but expressed concern about exchange control leakage. So the Bank suggested:

> We need, therefore, to be quite sure that the possible proliferation of trust companies, banks, etc., which in most cases would be no more than brass plates manipulating assets outside the islands, does not get out of hand. *There is, of course, no objection to their providing boltholes for non-residents.* (emphasis added)

The archives reveal a confusion of attitudes between different parts of the UK state. The Inland Revenue fulminated against tax losses to the Exchequer; the departments responsible for foreign aid seem to have encouraged the British OTs to become secrecy jurisdictions in order to reduce their financial dependence on Whitehall – while ignoring the spillover impacts these jurisdictions inflicted on other countries. The Bank of England appears to have been positively comfortable with the growth of British secrecy jurisdictions, even to the point of openly colluding with tax avoidance. It is not clear whether successive UK governments were actively encouraging these developments or were more like passive bystanders, stymied by inter-departmental conflict and lobbying from City interests.[20]

Whatever the dynamic behind this growth of secrecy jurisdictions, governments elsewhere were becoming increasingly unhappy. A confidential report prepared jointly in 1971 by HM Treasury, the Foreign and Commonwealth Office and Inland Revenue noted in connection with concerns about the exploitation of double taxation agreements by tax havens that:

> There is a difference between actually concluding and operating an agreement which leads to loss of tax and acquiescing, however reluctantly, in a tax loss about which we can do nothing. The distinction has been noted by some O.E.C.D. member countries including the U.S.A. which deplores the United Kingdom's 'encouragement' of tax havens, and France, which has animadverted on the prevalence of 'paradis fiscaux' as yet another undesirable feature of the Sterling Area.[21]

Still, successive UK governments for decades did little to rein in their offshore territories. Indeed, UK governments have generally shielded the OTs and CDs from all but the most superficial measures to tackle secrecy, and the majority of OTs and CDs remain largely uncooperative and non-compliant with best practice,[22] challenging Prime Minister David Cameron's statement to Parliament in September 2013:

> I do not think it is fair any longer to refer to any of the overseas territories or Crown dependencies as tax havens. They have taken action to make sure that they have fair and open tax systems. It is very important that our focus should now shift to those territories and countries that really are tax havens.[23]

To be fair, we must allow for time lags as British secrecy jurisdictions rewrite their laws and adapt to the rapidly changing international mood favouring more transparent financial markets and stronger information exchange processes between governments. Seismic changes might be underway as secrecy jurisdictions accede to the emergence of automatic tax information exchange as the new global best practice, but the offshore finance industry, led by the powerful British lobby of the Society of Trust and Estate Practitioners, is fighting to ring-fence trusts from information exchange. If they succeed, they will drive a coach and horses through global attempts to tackle tax havens.

Reframing Corruption

Revelations about LIBOR and exchange rate manipulations by Barclays and other major London banks, PPI mis-selling, sub-prime mortgage frauds, the money-laundering antics of banking giant HSBC, and other scandals have shaken public confidence in Britain's banks and financial institutions (see Chapter 13). Combine this with media phone hacking, match rigging in the Premier League, fraud in public/private partnerships (G4S, for example), elaborate tax dodging by major transnational corporations, and it is clear that institutional corruption within the private sphere in Britain is a systemic problem.

Greed, exemplified by unjustifiable bankers' bonuses, is widely identified as the driving impulse behind these abuses, but other factors play a role, notably the neoliberal ideological project which demands that the role of the state must be reduced to policies that encourage markets to weave their magic.

Following the analysis of 'counter-corruption' discourse set out in the Introduction to this book, it is striking to note that some of the 'cleanest' performers in widely cited corruption indices, such as Transparency International's Corruption Perceptions Index and the World Bank's corruption scores, include Switzerland, Singapore and the United Kingdom; precisely those that the Tax Justice Network's Financial Secrecy Index identifies among the world's most important secrecy jurisdictions. This apparent paradox can be understood by considering the two conflicting incentives that face tax havens: on the one hand, they want to be considered clean, trustworthy and reliable places that won't steal investors' money; on the other hand, the profitability of offshore 'wealth management' provides these jurisdictions with strong incentives to attract the greatest possible quantities of dirty cash from around the world, with few questions asked.

Both kinds of ranking have validity in certain circumstances, but the contrast between them shows that we need to develop utterly new understandings about what corruption is, and how and where it happens.

Jurisdictions' attempts to compartmentalise these two opposing offshore incentives and keep them apart are futile: the stink will leak from the dirty into the clean, infecting not just the entire financial sector but ultimately the political establishment that gives it legitimacy. Offshore tax avoidance by transnational corporations – whether legal or not – extracts wealth from other taxpayers, for the benefit of wealthy owners of capital, creating market distortions that ultimately corrupt those markets and people's trust in them. More generally, 'socially useless' wealth-extraction involves certain interests bypassing accepted norms, taking advantage of rules made available to them but not to poorer people and small companies. Tax avoidance invariably involves insiders operating in covert, secretive ways, without restraint. It is highly anti-social and corrodes public confidence in the tax system, the rule of law, and in democracy itself. The lax regulation and abusive tax practices of offshore – and the anti-state, anti-democratic ideology that accompanies it – inevitably stimulate race-to-the-bottom responses from politicians in mainstream states, undermining regulation and making tax regimes increasingly regressive. Faced with structural deficits and rising inequality, the United Kingdom has been kidding itself that it can survive its offshore-based strategy.

Public anger in Britain has been easily distracted from the corrupt practices of the City of London. For example, the UK government announcement that £1.2 billion was lost to benefit fraud by job-seekers in 2012/13 fuelled perceptions that benefit fraud is widespread. But another estimate has revealed that annual revenue losses as a result of evasion, avoidance and failure to collect taxes due amount to £120 billion: 100 times greater than the losses through benefits fraud and clearly a far greater scandal in an era of austerity measures targeted at unemployed and low-paid working people.[24] Nonetheless, the government and its supporting media have focused far more on benefit fraud, and it has been civil society agencies that have led the charge against personal and corporate tax abuses.

The anti-corruption spotlight now needs to focus on:

- the role of the UK and OT/CD governments which purposefully and knowingly supply the secrecy spaces through which the proceeds from high-level corrupt practices flow
- the intermediaries: the bankers, lawyers, tax accountants, company directors and other professionals whose activities facilitate corrupt financial practices.

Steadily, stealthily, the British tax system and broader economy has been reconfigured since the 1950s to serve the interests of a class of unaccountable, untouchable offshore-diving super-rich (this is developed in Chapter 12).[25] Huge effort and corporate resource goes into lobbying politicians on tax, and swathes of the British political class are deeply embedded in offshore secrecy, either personally or through party political funding from City and offshore sources. For all of David Cameron's moralising about the harm caused to poorer countries by tax havens (which no one could dispute), it is worth recalling that he is part of an offshore dynasty: his father chaired an offshore investment firm based in Jersey and co-founded an investment company registered in Panama. Many of his fellow Cabinet members and coalition colleagues share similar connections.

The United Kingdom has played a large role in furnishing the supply side of the global market for secrecy. This has helped entrench corruption in countries around the world – and in British politics too. The moment has come to confront Britain's empire of secrecy jurisdictions.

Notes

1   Christensen, J. E. (2012) 'The hidden trillions: secrecy, corruption, and the offshore interface', *Crime Law and Social Change*, vol. 57, pp. 325–43.
2   Brooks, R. and Bousfield, A. (2013) 'Where there's muck … there's brass plate', *Private Eye*, issue 1340, May.
3   Albert, E. (2014) /L'argent russe de "Londongrad" influence le pouvoir britannique', *Le Monde*, 10 March.
4   Henry, J. (2012) *The Price of Offshore Revisited*, London: Tax Justice Network.
5   Shaxson, N. (2012) *Treasure Islands: Tax Havens and the Men Who Stole the World*, London: Vintage, pp. 103–23.
6   Shaxson (2012) , p. 104.
7   Henry (2012).
8   Piketty, T. (2014) *Capital in the Twenty-First Century*, Boston, Mass.: Belknap Press of Harvard University Press, pp. 515–39.
9   Fuentes-Nieva, R. (2014) *A Tale of Two Britains: Inequality in the U.K.*, London: Oxfam.
10 Hampton, M. P. (1996) *The Offshore Interface: Tax Havens in the Global Economy*, Basingstoke: Macmillan. p.77.
11 Cain, P. J. and Hopkins, A. G. (1993) *British Imperialism: Crisis and Deconstruction, 1914–1990*, London: Longman, p. 293.
12 Christensen, J. E. (2011) 'The looting continues: tax havens and corruption', *Critical Perspectives on International Business*, vol. 7, no. 2, pp. 177–96.
13 Kar, D. and Le Blanc, B. (2013) *Illicit Financial Flows from Developing Countries: 2002–2011*, Washington DC: Global Financial Integrity.
14 Shaxson, N. and Christensen, J. (2013) *The Finance Curse: How Oversized Financial Sectors Attack Democracy and Corrupt Economics*, London: Commonwealth Publishing.
15 For more information about the Dutch disease see: http://blogs.worldbank.org/growth/dutch-disease-theory-and-evidence.
16 Arguably, City interests have diverged from those of the wider British economy for decades: the Macmillan Committee on Finance and Industry appointed in 1929 to report on Britain's post-crash plight reported that 'in some respects the City is more highly organised to provide capital to foreign

countries than to British Industry'. *Report of the Committee on Finance and Industry*, CMD 3897, para. 397.

17 Shaxson and Christensen (2013).

18 Nairn, T. (1997) *Faces of Nationalism*, London: Verso,

19 Sagar, P., Christensen, J. and Shaxson, N. (2013) 'British government attitudes to British tax havens', in Leaman, J. and Waris, A. (eds), *Tax Justice and the Political Economy of Global Capitalism, 1945 to present*, Oxford: Berghahn.

20 Sagar et al. (2013), p. 129.

21 Confidential report of the Treasury, Foreign and Commonwealth Office, and Inland Revenue on British Dependent Territories and Tax Haven Business, circulated 13 July 1971, held on Bank of England West Indies file OV121/23.

22 www.financialsecrecyindex.com/faq/britishconnection

23 Hansard, 9September 2013, col. 700.

24 Murphy, R. (2008) *The Missing Billions: The UK Tax Gap*, London: Trade Unions Congress.

25 Lansley, S. (2006) *Rich Britain: The Rise and Rise of the New Super-Wealthy*, London: Politicos.

12

Accounting for Corruption in the 'Big Four' Accountancy Firms

Prem Sikka

This chapter looks at the involvement of the 'Big Four' accountancy firms – Deloitte & Touche, PricewaterhouseCoopers (PwC), Ernst & Young (EY) and KPMG – in corrupt practices. The Big Four originated in the United Kingdom. Through a series of international mergers they have become 'too big to close' and wield enormous financial and political resources to resist reforms and effective regulatory action. During 2013, they employed over 717,000 people worldwide and their combined global revenues[1] were around US$115 billion (£72 billion), of which some $65 billion (£41 billion) came from consultancy services, including selling tax avoidance schemes. In 2013, they generated revenues of about £8.25 billion in the United Kingdom,[2] of which £1.83 billion came from audit fees and £6.42 billion related to consultancy services.

The firms play a central role in the construction and operation of regulatory arrangements for corporations and global financial markets through governance arrangements, such as those relating to accounting and auditing. They have been key players in the development of the post-1970s neoliberal hegemony and have been major beneficiaries from the financialisation of the economy. They have become adept at bending the rules to advance their economic interests. The culture of sleaze affects every part of their operations as the firms chase profits from auditing, consultancy and tax avoidance. This chapter provides a brief glimpse of some of their corrupt activities.

A Culture of Sleaze

The websites of the Big Four firms are full of claims about ethical conduct,[3] but this veneer of respectability is routinely punctured by revelations of involvement in malpractices.[4] In 2013, the Big Four became the subject of a hearing into their tax avoidance practices by the House of Commons Committee of Public Accounts.[5] Just before the hearing the Committee received evidence from a former senior PwC employee stating that the firm's policy was that it would sell a tax avoidance scheme which had only a 25 per cent chance of withstanding a legal challenge, or as the Committee chairperson put it, 'you are offering schemes to your clients – knowingly marketing these schemes – where you have judged there is a 75% risk of it then being deemed unlawful'.[6] The other three firms admitted to 'selling schemes that they consider only have a 50% chance of being upheld in court'.[7] The full extent of the involvement of the firms in the tax avoidance business is not known, but a 2005 internal study[8] by Her Majesty's Revenue and Customs (HMRC) concluded that the Big Four accounting firms were behind almost half of all known avoidance schemes. In 2012, HMRC was scrutinising some 41,000 tax avoidance schemes,[9] though the proportion of this number attributable to the Big Four is not known.

In one particularly notorious example, Deloitte designed a scheme for the London office of Deutsche Bank, to enable its staff to avoid income tax and national insurance contributions (NIC) on bonuses adding up to £92 million.[10] More than 300 bankers participated in the scheme, which operated through a Cayman Islands-registered investment vehicle. In 2011 the scheme was declared to be unlawful by the courts. The judge in the case said that 'the Scheme as a whole, and each aspect of it, was created and coordinated purely for tax avoidance purposes'.[11] The case of Explainaway Limited v HMRC [2012] UKUT 362 (TCC) further showed that Deloitte designed an avoidance scheme which used a series of paper transactions in company shares, futures and derivatives contracts to generate an artificial loss and make the client's tax liability vanish. The judge declared the scheme to be illegal because there was no real loss.

In another tax avoidance episode, Deloitte became embroiled in the acquisition of the German telecoms operator Mannesman by London-based Vodafone. Some estimated that about £6 billion of tax was unpaid by Vodafone, although the details have never been made public. Coincidentally, Deloitte showered hospitality upon HMRC boss Dave Hartnett.[12] Between 2006 and 2010, Dave Hartnett had no less than 48 meetings with Deloitte UK chairman David Cruickshank to resolve Vodafone's dispute with HMRC. In 2010 Vodafone's tax liability shrank and the actual settlement was a lump sum of £800,000 and a further £450,000 spread over five years.[13] A 2012 report by the National Audit Office[14] (NAO) said that the settlement was 'reasonable', but criticised

HMRC for failing to follow its own procedures, which included keeping notes of key meetings, consulting independent experts and seeking legal advice. In May 2013, Dave Hartnett joined Deloitte & Touche as a specialist adviser.[15]

Ernst & Young designed schemes including one that enabled the directors of Phones 4U to avoid NIC by paying themselves in gold bars, fine wine, and platinum sponge.[16] No sooner had legislation been passed to outlaw that scheme than Ernst & Young had devised another scheme. This time, the scheme enabled executives and directors of Phones 4U to avoid NIC and income taxes by securing payments through an offshore employee benefit trust in Jersey. The firm told directors the scheme 'will be viewed by the Inland Revenue as aggressive',[17] but still sold it. The House of Lords judgment in HM Inspector of Taxes v Dextra Accessories Ltd [2005] UKHL 47 (07 July 2005) declared the scheme to be unlawful.

In May 2012, BBC's *Panorama* programme[18] showed how PwC devised schemes to enable multinational corporations such as GlaxoSmithKline (GSK) and Northern & Shell[19] to shift profits to offshore tax havens via Luxembourg. The schemes involved intergroup loans, contrived interest payments and transfer pricing arrangements to reduce taxable profits in the United Kingdom and avoid corporate taxes.

These brief examples give us more than enough evidence to show how helping the rich and powerful at the expense of the rest of us is the norm at the Big Four. For a fee of £200,000 a millionaire bought a scheme from PwC, which manufactured losses through a series of circular transactions and made his profit of £10 million from the sale of a business vanish into thin air. The case of Schofield v Revenue & Customs (Rev 1) [2010] UKFTT 196 (TC), declared the scheme to be unlawful. Former Libyan dictator Muammar el-Qaddafi amassed a vast personal fortune from oil revenues with western financial institutions,[20] and invested it through the Libyan Investment Authority (LIA).[21] The LIA was advised by the London office of KPMG.[22]

A PwC partner has submitted a report to the Jamaican government[23] listing the steps it needs to take to become a tax haven. PwC is credited with developing Ireland[24] as a tax haven and particularly refining a scheme known as the Double Irish Dutch sandwich.[25] The scheme enables multinational corporations to shift profits to low/no tax jurisdictions through complex corporate structures, royalty payments for intellectual property and the use of transfer pricing. Companies such as Apple, Facebook, Google, Intel, LinkedIn and Microsoft are known to use the scheme and avoid taxes in many countries.

Private profiteering is defended in numerous other ways. Ernst

& Young collected $21 million in 2012 from acting as Google's global auditor and tax adviser, including $5.5 million for tax advice. Google routes its UK business through Ireland and Bermuda, with the result that UK taxes virtually disappear. For the period 2006 to 2011, Google's UK operations generated revenues of $18 billion (£11.5 billion), but the company paid just $16 million (£10 million) in corporate taxes.[26] The company's accounts always receive a clean bill of health even though they provide no information about tax avoidance strategies. During one of its hearings, the chair of the House of Commons Public Accounts Committee asked an Ernst & Young partner to explain the firm's role in Google's tax games. The partner replied, 'I am not able to comment on the specifics.'[27] Following information provided by whistleblowers, the Committee recalled Google and admonished Ernst & Young for being economical with information,[28] but the firm cited client confidentiality and refused to provide any further information.

Auditors for Hire

The Big Four audit 99 per cent of the FTSE100, 96 per cent of FTSE250 companies and 78.8 per cent of all UK main market listed companies.[29] Auditors are supposed to be independent of companies and avoid conflict of interests, but that is clearly not the case. The case of Iliffe News and Media Ltd & Ors v Revenue & Customs [2012] UKFTT 696 (TC) (01 November 2012) drew attention to an Ernst & Young tax avoidance scheme for an audit client. This company's directors were concerned that in view of its high profits its workers would want higher wages, and sought advice from Ernst & Young. The company owned a number of newspaper titles and Ernst & Young advised it to treat mastheads as a new asset. These were transferred to the parent company for a nominal sum and then immediately leased back to the subsidiaries for annual royalties. Over a five-year period, the subsidiaries paid royalties of £51.6 million to deflate their profits. This transaction did not result in any transfer of cash to an external party, but the subsidiaries claimed tax relief on the royalty payments. The company's board minutes, as reproduced in the court papers, noted that:

> [E&Y] had confirmed that if the newspaper titles and/or mastheads were registered as trade marks in the ownership of [INML[30]], it was possible for the latter [i.e. INML] to charge the newspaper companies a fee for the use of the former in a tax efficient manner that would significantly lessen the

transparency of reported results. It was agreed to progress this matter in consultation with [E&Y].[31]

The avoidance scheme was declared to be unlawful.

The conflict of roles that the Big Four are expected to perform was dramatically exposed by the 2007–08 banking crash. Just before the crash, all of the distressed UK banks received a clean bill of health from their auditors.[32] Lehman Brothers was no exception. For every £1 provided by shareholders, Lehman Brothers borrowed £30 to finance its operations, giving it a leverage ratio of more than 30 to 1.[33] With this leverage, a 3.3 per cent drop in the value of assets would wipe out its entire long-term capital and make the bank technically insolvent. The bank collapsed in 2008 and a subsequent investigation showed that with advice from auditors, Lehman Brothers used questionable accounting practices to massage its accounts. Auditors Ernst & Young collected $31 million (£19.4 million) in fees in 2007. A subsequent US investigation concluded that 'the firm's outside auditor, was professionally negligent'.[34] In 2010, the firm was charged with 'a massive accounting fraud' by the state of New York,[35] and eventually settled the allegations by paying $99 million.[36] Amidst intense media scrutiny, the UK regulator, the Financial Reporting Council (FRC), announced that it has begun an investigation into the Lehman audits.[37] In 2012, without ever publishing a report or public provision of evidence in its possession, the FRC announced that 'no action should be taken against Ernst & Young LLP or any individuals in connection with their conduct in this matter ... there is no realistic prospect that a Tribunal would make an adverse finding against Ernst & Young LLP in the UK or Members within that firm'.[38]

The burying of investigations into the practices of Big Four accountancy firms in this way is not unusual. On 1 March 2010, BAE Systems plc (BAE) pleaded guilty to conspiring to defraud the United States by impairing and impeding its lawful functions and making false statements about its Foreign Corrupt Practices Act compliance programme. The company paid secret commissions to third parties through shell companies to secure contracts in Saudi Arabia, Hungary and the Czech Republic. BAE paid a $400 million criminal fine.[39] One aspect of the revelations related to a $40 million contract to sell an air traffic control system to the Government of Tanzania.[40] BAE paid £29.5 million to the Tanzanian government and a UK fine of £500,000. The court order noted that secret commissions were recorded in accounting records as payments for the provision of technical services by agents.[41] This was the result of a deliberate decision by officials. The company admitted that it failed to 'keep adequate accounting records',[42] a statutory requirement under Section 221 of the Companies Act 1985 (now part of the Companies Act 2006). Even in the absence of adequate accounting records, BAE's annual accounts continued to receive clean bill of health from its auditors.

Amidst media attention, the FRC announced that it would investigate audits and professional services advice provided by KPMG to BAE in the period 1997 to 2007. In 2013, the investigation was suddenly abandoned because:

> proper assessment of KPMG's conduct would require consideration of work undertaken in earlier years. Because there is no realistic prospect that a Tribunal will make an adverse finding in respect of a complaint relating to work done so long ago it has been concluded that it is not in the public interest to extend the investigation to the years preceding 1997.[43]

Regulatory Inertia and Revolving Doors

Some countries, most notably the United States, are beginning to focus on the corrupt practices of the Big Four firms. For example, PwC, Ernst & Young and KPMG have all been found by one US Senate subcommittee to be selling potentially abusive and illegal tax shelters.[44] KPMG has admitted 'criminal wrongdoing'[45] to the Department of Justice and paid a fine of $456 million. A number of its former personnel received prison sentences. In March 2013, Ernst & Young paid a fine of $123 million to avoid prosecution over 'the wrongful conduct of certain partners and employees'.[46] Former partners of Deloitte have been fined for insider trading and sent to prison for securities frauds.[47] Just over a year later, Ernst & Young paid a fine of $4 million for violating auditor independence rules.[48] In sharp contrast, there is little effective retribution in the United Kingdom. How is this to be explained?

The Big Four firms and their clients have a significant presence on the FRC[49] and its various committees to enable them to exercise significant influence on regulatory matters. They have also become part of the state through a close relationship with politicians, civil servants and public policy makers. For example, before the 2010 general election, the Big Four firms gave £3.5 million to the Conservative Party and provided advisers and consultants to shape party policies.[50] In previous elections, they have also done the same for the Labour Party, notably when the polls have suggested a high probability of victory. The Big Four firms are prolific spenders on civil servant hospitality, something which secures the ear of policy makers.[51]

The elevation of personnel from the accounting firms to senior policymaking positions – the so-called revolving door – has enabled the penetration of the state by the Big Four. In October 2010, Sir Michael Rake, former chairman of KPMG International, became an advisor to Prime Minister David Cameron. Nick Gibb MP, a former KPMG staffer, has held senior positions in the Conservative Party and was the minister of state for schools from 2010 to 2012. In June 2012, KPMG UK chairman John Griffith-Jones was appointed non-executive chairman of the Financial Conduct Authority. In July 2012, Ian Barlow, a former KPMG senior partner became the lead non-executive director and chair of the HMRC board.

The above examples are not isolated. All of the Big Four are deeply implicated in this process. The following revolving door appointments involve PwC personnel.

- Former PwC staffer Mark Hoban became treasury minister responsible for oversight of tax laws (2010–12) and subsequently moved to the Department of Work and Pensions.
- In June 2009 former PwC partner Amyas Morse was appointed UK comptroller and auditor general and became responsible for directing the National Audit Office (NAO). There he is accompanied by another former adviser to the Treasury, Dame Mary Keegan, also a former PwC partner.
- In May 2010 another PwC alumnus, Justine Greening, became economic secretary to the Treasury, followed in October 2011 by her appointment as secretary of state for transport and then, in September 2012, as secretary of state for international development. A PwC partner, Richard Abadie, has been the head of private finance initiative (PFI) policy at the Treasury and has been accompanied by ten or more colleagues.[52]
- In June 2011 another former PwC partner John Whiting became the director of the newly established Office of Tax Simplification (OTS), advising the government on simplification of tax laws; and since 1 April 2013 he has been a non-executive director of HMRC.[53] Chris Tailby, one-time tax partner at PwC, was head (until 2009) of Anti-Avoidance at HMRC.

The door revolves both ways (see Chapter 10). In July 2009 former Labour health minister Lord Norman Warner of Brockley became a strategic adviser to Deloitte's public sector practice. In May 2013, former HMRC director Dave Hartnett joined Deloitte as a consultant (see above). Former Labour business secretary Lord Mandelson resigned from government in 1998, but was soon hired by Ernst & Young. Since 1999, former Conservative minister Sir Malcolm Rifkind has been an adviser to PwC. In June 2011, former Labour home secretary Jacqui Smith became a consultant for KPMG. No doubt, all of those politicians are eager to serve the public interest, but their conception of 'public interest' is no doubt influenced by their wealth and their business interests.

Summary

This chapter has provided a brief glimpse of some of the anti-social practices of accountancy firms relating to tax avoidance, tax evasion, company audits and consultancy work. With full cooperation of regulators, the firms have developed skill in bending the rules to advance their economic interests. The banking crash of 2007–08 has not led to any investigation of failed audits. On a number of occasions, tax avoidance schemes marked by the firms have been declared to be unlawful by the courts. Yet not a single accountancy firm or its partners have ever been disciplined by any UK professional accountancy body for designing, marketing or implementing tax avoidance schemes. The UK government has failed to investigate, prosecute, or fine any firm or its partner, although numerous public contracts are awarded to the Big Four firms. Those firms have become central to the neoliberal project championed by major political parties, and have played a leading role in the privatization of the state-owned enterprises, the National Health Service (NHS) and expansion of market logics through PFI. Such relationships have yielded vast financial benefits to accountancy firms, but the accompanying sleaze is also incubating a deepening economic and social crisis.

Notes

1   Data collected by the author from the annual reviews published by the firms.
2   Financial Reporting Council (2014) *Key Facts and Trends in the Accountancy Profession*, London: FRC.
3   Sikka, P. (2010) 'Smoke and mirrors: corporate social responsibility and tax avoidance', *Accounting Forum*, vol. 34, no. 3/4, pp. 153–68.
4   Mitchell, A. and Sikka, P. (2011) *The Pin-Stripe Mafia: How Accountancy Firms Destroy Societies*, Basildon: Association for Accountancy and Business Affairs.

5   UK House of Commons Committee of Public Accounts (2013a) *Tax Avoidance: The Role of Large Accountancy Firms*, London: The Stationery Office. www.publications.parliament.uk/pa/cm201213/cmselect/cmpubacc/870/870.pdf

6   UK House of Commons Committee of Public Accounts (2013a), Ev4.

7   UK House of Commons Committee of Public Accounts (2013a), p. 5.

8   *Guardian*, 7 February2009, www.guardian.co.uk/business/2009/feb/07/tax-gap-avoidance-schemes

9   National Audit Office (2012) *Tax Avoidance: Tackling Marketed Avoidance Schemes*, London: The Stationery Office.

10   Deutsche Bank Group Services (UK) Ltd v Revenue & Customs [2011] UKFTT 66 (TC).

11   UKFTT 66 (TC), para 112.

12   *Daily Mail*, 27 March 2011, www.dailymail.co.uk/news/article-1370365/Revenue-boss-entertained-Vodafone-accountants-weeks-6bn-tax-deal.html

13   Brooks, R. (2013) *Britain Became a Tax Haven for Fat Cats and Big Business*, London: Oneworld Publications.

14   National Audit Office (2012) *Settling Large Tax Disputes*, London: The Stationery Office.

15   *Independent*, 28 May 2013.

16   *Mail on Sunday*, 15 February 2004; see also www.thisismoney.co.uk/money/news/article-1514887/1636m-tax-threat-to-Phones4U-founder.html (accessed 27 August 2012).

17   Para 15(2) of Dextra Accessories Ltd & Ors v Inspector Of Taxes [2002] UKSC SPC00331).

18   *BBC News*, 11 May 2012, www.bbc.co.uk/news/business-17993945

19   The Northern & Shell business empire includes newspapers (such as the *Daily Express, Sunday Express, Daily Star* and *Star on Sunday*), magazines (such as *OK!, New!, Star* and *TV Pick*) and television stations (such as Channel 5, 5*, 5USA, Television X and Red Hot TV).

20   *New York Times*, 26 May 2011, www.nytimes.com/2011/05/27/world/africa/27qaddafi.html

21   Libyan Investment Authority Management Information Report, 30 June 2010, www.globalwitness.org/sites/default/files/library/Libyan%20Investment%20Authority%20funds%20as%20of%20September%202010.pdf

22   Libyan Investment Authority Management Information Report, 2010 (see note 21); *New York Times*, 2011 (see note 20).

23   *Jamaica Gleaner*, 3 October 2008, http://jamaica gleaner.com/gleaner/20081003/business/business3.html

24   Bloomberg, 28 October 2013, www.bloomberg.com/news/2013-10-28/man-making-ireland-tax-avoidance-hub-globally-proves-local-hero.html

25   For an overview of schemes see International Monetary Fund (2013) *Fiscal Monitor 2013: Taxing Times*, Washington DC: IMF, www.imf.org/external/pubs/ft/fm/2013/02/pdf/fm1302.pdf

26   Reuters, 1 May 2013, http://uk.reuters.com/article/2013/05/01/uk-tax-uk-google-specialreport-idUKBRE94005R20130501

27   House of Commons Committee of Public Accounts 2013a, Ev10.

28   House of Commons Committee of Public Accounts (2013b), *Tax Avoidance: Google*, London: The Stationery Office.

29   Financial Reporting Council (2014) *Key Facts and Trends in the Accountancy Profession*, London: FRC.

30   This is a reference to Iliffe News and Media Ltd.

31   Paragraph 54 of Iliffe News and Media Ltd & Ors v Revenue & Customs [2012] UKFTT 696 (TC) (01 November 2012).

32   Sikka, P. (2009) 'Financial crisis and the silence of the auditors', *Accounting, Organizations and Society*, vol. 34, no. 6/7, pp. 868–73.

33   As per the annual financial statement filed with the SEC for the year to 30 November 2007.

34   US Bankruptcy Court Southern District of New York (2010) In re Lehman Brothers Holding Inc.: Report of Anton R. Valukas, p. 750. http://jenner. com/lehman/VOLUME%203.pdf

35   The charge sheet is available at http://amlawdaily.typepad.com/032312e%26y-complaint.pdf

36   Bloomberg, 28 November 2013, www.bloomberg.com/news/2013-11-28/ ernst-young-settles-lehman-investor-suit-for-99-mln.html

37   FRC (2010) 'AADB investigating auditors' role in relation to Lehman Brothers' compliance with FSA client asset rules', press release, 4 October, https://frc.org.uk/News-and-Events/FRC-Press/Press/2010/October/AADB-Investigating-Auditors-Role-in-Relation-to-Le.aspx

38   FRC (2012) 'Lehman Brothers International (Europe),' press release, 22 June, https://frc.org.uk/News-and-Events/FRC-Press/Press/2012/June/ Lehman-Brothers-International-(Europe).aspx

39   US Department of Justice (2010) 'BAE Systems PLC pleads guilty and ordered to pay $400 million criminal fine', press release, 1 March, www. justice.gov/opa/pr/2010/March/10-crm-209.html (accessed 3 June 2014).

40   Serious Fraud Office (2010) 'BAE fined in Tanzania defence contract case', press release, 21 December, www.sfo.gov.uk/press-room/press-release-ar-chive/press-releases-2010/bae-fined-in-tanzania-defence-contract-case.aspx (accessed 2 June 2014).

41   R and BAE Systems PLC [2010] EW Misc 16 (CC) (21 December 2010), www.bailii.org/ew/cases/Misc/2010/16.pdf (accessed 3 June 2014).

42   This was a statutory requirement under Section 221 of the Companies Act 1985.

43   FRC (2013) 'Closure of investigation into the conduct of: KPMG Audit plc, member firm of the ICAEW', press release, 1 August, www.frc.org.uk/News-and-Events/FRC-Press/Press/2013/August/Closure-of-investigation-into-the-conduct-of-KPMG.aspx (accessed 31 May 2014).

44   US Senate Permanent Subcommittee on Investigations (2003) *US Tax Shelter Industry: The Role of Accountants, Lawyers, And Financial Professionals – Four KPMG Case Studies: FLIP, OPIS, BLIPS and SC2*, Washington DC: USGPO; US Senate Permanent Subcommittee on Investigations (2005) *The Role of Professional Firms in the US Tax Shelter Industry*, Washington DC: USGPO.

45   US Department of Justice (2005) 'KPMG to pay $456 million for criminal

violations in relation to largest-ever tax shelter fraud case', press release, 29 August, www.justice.gov/opa/pr/2005/August/05_ag_433.html

46   US Department of Justice (2013) 'Manhattan U.S. attorney announces agreement with Ernst & Young LLP to pay $123 million to resolve federal tax shelter fraud investigation', press release, 1 March, www.justice.gov/usao/nys/pressreleases/March13/EYNPAPR.php

47   SEC (2010) 'SEC charges former Deloitte partner and son with insider trading', 4 August; *Chicago Business News*, 26 October 2012; SEC (2010) 'SEC charges former Deloitte partner and wife in international insider trading scheme', 30 November.

48   SEC (2014) 'SEC charges Ernst & Young with violating auditor independence rules in lobbying activities', 14 July, www.sec.gov/News/PressRelease/Detail/PressRelease/1370542298984.

49   See www.frc.org.uk/

50   For example, *Independent*, 29 July 2009, www.independent.co.uk/news/uk/politics/windfall-for-tories-as-firms-eye-1634bn-contracts-1764007.html; *Guardian*, 10 July 2012, www.theguardian.com/politics/2012/jul/10/lobbying; *Financial Times*, 28 May 2013, www.ft.com/cms/s/0/a7574dbc-c7aa-11e2-be27-00144feab7de.html#axzz31aPEpjl9

51   *Accountancy Age*, 13 February 2009, www.accountancyage.com/aa/news/1776133/kpmg-tops-whitehall-schmooze-league; *Guardian*, 7 June, www.theguardian.com/business/2010/jun/17/hmrc-head-tax-corporate-entertainment

52   House of Commons Treasury Committee (2011) *Private Finance Initiative*, London: TSO.

53   *Accountancy Age*, 17 January 2013, www.accountancyage.com/aa/news/2237104/whiting-takes-nonexec-role-with-hmrc

13

Corporate Theft and Impunity in Financial Services

Steve Tombs

Introduction: Routine Theft and Fraud

Since 2008, public criticism and condemnation of 'the banks' has been commonplace. Beyond the rhetoric, however, and despite a massive transfer of national wealth to the sector which has restored profitability, what has been most striking has been nation-state failures to examine – let alone act upon – their harmful and criminal risk-taking. The focus of the state has been to impose class-targeted austerity to meet the cost of socialised private debt. But even this stunning achievement notwithstanding, retail banking has continued, at least in the United Kingdom, to steal and defraud on a massive scale with relative impunity.

In the past 30 years, and particularly since the 'Big Bang' deregulation of the Financial Services Act (1986), consumers of financial services firms have been victims of three major waves of offences in the United Kingdom. These have involved many of the same (well-known) financial services companies. First, personal pension frauds emerged in the 1980s, in which as many as 2.4 million victims lost their pensions after replacing their occupational schemes with high-risk private schemes;[1] second, the endowment mortgage frauds of the 1990s – mis-selling a particularly risky mortgage product to high-risk customers – created as many as 5 million victims;[2] and third, the 'mis-selling' of payment protection insurance has been estimated as affecting almost 5 million people,[3] with the volume of claims still increasing in 2013.[4]

In each of these crime waves, we find very similar patterns: in their origins, in the way in which each unfolds over several years after their initial exposure, in the scale of harm in terms of victims and financial amounts, and in the identity of the key actors involved. These common features suggest a pattern of systematic crime and harm emanating from across the sector. In each case, we see in the background government policy creating an opportunity structure for crime and harm. Products are then sold in a deregulated market to further boost super-profits, despite the products being unsuitable for those customers to whom they are sold. This results in widespread financial hardship, mass complaints, regulatory actions against the companies involved, and long-term dissembling on the part of companies in the process of reaching settlements with victims. In each case, the products continued to be sold long after widespread concerns had been established about them. Each involved all of the main actors in their markets, and indeed many of the same companies were involved across all three waves of scandal. In all three forms of mis-selling, the key combination of formal deregulation, and the subsequent inability or unwillingness of governments to enforce compliance with regulation, combined to implicate the state intimately in the harms produced.

The First Crime Wave: Pensions

Academic Michael Clarke[5] has documented how the gradual withdrawal of the Conservative government from pension provision, coupled with deregulation of the retail financial services sector in the United Kingdom in the latter half of the 1980s, contributed to the 'biggest scandal of them all' in the sector. Pensions providers launched into a hard sell, targeting many public sector workers in well-developed pension programmes, wrongly advising many to cash in their contributions and transfer them to a new, private scheme about which they received false information. One survey conducted by the Securities and Investments Board found that only 9 per cent of pension companies had complied with legal requirements when originally advising on these pension transfers.[6] Moreover, once the mis-selling was exposed:

> the industry proved extremely reluctant to admit wrong doing, even by way of over-selling, still less mis-selling. Enquiries by the supervisory regulator, the Securities and Investments Board in the early 1980s, eventually produced an estimate that 1.4 million people may have been mis-sold personal pensions and had a right to have their cases reviewed and awarded compensation as appropriate; the costs of this were estimated at between £2 and £4 billion.[7]

Indeed, despite the establishment of a timetable for reviewing cases, and if necessary compensating the victims, pensions providers consistently missed deadlines, ignored regulatory cajoling, and proved relatively resistant to government threats. While breaches had been first uncovered in 1990,[8] a KPMG survey of pensions advice given from 1991–3, revealed, quite incredibly, that in 'four out of five cases' pensions companies were still giving advice which fell short of the legally required minima.[9] This was in the period after the mis-selling had been first exposed. Many of the offending companies had resolved less than 10 per cent of the cases under review by 1997.[10] In July of that year, Treasury economic secretary Helen Liddell began resorting to consistent but apparently fruitless efforts to 'name and shame' the most recalcitrant offenders, with the first 24 companies named including Allied Dunbar, Abbey Life, Sedgwick, the French insurer GAN, Colonial and Hogg Robinson, Barclays Life, Pearl, Prudential, Royal London, Legal & General, Norwich Union and Lloyds/TSB Group.[11]

The sum involved in this series of offences was, by the end of 1997, consistently being referred to as £4 billion,[12] and the scandal involved 2 million or more victims.[13] Early in 1998, the then new regulatory body, the Financial Services Authority (FSA), cited research which estimated the final costs as 'up to £11 billion, almost three times the original estimate. The number of victims could be as high as 2.4 million.'[14] As the cost of one particular series of crimes, this figure of £11 billion – even if ultimately an over-estimate, even though it was not an annual but a 'once and for all' cost – dwarfs the costs of almost all estimates of all forms of 'street' crimes put together.

The Second Crime Wave: Endowment Mortgages

At the end of the 1990s, evidence of widespread mis-selling of endowment mortgages had also begun to emerge. Following the end of state house-building and government encouragement for people to buy their homes, millions of such policies had been sold through the 1980s and 1990s, based on the claim that on the maturity of the endowment policy, the sum returned to an investor would pay off the mortgage on their home, a claim which often proved to be false.[15] The saga is uncannily similar to that of pensions mis-selling.

First, the list of companies involved in each is very similar. Among the companies known to be mired in the endowment mortgages episode were virtually all of the main high street providers of financial services. These included Prudential, Norwich Union, Legal & General, Bradford

& Bingley, Lloyds TSB (which at the time included Cheltenham & Gloucester) and HBOS, CGU (formed by a merger of the Commercial Union plc and General Accident plc), Nationwide and HSBC, Royal & Sun Alliance, Standard Life and Scottish Widows, Allied Dunbar, Scottish Amicable, Abbey Life and Friends Provident.[16]

Second, the endowment mortgage scandal was characterised by long-term obduracy on the part of companies in the sector, which were not prepared initially to admit any wrongdoing, then subsequently to compensate victims. Even in 2006, for example, the FSA was still responding to reports from the Financial Ombudsman to complaints that cases for compensation had been rejected by mortgage providers.[17] Six years after the scandal was first uncovered,[18] the FSA began, in July 2005, to investigate further 'the procedures of 52 firms which accounted for 90% of all the endowments mortgages that have been sold'. It claimed that this led to 75 per cent of rejected claims being re-adjudicated in favour of the customer.[19]

The Third Crime Wave: Personal Payment Protection Insurance

A virtually identical sequencing of events as had occurred in both pensions and endowment mortgages mis-selling then unfolded with respect to personal payment protection insurance (PPPI). PPPI policies were widely marketed and sold at the start of this century, at the height of the credit boom. Financial services firms targeted customers with debts such as mortgages, credit cards or loans insurance against a future inability to meet repayments. But again, these products were often sold when they were unnecessary, or without customers' knowledge, or indeed were to prove invalid in the event of customers claiming against them.[20] In 2005, the Citizens Advice Bureau (CAB) filed a 'super-complaint' relating to PPPI mis-selling to the Office of Fair Trading; and by this year, the FSA had 'already fined several smaller firms for mis-selling'.[21]

As in pensions and mortgages, the uncovering of PPPI mis-selling did not stop companies continuing to engage in a business they knew to be illegal. Thus, some 16 million PPPI policies have been sold since 2005.[22] Indeed, in 2007, two years after the CAB's super-complaint was filed, 'The reliance on PPPI insurance sales was at its highest', and analysts have 'estimated 14% of Lloyds' [Banking Group] group profits were generated from the product',[23] as was the case for most High Street banks.[24] Only in 2011 did the British Bankers Association abandon a legal challenge to an FSA ruling on compensating victims.[25] Moreover, the companies embroiled in the mis-selling of PPPI included many of the by now 'usual suspects', such as the Royal Bank of Scotland, Barclays, HSBC, Santander, MBNA, NRAM (Northern Rock and Bradford & Bingley), Yorkshire and Clydesdale banks, the Co-op Bank, Nationwide, Capital One, Welcome Financial, Principality Building Society – and Tesco.[26]

Again the Financial Ombudsman Service has dealt with hundreds of thousands of complaints from consumers whose claims for compensation have been turned down by companies, and about 70 per cent of its rulings have been in favour of the customer.[27] In the first six months of 2012, the Ombudsman upheld the following percentages of complaints against individual firms: Lloyds TSB (98 per cent of complaints upheld), MBNA (97 per cent), Barclays (93 per cent), CitiFinancial (93 per cent), Welcome Financial (92 per cent), Bank of Scotland (90 per cent), HFC (part of HSBC, 90 per cent) and NatWest (89 per cent).[28] By the end of 2012, £12.9 6billion had been set aside by companies to deal with compensation claims, and an estimated 4 to 4.75 million people had been, or were due to be, compensated.[29] Yet even in January 2013, the Financial Ombudsman expected an annual tripling of complaints to be dealt with as companies, in the words of the deputy Ombudsman, 'continue to frustrate their customers with delays and inconvenience'.[30]

In other words, the same companies acted in the same way that they had in response to consumer complaints around pensions and endowment mortgage mis-selling – rejecting the vast majority of claims for compensation, only to have these decisions overturned in favour of the complainant.

The Next Crime Wave?

These will not be the last 'scandals' associated with the retail financial services sector and its direct targeting of individual consumers[31] – quite apart from the wider allegations of crime and risk-taking such as those associated with the fixing of LIBOR, sanctions busting, money laundering, cartelisation, and insider trading. In combination, such phenomena are likely to generate greater media and popular, if not political and regulatory, scrutiny of the sector; and this, in turn, will bring to light further categories of mis-selling. Amongst the contemporary candidates for the next major mis-selling scandal are several that bear a remarkable similarity to the waves of mis-selling reviewed above – for they include further pensions,[32] mortgages[33] and credit card identity-theft protection[34] mis-selling. There is no reason to believe that, when the next wave of consumer victimisation is revealed, the companies involved – which will doubtless be more or less the same companies – will behave any differently than they have in the previous three waves: they will deny the offence, continue to sell the product, ignore adverse legal judgements and regulatory censure, then deny claims for compensation, only to be dragged kicking and screaming ultimately into a slow trickle of payments.

It is worth emphasising that the three waves of mis-selling analysed in this chapter occurred in the retail arms of financial services companies – which, in political and popular rhetoric, have, since the events of 2008, been generally represented as the 'clean' or 'safe' ('good') side of banking when contrasted with the 'bad', risk-hungry, profit-maximising investment banking arms. This distinction has been so thoroughly accepted that the key legislative response to the banking crisis in the United Kingdom is Vickers' proposal to erect an admittedly rather thin fence between these two forms of banking. State and governmental myopia about the harm caused by retail financial services appears to be entrenched. If this wall between the two parts of the sector has any effect at all, one consequence will in fact be to insulate the retail parts of businesses, bolstering their impunity.

The Social Costs of Routine Corporate Theft and Fraud

This chapter has detailed one small sub-set of routine, systematic, corporate harms. These harms involve more or less the same companies. They affect millions of people in ways that are diffuse. Moreover, they have generated a series of forms of victimisation and social harms.

First, these products and their markets were regulated – albeit not adequately – but state expenditures were consumed in the various stages of this regulatory process, expenditures sourced by general taxation and thereby unavailable for other uses. This is hardly a minor observation in the context of 'austerity' and significant pressures on every aspect of government spending, the effects of which are differentially experienced.

Second, while millions of individuals did receive compensation, this cannot take account of any emotional or psychological costs that they or their families may have incurred in this process, not least where claims for compensation across each form of mis-selling were, routinely and falsely, initially denied.

Third, new market opportunities for business emerged around these waves of mis-selling. These markets are defined by the proliferation of 'claims management' firms, private sector companies which pursue claims on behalf of individuals – on the basis of a percentage of the settlement. Thus, private profits were created, and individuals were not fully recompensed.

Fourth, the costs incurred by financial services companies in compensation must be offset elsewhere, through raising prices or charges for other products they sell. In other words, the costs of offending are dispersed to existing and future customers. This response is much more likely when the 'need' to recover costs is spread so widely across all the major actors in a market – virtually removing any ability of consumers to exercise 'choice' and avoid such costs.

Fifth, the 'burden' of compensation may help partly to 'explain' why banks have not responded to cash injections from central government by increasing lending to individuals and businesses in order to generate economic growth. For example, it is estimated that virtually all of the £200 million created by the Bank of England in the first round of quantitative easing did not make its way into the economy via increased bank lending, which declined. In fact it was hoarded by banks to restore their profitability.[35]

In sum, these processes underscore the fact that this is a dysfunctional sector, certainly when these scandals are set alongside the higher-profile harms of the investment banking industry. They further undermined social trust in banking, a basic and at present necessary social function.

Perhaps most significantly of all, taking these waves and layers of harms together, a combined effect of them may be to generate popular anger, anxiety or apathy. Each effect – and they are not mutually exclusive – appears to be a logical or at least a comprehensible response to evidence of ongoing harms produced by the corporate sector, in which the state either colludes or at best 'fails to act'. The routine and seemingly endless production of harms may inure people to their malevolence, as the population becomes anaesthetised to such harm. Thus, perhaps the most pernicious effect is that harm and crime become virtually normalised, part of what 'banks' do, seemingly inevitable and unstoppable. What can now surprise us about the corporate world? About the state? And is not a reasonable response simply to slide into apathy, alienation and atomisation?

These harms, then, have potentially significant political effects – in a sense, they are both inadequately known but are also all too well known. The waves of mis-selling to which this chapter has pointed may, in the current conjuncture, simply be consigned with a collective sigh to the generalised problem of 'the banks', seemingly an inherent fixture of contemporary capitalism. Critics of corporate power often see their task as uncovering hidden social phenomena, not least harms and injustices, bringing these to light, making them visible. But the problem here is not necessarily the invisibility of the harm routinely inflicted – it is in some ways their very visibility through their 'ceaseless repetition'.[36] Harm produced from the financial services sector is now so common, so ubiquitous, it is virtually normalised (see also Chapter 2). Literally, 'normal' business, as the Introduction to this book shows, is now corrupt business. Challenging these anaesthetising effects of the routine nature of bank crime and harm represents a significant academic, and most of all a pressing political, challenge for those who would resist such harms.

Notes

1   Slapper, G. and Tombs, S. (1999) *Corporate Crime*, London: Longman.
2   Fooks, G. (2003) 'In the valley of the blind the one eyed man is king: corporate crime and the myopia of financial regulation', in Tombs, S. and Whyte, D. (eds), *Unmasking the Crimes of the Powerful*, New York: Peter Lang.
3   Pollock, I. (2012) 'Q&A: PPPI claims – how high could they go?', BBC News Online, 5 November 2012, www.bbc.co.uk/news/business-20204593 (all URLs were last accessed 1 May 2014).
4   Bachelor, L. (2013) 'PPPI payouts expected to rocket in 2013', *Guardian*, 10 January, www.guardian.co.uk/money/2013/jan/10/ppi-payouts-rocket-2013.
5   Clarke, M. (1996) 'The regulation of retail financial services in Britain: an analysis of a crisis', paper presented at the conference Regulation and Organisational Control, Liverpool, 20 November.
6   Black, J. (1997) Rules and Regulators, Oxford: Clarendon Press: 178.
7   Clarke (1996), p. 14.
8   *Guardian*, 9 October 1997.
9   Cited in Black (1997), p.178 and fn 143.
10 *Guardian*, 10 July 1997.
11 Cicutti, N. (1997) 'Liddell names the worst 24 pension firms', *Independent*, 10 July, www.independent.co.uk/news/business/liddell-names-the-worst-24-pension-firms-1249929.html
12 *Financial Times*, 19 September 1997.
13 *The Times*, 20 September 1997.
14 *Guardian*, 13 March 1998.
15 BBC News Online, 27 July 1999, http://news.bbc.co.uk/1/hi/business/404872.stm
16 See respectively BBC News Online, 27 April 2005, http://news.bbc.co.uk/1/hi/business/4489023.stm; BBC News Online, 3 October 2005, http://news.bbc.co.uk/1/hi/business/3621044.stm; Kollewe, J. (2007) 'Bradford & Bingley stung by mis-selling costs', *Guardian*, 13 February 2007,

www.guardian.co.uk/business/2007/feb/13/bradfordbingleybusiness.endow-ments?INTCMP=SRCH; Treanor, J. (2005) 'Lloyds pays customers £150m for endowment mis-selling', *Guardian*, 13 December 2005, www.guardian.co.uk/money/2005/dec/13/endowments.lloydstsbgroup?INTCMP=SRCH; Collinson, P. (2000) 'CGU endowment policy holders win reprieve', *Guardian*, 28 January 2000, www.guardian.co.uk/business/2000/jan/28/7?INTCMP=SRCH; Financial Services Authority (2003) 'Friends Provident fined 675,000 for mis-handling of mortgage endowment complaints', press release, 17 December, www.fsa.gov.uk/library/communication/pr/2003/135.shtml

17 BBC News Online, 11 December 2006, http://news.bbc.co.uk/1/hi/business/6168813.stm

18 BBC News Online (1999) (see note 16).

19 BBC News Online (2006) (see note 17).

20 Pollock (2012).

21 S. Neville, 'Scale of PPPI mis-selling overtakes private pensions scandal, says Which?', *Guardian*, 1 November 2012, www.guardian.co.uk/money/2012/nov/01/ppi-mis-selling-scale-which?INTCMP=SRCH

22 Pollock (2012).

23 Neville (2012).

24 Pollock (2012).

25 Hickman, M. (2011) 'Three million customers due for payout over banks' PPPI policy', *Independent*, 10 May, www.independent.co.uk/news/business/news/three-million-customers-due-for-payout-over-banks-ppi-policy-2281588.html

26 Pollock (2012).

27 Pollock (2012).

28 Pollock (2012).

29 Pollock (2012).

30 Bachelor (2013).

31 Osborne (2012) 'Bank staff "still feel pressured into selling unsuitable products"', *Guardian*, 7 December, www.guardian.co.uk/money/2012/dec/07/bank-staff-pressured-selling-unsuitable-products

32 Simon, E. (2012) 'A £20bn pension mis-selling scandal?', *Telegraph*, 4 March, www.telegraph.co.uk/finance/personalfinance/pensions/9120476/A-20bn-pension-mis-selling-scandal.html; BBC News Online, 11 October 2012, www.bbc.co.uk/news/business-19901572

33 Bachelor, L. (2012) 'Claims management firms turn from PPPI to mortgage mis-selling', *Observer*, 28 October, www.guardian.co.uk/money/2012/oct/29/claims-firms-mortgage-mis-selling

34 Bachelor, L. and Treanor, J. (2012) 'Banks braced for exposure to CPP mis-selling investigation', *Guardian*, 15 November.

35 Murphy, R. (2010) *Green Bricks in the Wall: Making Quantitative Easing Green*, Downham Market: Finance for the Future, p. 2.

36 Dilts, A. (2012) 'Revisiting Johan Galtung's concept of structural violence', *New Political Science*, vol. 34, no. 2, p. 192; Winter, Y. (2012) 'Violence and visibility', *New Political Science*, vol. 34, no. 2, pp. 195–202.

14

High Pay and Corruption

Luke Hildyard

The runaway growth of top pay for corporate executives has been a vexatious issue in public debate since the Thatcher era. The huge windfalls for executives of privatised utilities provoked outrage in the late 1980s and early 1990s, leading to the publication of the *Cadbury Report* (1992)[1] and the *Greenbury Report* (1995),[2] and changes in the way that pay for the senior managers of publicly listed businesses was set. Following the onset of the financial crisis in 2007, the continuing growth of executive pay, in contrast with falling wages and declining living standards across most of the UK population, has again become a source of much public anger.

Research from the High Pay Centre provides the statistical underpinning for the public concern. Average pay for a FTSE 100 chief executive (CEO) has risen from around £100–200,000 in the early 1980s, to just over £1 million at the turn of the 21st century, to £4.3 million in 2012.[3] This represented a leap from around 20 times the pay of the average UK worker in the 1980s, to 60 times in 1998, to 160 times in 2012. (See Table 14.1.)

Over the same period, the share of total UK income accruing to the

Table 14.1

Year	FTSE 100 CEO pay	FTSE 100 employee pay	Pay ratio (FTSE CEO: employee)	Average UK worker	Pay ratio (FTSE 100 CEO:UK worker)
1980	£115,000*	n/a	n/a	£6,500	18:1
1998	£1,000,000	£21,500	47:1	£17,400	57:1
2012	£4,300,000	£33,967	127:1	£26,500	162:1

- Based on the High Pay Commission's analysis of six leading UK companies: High Pay Commission (2012) 'Cheques with balances: why tackling high pay is in the national interest', London: High Pay Commission, p. 23.

richest 1 per cent of the population has more than doubled from 6 per cent in 1979 to 13 per cent in 2011 (the most recent year for which the World Top Income database contains records). Research from the Organisation for Economic Co-operation and Development (OECD) shows that the United Kingdom is now the seventh most unequal of the 32 advanced economies that comprise membership of the OECD.[4]

The response from both government and company owners has been weak, and has failed to reflect the public appetite for reducing the pay gap between top executives and the rest of the population. The UK government introduced the 2013 Business, Enterprise and Regulatory Reform Act, giving shareholders a veto over companies' executive pay policy. However, this is hardly likely to provide an effective restraint. Even during the so-called 'shareholder spring' of 2012 the average number of company shareholders who used their non-binding vote to oppose pay policy was just over 7 per cent[5] – a negligible percentage. By contrast Polling for the High Pay Centre in April 2014 found that 80 per cent of people think that pay gaps in the United Kingdom are still too large.[6]

But while levels of top pay continue to exercise public opinion, the issue of high pay is rarely framed as an issue of corruption, as opposed to injustice or unfairness. This framing is important because 'corruption' is a stronger term – practices considered corrupt require urgent redress. People seem willing to accept a degree of unfairness in society but are less tolerant of corruption. Many children will have been told by a parent or teacher that 'life isn't fair' but it would take an unusually misanthropic adult to tell a child that 'life is inherently corrupt'.

Yet even if we were to adopt the definition of corruption used by Transparency International – 'the abuse of entrusted power for private gain' – this narrow definition would amply cover examples of excessive top pay (see the Introduction, and Chapters 1 and 11 of this book). So why has the corruption narrative has failed to take hold? There are three possible reasons.

First, there is a tendency to think of corruption in terms of the law. Multi-million-pound pay packages for the FTSE 100 executives, top bankers, city lawyers and the like are not illegal. As such, there is a clear distinction between these and bribes, cover-ups and slush funds. Egregious pay packages such as the £350,000 annual pension awarded to former RBS CEO Fred Goodwin after he had reduced the bank to dependency on a government bail-out; the £2.4 billion bonus pool at Barclays, three times the size of its dividend pay-out in a year of falling profits; or the £400 million incentive offered to a handful of directors at the building firm Persimmon may attract widespread condemnation.

But this is criticism of the morality rather than legality of the actions of these companies and individuals. It is a different kind of criticism from the cover-up over police conduct during the Hillsborough disaster (see Chapter 5); the alleged case of bribery involving BAE Systems and the sale of weapons to the Saudi Arabian government (see the Introduction to this book); or the expropriation of public money by officials in the developing world.

Second, each of these examples of high-profile corruption cases involves corrupt state officials. Executive pay is ostensibly a free-market transaction between two willing partners – the owners of the business, the shareholders, on the one hand, and the executives they employ, on the other, with no ostensible role for the state. The doctrine of 'the market' – hegemonic in UK political discourse to the extent that even the supposedly apolitical permanent secretary of the Treasury can declare the belief that 'markets work' to be a non-contentious, apolitical assertion – suggests that if an individual employee is overpaid, 'market forces' will inevitably correct the anomaly.[7] The employer can secure either a fairer price or a better service from an alternative employee.

Finally, there is the matter of transparency. Many high-profile corruption allegations – like the Hillsborough case and the relationship between News International and the Metropolitan Police over the phone-hacking scandal – involve the suppression of information. By contrast, top pay – at least at UK listed companies – is, in theory at least, highly transparent and accountable. Information on top executives' pay is placed in the public domain via the companies' annual remuneration reports. It is available for scrutiny by the media, campaigners and other analysts. Shareholders, the owners of the company and – according to the UK 2006 Companies Act – the beneficiaries whose interests UK company directors must represent, can use their binding vote to veto pay packages of which they disapprove.

Of course, it is not the case that all forms of corruption fall into at least one of these categories. Moreover, the runaway growth of top pay that has occurred in recent years cannot be attributed to illegal activities, corrupt government officials or cover-ups. This perhaps explains why even the most trenchant critics of the rampant growth of executive pay in recent decades have tended not to frame it as an issue of corruption.

Institutionalisation of corporate power

But if we consider the wider structures that enable corruption in developing economies and the negative consequences for those societies as a result of corruption, there are many similarities with the conditions that have enabled the incomes of the highest-paid to accelerate away from the rest of the population in the United Kingdom.

One of the most frequently cited causes of corruption is a lack of democratic accountability. The United Kingdom is not a dictatorship. People who speak out against the government do not fear for their safety. The press can expose government misdoings without fear of censorship.

At the same time, however, most national UK newspapers are owned by multi-millionaire businessmen. While they may sometimes publish news stories critical of individual bankers' bonuses or executive greed, the right-wing national papers (which constitute the overwhelming majority of total sales) support a wider narrative that identifies individual businesspeople as 'wealth creators' and suggests that any attempt on part of government to achieve a more equal distribution of incomes is a threat to the economy and a punishment for success.[8]

Similarly, corporate power has become so entrenched in the United Kingdom that it arguably functions as a governing institution in its own right, with the political parties' policy programmes confined within boundaries determined by corporate interests. Stephen Wilks, professor of politics at Exeter University, notes some of the ways in which those who benefit from high top pay and rampant inequality strongly influence if not control the democratic process:

- The two major political parties in the United Kingdom, particularly the Conservatives, but also the Labour Party, depend on contributions from the super-rich to fund their campaign budgets. As such, both would instantly weaken their chances of electoral success if they adopted policies designed to curtail the incomes of the super-rich.
- The media – as previously noted, largely owned and managed by highly paid business leaders – frequently reinforces a narrative of the interests of big businesses, as articulated by highly paid business leaders, as being consistent with the United Kingdom's national interests. For example, a group of CEOs wrote to a newspaper in the run-up to the 2010 general election to argue against a tax on employers that would have funded public services. Their letter dominated news coverage for days, with the opinions of these 'wealth creators' elevated to that of oracles of the United Kingdom's economic prospects. Politicians must operate in this context.
- A large proportion of civil servants now serve two masters – government and corporations. In addition to the 'outsourcing' of government services, under the Coalition government over 60 non-executive

directors advise government departments. For example, Sir Andrew Witty, the CEO of GlaxoSmithKline, who was paid £7 million in 2013, served as lead non-executive director of the Department for Business, Innovation and Skills, the department responsible for legislation on executive pay. Central government paid £1.2 billion for advice from consultants in 2009–10. This represents over 40 per cent of staff costs in five departments, effectively meaning that policy was influenced by individuals employed by major consultancies where pay packages hundreds of times those of the average worker are commonplace. These consultants are generally both highly paid themselves and highly qualified individuals with an enviable academic or professional record, appointed after a competitive recruitment process. As such, their pay levels raise the pay expectations of senior civil servants, and widen the gap between them and lower-paid employees. Together, highly paid senior civil servants and private sector consultants are likely to share a vested interest in defending policies that maintain higher pay for those at the top.

- The global economy means that the biggest companies operating in the United Kingdom are transnational in nature. They could relocate to other jurisdictions with relative ease, at the cost of jobs and tax revenue to the United Kingdom. Given the economic affiliations of the UK media, this would probably be presented as a blow to the credibility of the governing party. Again, this means that politicians are under pressure to enact policies that are favourable to highly paid business leaders. For example, the Conservative Party has frequently invoked the language of 'the global race' since 2010 – the need to attract businesses to the United Kingdom with low tax rates and a lack of workplace regulation, policies which are all likely to aid the accumulation and concentration of wealth by top executives and business leaders.[9]

It is instructive to compare how the institutionalisation of corporate power has coincided with policies that enable the growth of top pay.

Throughout the 1980s and 1990s a series of measures were taken to reduce the power and influence of trade unions, while the top rate of tax was reduced from a high of 98p in the pound in the 1970s to 40p in 1988. In the late 1990s the Corporate Governance Code recognised the principle of 'performance-related pay', effectively licensing the payment of bonuses and incentive payments, which became commonplace in the 21st century. Despite many on the left arguing that capital gains tax should be taxed at the same rate as income tax, it was lowered in 2008 to just 18 per cent, meaning that executives pay a lower rate when selling on share awards than ordinary workers pay on their incomes.

Over the same period, dwindling party membership has increased the importance of wealthy donors to party funding. The economy has become increasingly globalised, with bigger companies enjoying greater political influence. The press have become increasingly politically active in support of the kind of economic policies that enabled the growth of top pay – in particular the *Sun*, the country's best-selling newspaper, moved from a more modest voice oscillating between Labour and the Conservatives in the 1970s to a much more strident advocacy of Thatcherite policies since 1979.

In this context, we begin to see how high pay in the United Kingdom might be considered a form of corruption. While politicians and media organs are not ostensibly prevented from speaking out against excessive top pay and social inequality, in practice they are largely influenced by undemocratic, unaccountable private interests. Thus, a tiny elite is able to use its political and economic power to facilitate its own self-enrichment, just as occurs in societies that are more widely considered to be corrupt.

Nepotism and appropriation

Although executive recruitment is in theory an open, meritocratic and non-discriminatory process, in practice high-paying jobs draw from an extremely narrow pool. There are, as of April 2014, just four female FTSE 100 CEOs out of 100. In 2007, the Sutton Trust found that 54 FTSE 100 CEOs were privately educated (compared with just 7 per cent of the population as a whole) while the figure is 51 per cent for leading bankers.[10] Privately educated pupils are 55 times more likely to attend Oxford or Cambridge universities and 22 times as likely to attend another top-ranked university than children who qualify for free school meals.[11]

Even beyond private education, income inequality is likely to prove self-reinforcing without counterbalancing political action. Research from the London School of Economics, analysing a range of international studies looking at the effects of household income on children's educational achievement, found that income had a significant effect, even when factors such as parental behaviour and school quality are taken into account.[12] So families with higher incomes are much more likely to obtain the education and qualifications necessary to reach executive positions.

The role played by non-advertised internships and family or school networks in career development has attracted criticism for giving young people from richer backgrounds an unfair advantage. Undoubtedly this kind of explicit nepotism could be understood as a form of corruption. But more widely, there is no great need for those in positions of power to adopt a direct system of patronage, offering well-paid jobs to friends and family rather than recruiting on merit. The in-built educational advantages enjoyed by the super-rich, resulting from an economic system that they control, mean that their children are likely to capture the lion's share of well-paid jobs, even when they are subject to a supposedly open and transparent application process. This is likely to worsen over time. Research shows that the earnings of children who grew up in the 1970s and 1980s were much more likely to be linked to their parents' earnings than those who grew up in the 1950s and 1960s.[13]

The same concern applies to the process by which remuneration committees set executive pay in the United Kingdom. 'Remcoms' were introduced following a recommendation of the *Cadbury Report*.[14] They are made up of non-executive directors who determine the size and structure of executive pay packages, with the aim of maximising value for shareholders.

A report by the High Pay Centre in 2012 found that 46 per cent of FTSE100 remcom members are CEOs of other companies.[15] Only 37 out of 366 FTSE100 remcom members have a professional background outside business or finance. Though remcom appointments are approved by shareholders, and the pay policy they implement is subject to a binding shareholder vote, in practice these decisions are controlled by wealthy investment professionals, rather than ordinary people with a savings account or pension plan. The *Financial Times* noted in 2014 that pay in the fund management sector now outstripped investment banking, with average pay – across all employees – standing at over £200,000 at three leading fund managers.

This means that executive pay in the United Kingdom is set by a narrow elite group who benefit or have benefited the most from a culture of high pay and pay inequality. Given that executive pay is set by benchmarking or references to 'the market', serving executives, in particular, have an indirect but powerful interest in encouraging higher pay packages when serving on remcoms.

The behavioural economist Cass Sunstein notes that people with similar opinions are prone to 'group-think', whereby more extreme decisions are reached when a group of individuals with shared backgrounds endorse each others' conclusions, rather than attempt to challenge them.[16] In the case of remcoms, we can see how this might manifest itself in terms of a consensus around contentious, if not ideological, and wholly untested assumptions such as the notion that executives are 'wealth creators' upon whom the organisation's success depends; that huge incentive payments are necessary to encourage a high level of performance; or that in a global marketplace it is necessary to pay a premium to attract and retain the best possible CEO.

Trends in CEO pay over the course of the 'remcom' era suggest theat these highly debatable assertions are treated as scientific fact. As detailed earlier, whereas executives were paid less than £1 million a year in the late 1990s, maybe 50 or 60 times the average worker, pay packages in 2012 had climbed to over £4 million, more than 160 times the average annual wage.

This has been achieved, not by illegally siphoning off company funds – there is no need to do so. Executives are able to access multi-million-pound pay packages by working within the boundaries of a corporate governance structure that renders the highly paid accountable only to other top earners.

Conclusion

This article has been chiefly concerned with CEO pay for the executives of listed companies, simply because the data are most readily available. But pay for corporate leaders sets a benchmark for bankers, city lawyers and top accountants too. Even senior managers in the civil service, universities and the BBC justify generous pay packages on the basis of comparisons with the city or major corporations. The net result is that a tiny proportion of the population have been able to capture an unearned, unnecessary and disproportionate slice of the United Kingdom's prosperity. Meanwhile living standards for ordinary people stagnate. Research from Eurostat shows that 30 of the United Kingdom's 37 regions are poorer than the EU average, because so much of the United Kingdom's total wealth is concentrated in London and the Home Counties.[17]

Although this chapter has not uncovered evidence of explicitly corrupt practices such bribery, coercion, nepotism and theft of company or state revenues, this is simply because inadequately regulated economic power achieves precisely the same ends. Yet can this be described as anything other than economic corruption? The people who determine top pay are drawn from the same executive class as those who benefit from it. Very often they are the same people. Access to this class is in practice restricted, as witnessed by the disproportionately high representation of people who were educated privately in top-paying jobs.

The implication for anti-corruption campaigners is clear. Political and economic inequality results in the abuse of power and responsibility, by the powerful and to the detriment of the powerless. This is corruption, and should be monitored and exposed as such when applied through soft power, as well as through more conventional forms of corruption.

Notes

1   *The Cadbury Report: Financial Aspects of Corporate Governance*, was a UK government commissioned report that sets out recommendations on the arrangement of company boards and accounting systems. The report was published in 1992; see: www.jbs.cam.ac.uk/cadbury/report/index.html

2   *Directors Remuneration: Report of a Study Group Chaired by Sir Richard Greenbury* was a report published in July 1995 by a committee convened by the Confederation of British Industry in order to establish good principles and practice for the pay of Directors of Public Limited Companies – see http://www.ecgi.org/codes/documents/greenbury.pdf'

3   High Pay Centre (2013) 'One law for them: how big companies flout rules on executive pay', London: High Pay Centre, p. 4.

4   OECD, *OECD Factbook 2011–2012: Economic, Environmental and Social Statistics*, www.oecd-ilibrary.org/sites/factbook-2011-en/03/05/01/index.html?itemId=/content/chapter/factbook-2011-31-en%20

5   High Pay Centre (2012) *The State of Pay: One Year on from the High Pay Commission*, London: High Pay Centre, p. 19.

6   High Pay Centre, 'UKIP supporters say tackling rich/poor gap is higher priority than taxes and benefits', 22 April 2014, http://highpaycentre.org/blog/ukip-supporters-say-tackling-rich-poor-gap-is-higher-priority-than-taxes-an

7   For 'the Treasury View' on markets see John Rentoul's account of a talk given by Sir Nick Macpherson, permanent secretary of the Treasury: *Independent*, 'The Treasury view', 20 January 2014, http://blogs.independent.co.uk/2014/01/19/the-treasury-view/

8   National newspapers supporting the Conservative Party at the 2010 general election comprised 71 per cent of UK newspaper sales, according to Wring, D. and Ward, S. (2010) 'The media and the 2010 campaign: the television election?' *Parliamentary Affairs*, vol.63, no. 4, pp. 802–17.

9   Wilks, S. (2013) *The Political Power of the Business Corporation*, Gloucestershire: Edward Elgar, pp. 77–9, 85–6, 96–7.

10 Sutton Trust (2007) 'The educational backgrounds of 500 leading figures', press release, 1 May 2007, www.suttontrust.com/news/news/the-educational-backgrounds-of-500-leading-figures/

11 Sutton Trust (2010), 'Private school pupils 55 times more likely to go to

Oxbridge than poor students', press release, 22 December 2010, www.sutton-trust.com/news/news/private-school-pupils-55-times/

12   Joseph Rowntree Foundation (2013) 'Does money affect children's outcomes? A systemic review', York: JRF, www.jrf.org.uk/sites/files/jrf/money-children-outcomes-full.pdf

13   Institute of Education (2014) *Education and Intergenerational Mobility: Help or Hindrance?* London: Institute of Education, http://repec.ioe.ac.uk/REPEc/pdf/qsswp1401.pdf

14   *Cadbury Report*, see note 1.

15   High Pay Centre (2012) 'The new closed shop: who's deciding on pay?' London: High Pay Centre, http://highpaycentre.org/pubs/publication-the-new-closed-shop-whos-deciding-on-pay

16   High Pay Centre (2012).

17   *Daily Mail*, 5 May 2014, www.dailymail.co.uk/news/article-2617938/Revealed-How-parts-Britain-poorer-POLAND-families-Wales-Cornwall-Europes-worst-off.html

Contributors

David Beetham is professor emeritus, University of Leeds. He has published widely on questions of democracy and challenges to it, and has authored and edited a number of books on those subjects.

John Christensen directs the global work of the Tax Justice Network. Trained as a forensic investigator and development economist, he has spent much of his career investigating Britain's tax haven empire. As part of his research he worked in offshore finance, spending four years working in offshore trust and company administration and 11 years serving as economic adviser to the government of Jersey.

Sheila Coleman has been involved in researching the aftermath of the Hillsborough Disaster for 25 years and is an active member of the Hillsborough Justice Campaign. She formerly worked as a senior lecturer and researcher in higher education, and currently works as a regional community coordinator for Unite the Union.

Joanna Gilmore is a lecturer in York Law School, University of York, where she teaches and researches the regulation of public protest and counter-terrorism policing. Her book *This is Not a Riot! Regulation of Public Protest and the Impact of the Human Rights Act 1998* will be published by Oxford University Press in 2016.

Chris Greer is professor of sociology at City University London. He is currently researching the multi-dimensional processes through which institutional child sex abuse scandals are activated and amplified – often after decades of silence, denial and/or cover-up – and the impact of these scandals on public policy and trust in public institutions.   His books include *Sex Crime and the Media* (Routledge, 2012) and his next book will be *Trial by Media* (with Eugene McLaughlin, Routledge 2016).

Luke Hildyard is deputy director of the High Pay Centre, a think-tank studying the social and economic effects of top pay and the super-rich. He has previously authored publications on executive pay, corporate governance and inequality.

Contributors

Paul Jones is a senior lecturer in sociology at the University of Liverpool. His research centres on the relationship between architecture and the political economy (particularly in periods of major social change), and he addressed these concerns in *The Sociology of Architecture* (Liverpool University Press, 2011).

Eugene McLaughlin is professor of criminology and co-director of the Centre for Crime and Justice Research. His books include *Out of Order? The Policing of Black People* (with Elliot Cashmore, Routledge, 2013) and *Trial by Media* (with Chris Green, Routledge, 2016).

Michael Mair is a senior lecturer in sociology at the University of Liverpool. His interests include politics, accountability, government and the state. Alongside ongoing studies of accountability in the context of live military operations, Michael has been investigating statecraft, market formation and the political economy of the local from a practice-oriented and ethnographically informed perspective.

David Miller is professor of sociology at the University of Bath and Global Uncertainties Leadership Fellow. He is a director of Public Interest Investigations (which is responsible for spinwatch.org and power base. info). His recent publications include *The Cold War on British Muslims* (with Tom Mills and Tom Griffin, Spinwatch, 2011); *The Britain Israel Communications and Research Centre* (co-authored with Tom Mills, Tom Griffin and Hilary Aked, 2013); and *Critical Terrorism Studies since 11 September 2001* (co-edited, Routledge, 2014).

Paul O' Connor works at the Derry-based human rights NGO, the Pat Finucane Centre. The Centre is named after a lawyer who was murdered in 1989 in Belfast by loyalist paramilitaries directed by RUC Special Branch and the security service MI5. He contributed to *Counter-Terrorism and State Political Violence* (Routledge, 2012).

Phil Scraton is professor of criminology in the School of Law at Queen's University Belfast He was principal author of the *Hillsborough Independent Panel Report*. His books include *Hillsborough: The truth* (Mainstream, 2009, 3rd ed.), *The Violence of Incarceration* (Routledge, 2010 with Jude McCulloch, 2010) and *The Incarceration of Women* (Palgrave Macmillan, 2014 with Linda Moore).

Prem Sikka is professor of accounting at the University of Essex, UK.

His research on accountancy, auditing, tax avoidance, tax havens, corruption, corporate governance, money laundering, insolvency and business affairs has been published in books, scholarly journals, newspapers and magazines. He holds the Accounting Exemplar Award from the American Accounting Association and Lifetime Achievement Awards from the British Accounting and Finance Association.

Steve Tombs is professor of criminology at the Open University. His work centres around corporate and state produced crime and harm, and responses to these. He is author of *Regulation After the Crisis: Social protection in an age of corporate barbarism?* (Policy Press, 2015) and co-author of *The Corporate Criminal* (with David Whyte, Routledge, 2015).

Waqas Tufail is a research fellow in the Department of Sociology, Social Policy and Criminology at the University of Liverpool. His research interests concern the policing of marginalised communities and the criminalisation of Muslim minorities.

David Whyte is professor of socio-legal studies at the University of Liverpool, where he teaches and researches the relationship between the rule of law and state-corporate power. His other books include *Crimes of the Powerful* (Open University Press, 2009) and *The Corporate Criminal* (with Steve Tombs, Routledge, 2015).

Jörg Wiegratz is lecturer in the political economy of global development at the University of Leeds. He teaches om the historical and contemporary relationship between the Global North and Global South and researches the political economy and moral economy of neoliberalism.

Stuart Wilks-Heeg is head of politics at the University of Liverpool. He has published widely on issues concerning UK politics, democratic integrity, party funding and electoral management. He was co-author of the 2012 *Democratic Audit of the UK* (with Andrew Blick and Stephen Crone).

Index